Narrowcast

Post 45 Florence Dore, Kate Marshall,
and Loren Glass, Editors
Post·45 Group, Editorial Committee

Narrowcast

Poetry and Audio Research

Lytle Shaw

Stanford University Press
Stanford, California

Stanford University Press

Stanford, California

Printed in the United States of America on acid-free, archival-quality paper

Library of Congress Cataloging-in-Publication Data

Names: Shaw, Lytle, author.

Title: Narrowcast : poetry and audio research / Lytle Shaw.

Description: Stanford, California : Stanford University Press, 2018. | Series: Post-45 | Includes bibliographical references and index.

Identifiers: LCCN 2017055027 (print) | LCCN 2017059718 (ebook) | ISBN 9781503606579 | ISBN 9780804797993 (cloth : alk. paper) | ISBN 9781503606562 (pbk. : alk. paper)

Subjects: LCSH: American poetry—20th century—History and criticism. | Sound—Recording and reproducing—History—20th century. | Sound recordings and the arts—United States— History—20th century. | Electronic surveillance—United States—History—20th century. | New Left—United States—History—20th century. | Oral interpretation of poetry. | Poetics.

Classification: LCC PS325 (ebook) | LCC PS325 .S49 2018 (print) | DDC 811/.5409—dc23

LC record available at https://lccn.loc.gov/2017055027

Cover design: Christian Fuenfhausen

Contents

Acknowledgments

This book was supposed to be short, more like an art-catalog essay than a decade-in-the-works scholarly tome. But the number of people I must thank already hints at just how successful my attempt at brevity was. Still, pausing to acknowledge those who have helped me realize this work gives me an opportunity also to admit that there would certainly be a lot more (mostly inadvertent) inaccuracies in *Narrowcast* had I not received so much assistance, encouragement, and practical information. Jimbo Blachly was near the origin of the project, as were the publishers Harry Blackett and Robin Kirkham of An Endless Supply in Birmingham, who in 2011 brought out a book of mine that pointed me in this direction. Since then, those colleagues, students, and friends who have contributed in various forms to this project include David Alworth, Tim Anderson, Kevin Attell, Jennifer Bartlett, Charles Bernstein, Art Blake, Andrea Brady, Brad Brown, Merritt Bucholz, Robert Byrd, Gerard Byrne, Una Chaudhuri, J. D. Connor, Jonathan Culler, Rhea Dall, J. Martin Daughtry, Patrick Deer, Steve Dibenedetto, Jeff Dolven, Stephen Duncombe, Lisa Gitelman, Ben Glaser, Phillip Brian Harper, George Hart, Lyn Hejinian, Fredric Jameson, Daniel Kane, Seth Kim-Cohen, Zane Koss, Shiv Kotecha, Joshua Kotin, Cynthia Lindlof, Zachary Lockman, Chelsie Malyszek, William Maxwell, Maureen McLane, John Melillo, Peter Middleton, Christopher Patrick Miller, Joe Milutis, Christine Mitchell, Anna Moser, Aryeh Neier, Tue Andersen Nexø, Peter Nicholls, Aldon Lynn Nielsen, Tomás Uraoyán Noel, Seth Perlow, Sonya Posmentier, Nate Preus, Anthony Reed, Dan Remein, Lisa Robertson, David Rothman, Sukhdev Sandhu, Robert Slifkin, Ada Smailbegovic, Kristen Tapson, Marvin Taylor, Simón Trujillo, Kazys Varnelis, Hayden White, Cameron Williams, Rachael Wilson, and Andrew Zuliani.

Quite a bit of *Narrowcast* draws on material from special collections, so I am grateful to a number of librarians: Amanda Watson and Kent Underwood from New York University; the whole staffs of the Avery Fisher media library and the Fales Special Collections at NYU; Elspeth Healey from University of Kansas Library; Bill O'Hanlon from Stanford University Library, Special Collections; Melissa Watterworth Batt from University of Connecticut, Storrs; Ross Mulcare from Harvard University Archives; Matthew C. Hanson and Herman Eberhardt from the Franklin D. Roosevelt Presidential Library; and Peter Hale from the Allen Ginsberg Project. I also thank Robert Morris and Renee Brown from the Castelli Gallery.

Infrastructural support from New York University has made this project much, much easier. It includes a Humanities Initiative Grant, a Global Research Institute Grant, and a Stein Grant, as well as support from my chairs, deans, and administrative staff. I am especially grateful to Thomas Augst, Ulrich Baer, Christopher Cannon, Georgiana Dopico-Black, Alyssa Leal, Taeesha Muhammad, Patricia Okoh-Esene, Jane Tylus, and Bennett Williams.

As the project has developed, I have received extremely helpful suggestions from the two anonymous readers for Stanford University Press and from my editor at Stanford, Emily-Jane Cohen, whose enthusiasm for this project had been crucial to its realization. I also thank Faith Wilson Stein at Stanford for her attention to details. I am indebted to my Post•45 series editors Kate Marshall and Loren Glass. And I want to single out Florence Dore from the Post•45 editorial group for her scrupulous, attentive, and challenging reading of the whole manuscript; the book's remaining faults are not for her lack of effort. Finally, I owe the greatest debt to Luca Clark-Shaw, Cosmo Clark-Shaw, and Emilie Clark.

Illustrations

Abbreviations

AB	Amiri Baraka, *The Autobiography of LeRoi Jones/Amiri Baraka*
BM	Amiri Baraka, *Black Music*
EC	Larry Eigner Papers, Thomas J. Dodd Research Center, University of Connecticut Library
EP	Larry Eigner, *The Collected Poems of Larry Eigner*
GG	Glenn Gould, *The Glenn Gould Reader*
H	Seymour Hersh, *The Price of Power*
JA	James Holzman, *James Jesus Angleton*
K	Niall Ferguson, *Kissinger 1923–1968*
MP	Charles Olson, *The Maximus Poems*
OC	Charles Olson Papers, University of Connecticut, Storrs

Narrowcast

Audio Research: A Theme Song

> listen to your present time tapes and you will begin to see who you are and
> what you are doing here mix yesterday in with today and hear tomorrow
> your future rising out of old recordings you are a programmed tape
> recorder set to record and play back
> —William S. Burroughs[1]

> our summer
> on the ground
>
> like last night another
> time
>
> in fragments
> —Larry Eigner[2]

Associated with the countercultural movements of the 1950s, and galvanized in
Donald M. Allen's 1960s anthology *The New American Poetry*, the body of writing that has come to be associated with the title of that book has been mislead-
ingly cast as committed, above all, to the thematization of spontaneity and the
mimetic depiction of everyday life. But New American poetry was, in large part,
a temporal project—though one that marshaled research and fieldwork from
anthropology, history, and what we might now call media studies to substantiate and extend its claims. These involved, in their most provocative instants,
the construction of a nonmonumental temporality like the fragmented time
proposed by Larry Eigner or the remixed time recommended by William S.
Burroughs with the aid of recording technology. Such new temporalities would
contest administered versions of national time—with its major events, shared
crises, and underlying narratives of progress. This normative time was, not surprisingly, the time of newspapers, magazines, television, and radio. It was, in
short, administered media time, a time that, as Burroughs put it, programmed
American subjects.

 Narrowcast is about the search for alternate temporalities that underlay
New American poets' engagement with tape recording and radio. In framing a
set of cassette tapes, LPs, and reel-to-reel recordings of poets within the post-

war mediascape, the history of poetics, the New Left, and state surveillance, the book is about the social life of tape and radio in the 1960s. But *Narrowcast* is also about critical and historical method. Through case studies of recordings by and of Allen Ginsberg, Larry Eigner, Charles Olson, Amiri Baraka, Glenn Gould, and R. Murray Schafer, this book reflects on the possibilities of audiotape as critical and historical evidence, the nature of context building in historical thinking, and the status and location of theoretical authority. At the literary critical or literary historical level, the argument is that tape recording within poetry should be understood neither (as poets themselves have sometimes proposed) as an efficient tool for generating textuality without the encumbrance of a typewriter, nor (as media theorists have often asserted) as a way of separating audio effects from the bodies in which they originate, nor again (as writers associated with recent experimental poetry have proposed) as a means of undoing the would-be foundational status of print by producing experiential singularities in performance.[3] Rather, in turning to the site-specific, often nonintentional and even nonhuman dimensions of tape recording, I frame a series of poet-generated audio works by the ways in which they engage with dominant American media—radio above all— paying particular attention to how these recordings contest radio's time and space: spatially its networks of news and advertising, its omnipresence and consequent suggestion of public relevance, common sense, and universality; temporally, its constitutive patterns of attention, its parceling of temporal units into both program lengths and into larger daily divisions (especially that between work and leisure), its construction of what counts (and demands a response) as a public event, and thus what drops below event-status into the condition of supposedly unremarkable ongoingness—a category, in fact, central to postwar poetics. But to mobilize this ongoingness as a real time of living and thinking, poets tended to use recording to insist on the specificity of a real *space* of enunciation—an environment that not only situated the speaker in a distinct location but also tended to interweave the speaker's sounds (including those nonintentional ones made by his body) with those of that environment.[4]

"Narrowcasting," then, is the term I use to designate this seemingly over-specific audio operation that, staged within the ostensibly boundless domains of recording and broadcasting, nonetheless insists almost perversely on grounding the speaker in a discrete space, often one that ambiguously merges body and environment. That the term "narrowcast" is, in everyday use, associated with niche marketing and "special interests" points to the normative evaluations I hope to question in my own recoding. Sketching the social and temporal dimensions of regimes of broadcast radio (from FDR's fireside chats to the emergence of FM radio in the 1960s) and to a lesser degree film (from the Luce corporation's the *March of Time* series, to spy thrillers from the 1970s), I take these poets' audio works not merely as offering critiques of normative national time but also as cultivating rich and various alternate temporalities whose implications I unpack in some detail. Yet some of the most compelling aspects of these poet-driven audio projects were not entirely embraced (or even, arguably, understood) by their makers and thus arrive to us in the present with something of an artifactual character, accounting for which, in turn, produces a few complications for the case studies that follow.

This book is organized by four connected senses of narrowcasting: the first, most obviously, is *spatial* and has to do with a conscious turn away from the would-be universal address of most media to the cultivation of a microclimate or countermedia space (a van, a porch, a kitchen table) in which the speaker's body in its sonic relation to its surrounding surfaces contests the nonsite of the media broadcasting studio. Here, narrowcasting involves the thematizing of an intimate, corporeal space that might ground media abstractions.

Second, hand in hand with this grounding operation is the *temporal* sense of narrowcasting that follows directly in these poets' works: the attempt to unplug from the national time of organized hours, days, weeks, months, years, decades, and centuries and their attendant attention patterns and reacquaint oneself with an immediate ongoingness not subject to the temporal parceling achieved by dominant media. Here the goal is not simply the familiar countercultural claim toward presence but the establishment of modes of duration that challenge the de facto temporal understanding and related production cycles effected by commercial and state media. This temporal sense of narrowcasting is not normally part of the word's semantic landscape. But I hope that, given what we will see and hear of the intimate ties between space and time in these poets' countermedia poetics, pursuing it as a corollary of spatial narrowcasting will ultimately make sense. It is in these two meanings of narrowcasting, spatial and temporal, that the poets I study perform research into the space and time of recording and broadcast media: its relation to bodies and sites, on the one hand; and to regimes of attention, social organization, control, on the other.

In the first chapter, on Ginsberg, narrowcasting is primarily spatial, and to the degree that it is temporal, time is in service of space; in the second chapter, on Eigner, the main concern is temporality, and the spatial narrowcasting that does happen (and here it is quite important) can be understood as supporting the poet's engagements with time. In the Olson and Baraka case studies, both models are in play. While the book's argument as a whole is more about temporal than spatial narrowcasting, the two modes must—I argue—be studied together because they inform and underlie one another. Bodies in Ginsberg, for example, must unplug from national time to claim the deinstrumentalized, nonviolent, erotic space proposed in his poetics; similarly, the finally temporal model of narrowcasting in Eigner emerges through close and persistent attention to a spatially limited frame—Eigner's porch and household, his street and neighborhood.

The third sense of narrowcasting transcends the threshold of intentionality and has to do with what I call an *artifactual* narrowcasting: by this I mean a tendency on the part of audiotape to embed within itself a series of abyssal gaps, noises, and registrations of contingent sound that challenge the medium's storage and retrieval protocols. What is *narrow* here is the literal tape its users would like to hear through to "voices" and "events" that would exist, as it were, on the other side, but that instead returns attention to its opaque, noisy sonic surface. But rather than understand this sonic noise merely as a failure or distraction, I will be listening, in what follows, for the ways this contingent bleed from the surrounding situation embeds revealing encrustations of period information onto the audio work.

Finally, within this umbrella of meanings is a *methodological* sense of narrowcasting whereby, in my own practices of reading and contextualization, I have sought to parallel my objects' adamant refusal to be subsumed by the dominant frames and hermeneutic modes of their moment. In response, I have tried to draw out how their own conceptual and theoretical models of corporeal space and ongoing temporality differed from those according to which the country was being run in the 1960s; moreover, I have also tried to avoid subsuming (even their resistance or radicality) within the ascendant theoretical models of my own moment. The suggestion here is that, in opening up method as well to a mode of narrowcasting, poets' tapes could themselves be understood as generators of theoretical propositions and not merely as passive cultural examples awaiting the conferral of authority typically granted by the discourses of philosophy, political theory, sociology, and so on.

Underlying this medial reframing of New American poetics is a proposition that poetry at a larger scale can be usefully understood as a mode of audio research—even if the sound studies frame that partly makes this possible only emerges in the 1970s and thus later than some of my case studies. But while sound studies, whose early years I consider in Chapter 4, may have lent terms and a degree of conceptual unity to a diverse array of practices that had previously been considered poetic or musical or technological, the site it came to inhabit, disciplinarily, was already one in which there was a great deal of overlap among these practices.

Poetry's relation to music, in particular, has been an area of intense and sustained concern. Let me therefore sketch two models of how this relationship might be conceived to set the stage for the third, quite different relationship between poetry and music pursued here. The most traditional and dominant account has it that the domain of sound, organized as music, provides the asymptote of excellence for the entire discipline of poetry, which always, as Walter Pater puts it, struggles "after the law or principle of music."[5] Narrative sequences, descriptive vignettes, even complex image patterns all give way, when this law or principle is in operation, to a reference-banishing play of sonic effects. However, when the earnest student of poetry tries to inquire further into this would-be basic law of her discipline (that it approach music) by asking how musicians and musicologists understand the essence of their discipline, she is in for disappointment. Though many musicians demonstrate interest in the most basic physical properties of their discipline—the physiology of sound—still they tend not to locate the transcendence of referentiality as the singular key to what they do. Far from it. Ethnomusicologists in particular simply could not operate without some, however attenuated, notion of reference. Even those musicians and music theorists most committed to the physiological dimensions of sound (we will name them, provisionally, the Deleuzians) still tend to describe the basic ontology of sound less as the kind of "law or principle" Pater had in mind than as a process. So poetry critics may be somewhat surprised, if not dismayed, to learn that, when asked to characterize the least referential, most Paterian moments of this process, musicians tend to wheel out the word: . . . poetic. Just as poetry's off-screen scene of transcendence gets mapped by the term "music," so music's Edenic nonrepresentational space tends, most commonly, to be evoked by a special power ostensibly lurking in the word from that other discipline, "poetry." What then to make of this reciprocal displacement operating at the would-be cores of these two disciplines? Self-loathing? Grass-is-always-greener syndrome? The embarrassed need for transcendence to occur while slumming in the unfamiliar territory of another discipline?

An alternate account of the period roughly from William Wordsworth to William Carlos Williams might see poets not so much as aspiring to the condition of music but rather behaving, at least in one way, very much *like* musicians. These poets, and their musical peers, were both sound collectors and audio researchers. Both were engaged in a process of roughening cosmopolitan hearing practices by a special kind of fieldwork that involved discovering, arranging, and presenting new sounds. Both challenged dominant cosmopolitan sounds by the provocative introduction of folk, regional, somehow marginalized, or previously uncelebrated aural archives. These new sounds could play nicely with the rest of the authorized acoustical standbys and thereby win audiences over politely to their plausibility as music or poetry, or they could be included in intentionally jarring ways—like two marching bands moving in opposite directions. Since Béla Bartók and Charles Ives and indeed since most strains of late nineteenth- and early twentieth-century musical modernism, the composer's role has often been that, first, of a sound collector, and, second, of advocate for the unheard or sonically underappreciated.

But while these earlier more classically ethnographic musicians and poets turned their ears outward toward direct encounters with folk traditions, rural idiolects, indigenous musical traditions, and so on, the poets in *Narrowcast* listen, instead, to how the outside world comes into the enclosures where they live and work. The attention they bring to this media saturation may at first seem casual or occasional and unconnected to what we normally think of as research. I hope, though, to build a case to the contrary: first, at a large scale, by sketching how much of the New American poetry can be understood as sharing a temporal project; and second, by drawing out how this pursuit of nonmonumental temporality extended crucially to media time in the poets I study here. If sociologists of science can perform "fieldwork" in neuroendocrinology laboratories, surely poets can turn a defamiliarizing ear to the sound-making devices in their immediate environments, studying not just the content and structure of these messages but also how these sounds interact with those made by their refrigerators, creaking furniture, relatives, wind, and the wheezing or gurgling of their own bodies. But these poets' goal was not primarily to make art from this contingency, as it often was, for instance, with more urban-oriented composers like John Cage and Pierre Schaeffer, who also, of course, worked extensively with tape recording. Rather, the poets in *Narrowcast* want to study the porosity of their own spaces: the ways their atmospheres could be at times overcoded by temporal, ideological, commercial signals from the outside. Though not programmatic or always even systematic, the poets in this book often used tape recording to perform research into, and develop critiques of, the media apparatus of radio itself: its time, its space, its hail, its logic, its common sense. Like traditional ethnography, the research in *Narrowcast* usually involves inquiry into discrete spaces. These, however, are not conceived as microcosms of cultures or regions but as points of contact with larger media networks, nodes on infrastructural maps whose analysis brings to light new ways of thinking about the social, spatial, and temporal dimensions of media grids.

But *Narrowcast*'s story is not only about the ways countercultural poets took up commercial and state media, about how the experimental spaces and temporalities of their poems contested widely broadcast models for feeling oneself as part of the space and time of the nation. In the course of gathering my materials (as the historians say), I became fascinated and disturbed by something for which I had not been looking: many of the New Left poets I was studying were *themselves* objects of state audio surveillance, often by the same portable reel-to-reel tape recorders whose liberatory potential they celebrated. This tension between sonic exploration and surveillance began to appear, increasingly, as a key aspect of the larger social life of tape recording in the 1960s. Adjusting my research plans to this unexpected contingency, I began to dip into the literatures of the Federal Bureau of Investigation (FBI, the Bureau) and the Central Intelligence Agency (CIA, the Agency).

Though this provided a more detailed picture of the state's attempts to control the New Left and contained occasional, enticing references to poets, as a whole this research appeared initially as a layer of popular history that might operate as the kind of inert cultural backdrop or normative model of "context" I hoped to avoid: the ham-fisted Bureau and Agency readers lost as they encountered the demanding cultural domain of experimental poetry, seeking (and failing) to turn it into so much thematic political content as

they invaded privacy and disrupted lives. Gradually, however, this simpli-
fied polarity began to collapse from within, in part with the help of James
Holzman's biography of James Jesus Angleton, chief of counterintelligence at
the CIA. The Angleton case provided a different picture of CIA interpretation, one with intimate ties to midcentury literary theory, and to poetry more
broadly, since Angleton was (among his many other ties to poetry) editor of a
magazine, *Furioso,* that published not just conservative modernists like Ezra
Pound, T. S. Eliot, and John Crowe Ransom but also figures like Williams,
Lorine Niedecker, and even Pablo Neruda. As I traced Angleton and his associates from their English educations at Yale through their work on the New Left
at the Agency, what became clear was not just that their literary educations
and ties to poets peeked through at discrete moments, as in the case of what
Holzman calls "pattern recognition," but that more fundamentally what the
CIA was doing when it was developing its research dossiers involved a mode
of literary-inflected historiography comparable to that undertaken by most
of us in the profession and, indeed, in this book as well.[6] But if the state, too,
was engaged in audio research, and if its historiography deserved comparison
with that of the poets and their critics, now the restricted scale of address and
distribution, generated by the illegality of these activities, was associated with
a symptomatic form of secrecy one would hardly want to include within the
umbrella of seemingly progressive narrowcasting operations. Yet the Bureau
and the Agency versions of narrowcasting, ghosting and in a sense parodying
that of the poets, is an inescapable component of what follows.

Nor did Agency operatives always neglect to theorize their work. We thus
encounter this second cast of characters (which includes canonical figures in
the history of surveillance like J. Edgar Hoover and Henry Kissinger as well
as lesser-known operatives like William R. Johnson and Sherman Kent) not
merely as practitioners of audio surveillance but also as its methodological
exegetes and research program directors. Though it is necessary at times to
extract theoretical propositions from practices (the Agency and the Bureau
often not wishing to commit their best thoughts to paper), still it is possible
to gather a rich body of thinking from this domain. The fact that *Narrowcast*
takes this corpus of theory seriously, as it does the poetics theory of the poets
I consider throughout, is an extension of its commitment to a methodological
form of narrowcasting: to position literary and cultural artifacts as generators of conceptual models on par with those provided by philosophy, soci-

ology, political theory, and other disciplines more typically used to anoint lowly literature with their prestige. *Narrowcast* practices a more horizontal model of theorization in which literary and historical texts are often reverse-engineered as articulations of conceptual models no less authoritative than those offered by the theoretical or philosophical discourses they frequently merely illustrate; the result, I hope, is that when historical and literary texts meet official theory in these pages, they tend to converse rather than simply instantiate and that this new kind of dialogue might lead to unexpected avenues of thought. Meanwhile, recognized theorists in these pages are often encountered not merely as disembodied fonts of authoritative model making but also as concrete characters acting within discrete layers of the historical narrative unfolded. The suggestion is not the journalistic one that isolated snapshots of theorists' lives will simply reveal the causal sources of their theories (usually of course to discredit them), but that attempting to imagine these intellectuals in concrete situations might open up new possible relationships with their thinking.

In Chapter 1, for instance, my models of lyric poetry, research hypotheses, evidence, intentionality, and tape recording's social power come equally from John Stuart Mill, the New Critics, and Fredric Jameson, on the one hand; and from Angleton, William Johnson, William S. Burroughs, J. Edgar Hoover, and his Counterintelligence Program (COINTELPRO) operatives, on the other; or others. These somewhat various authorities help us contend with the works and surveillance cases of Allen Ginsberg and LeRoi Jones (Amiri Baraka). My interest in rethinking the status of theory extends also into the domain of poetics where we have, for too long, tended to read various individual figures as simple exemplars of the most canonical theoretical statements of the movements to which they have been assigned: Charles Olson's "Projective Verse" essay for all poets grouped within the "Black Mountain" section of the Allen anthology (or indeed any open field poetics); Ron Silliman's "The New Sentence" for the entirety of Language writing; Amiri Baraka's "Black Art" for the Black Arts movement; Allen Ginsberg's "First Thought, Best Thought," for a Beat poetics; and so on. Meanwhile, poetry critics have tended to assume that if a group does not have a canonical statement of poetics, then its work simply has no theoretical implications: despite some half-hearted attempts to make O'Hara's "Personism" play this role, such has largely been the case for studies of the New York school. Thus, when I turn to the writings of Larry

Eigner in Chapter 2, I seek to distinguish his own quite remarkable poetics both from Olson's model of open field poetry and equally from the appropriations of Eigner undertaken by Allen Ginsberg and Ron Silliman, Beat and Language oriented, respectively.

My attempt to explore the gaps and discontinuities between literary texts and theoretical models (be they philosophical, theoretical, or from the domain of poetics) is not based on the belief that one can simply forget the larger theoretical contexts that have framed reception histories and approach literary works through pure induction. For Fredric Jameson, in a moment near the beginning of *The Political Unconscious*, these theoretical contexts simply *are* the content and context of our reading: "We never really confront a text immediately, in all its freshness as a thing-in-itself. Rather, texts come before us as the always-already-read; we apprehend them through sedimented layers of previous interpretations, or—if the text is brand-new—through the sedimented reading habits and categories developed by those inherited traditions." Thus, what we do, in an operation Jameson names "metacommentary," is map one of these layers, methodologically, against another: "Our object of study is less the text itself than the interpretations through which we attempt to confront and appropriate it."[7] *Narrowcast*, too, is concerned with recoding, and thus offering a metacommentary on, a string of methodological and historical precedents. But a key part of this recoding emerges, nonetheless, by turning to the audio works "themselves"—which, as primary texts, are among those mysterious objects Jameson sees as "always-already" having vanished beyond the realm of accessibility. If one can agree with Jameson that reception histories and the larger critical terrain they drag with them belie the notion of reading as a tabula rasa, one might wonder, nonetheless, why these histories must always neatly *contain* the literary object—why, that is, none of a text or a recording's hitherto unconsidered terms or features might be marshaled as part of a new, more powerful metacommentary. We might then ask why the particularities of texts seem never to trouble, and thereby extend, our theoretical models themselves. The belief that description can have more intimate ties to theorization was one reason for my turning to materials—audiotapes—that exist in a netherworld even of description and almost entirely without theorization.[8]

It's not, however, that critics of contemporary poetry have completely ignored recordings. In fact, arguments based on recordings have been increasingly common in the poetry criticism of the last twenty years. Michael Davidson, for instance, in one chapter of his *Ghostlier Demarcation* (1997) both sketches a technological and social history of poets' use of tape recording and develops a series of generative theoretical arguments about why attending to that history might allow us to read postwar poets' recordings against the same poets' claims about unmediated presence.[9] Six years later, Daniel Kane made excellent use of recordings in his history of the emergence of the poetry scene in the Lower East Side in New York (2003).[10] More recently (2014), Tomás Uraoyán Noel makes the analysis of both video and audio recordings fundamental to his account of the rise of the Nuyorican scene in New York City.[11] The increasing centrality of recording to the arguments of these three books (and many others could be cited) points not only to a growing interest in performance and the reading more generally as objects of study but also to our wider and more immediate access to digital archives of such recordings.

The largest, most important archive of poet recordings, PennSound (coedited by Al Filreis and Charles Bernstein), was launched in January 2005. As the site has expanded in its holdings and postings and begun to lodge itself on syllabi and at key junctures in recent debates about poetry, PennSound has done something more than make critics and historians of poetry aware of readings and recordings more broadly as objects of study. Its very existence has pressed the question of just what this awareness might mean for our understanding of poetry, for our attempts to think it historically and theoretically. We can thus trace a kind of tipping point even within the brief genealogy of poetry criticism I've just sketched: over the last few years recordings have, in some instances, stopped offering new windows onto what are finally readings of texts and become instead primary objects of study in themselves, so Uraoyán Noel's account of the Nuyorican scene, for instance, tends to be *about* recorded performances as events rather than as instantiations of more authoritative, prior texts. From the perspective of methodology, this is not a simple improvement. But it is a development worthy of more attention than it has so far received, especially inasmuch as it presents a series of difficult questions about what and how poetry critics study and about where they locate this study in culture and history.

Consider, for instance, Raphael Allison's *Bodies on the Line: Performance and the Sixties Poetry Reading* (2014), a book that not only takes up recordings of three poets studied here (Ginsberg, Olson, and Eigner) but also understands these recordings *themselves* as its central scholarly objects. If my own earlier sketch would seem to confirm Allison's claim that "poetry in performance has moved from the periphery of mainstream interest toward its center," we remain in need, nonetheless, of more theoretical attention to what happens when recordings vie for central attention within the discipline.[12] Happily, Allison offers some. For him, recorded poetry complicates distinctions between rhetorics of presence or immediacy and modes of distance or disaffection, between the earnest desire to emote traditionally associated with poetry and the more analytical drive to inquire into the conventions and bases of such claims to the successful transfer of feeling. The surprising insight of his study, however, is that he does *not* simply attribute the emotive position to Confessional poets and Beats, and the latter to cooler avant-gardists like John Ashbery. Rather, with a nod to deconstruction, Allison teases out a not-quite-controllable dynamic between these poles in *all* the readings he studies. While Ginsberg, for instance, may emphasize "authenticity and the power of physical presence of body and voice," nonetheless Allison helps us hear a "skeptical counterforce . . . audible in the Dharma Lion himself."[13]

Rare within this widespread turn to recording, Allison's two-pole model of presence and skepticism suggests a larger interpretive matrix that transcends the individual case study. The specific terms of Allison's model, in its attention to the slippery relation between claims about presence and modes of addressing, enacting, or simply being subject to technological mediation, could be understood to amplify and elaborate Davidson's brief argument about tape recording in *Ghostlier Demarcations*, which, though the book as a whole is only partly about recording, nonetheless pioneered ground by outlining something very close to this dialectic of technology in New American poetry. Though Peter Middleton's writing on the history of the poetry reading is also only partly on recording, it too deserves mention in this context as a rare work that offers theoretical propositions about what critics might do with the expanding archive of recorded poetry. Rather than understand poets simply as poor performers who always tap on their mikes, produce feedback, and read without the dramatic consistency of stage actors, Middleton suggests that "the hissing background is a constant reminder that readers and audience have taken hold of a space defined by the dominant culture" and thus that the poetry reading itself is a kind of ritual misuse of that space, and its sound equipment, that thematizes the tenuous social existence of poetry and its cultures.[14] Like Davidson, Middleton evocatively traces a set of dynamics between the internal mechanism of the reading or the recording and a larger cultural or social situation. Pushing further on this line of relating the micro-scene of the recording to the macro network of social life, *Narrowcast* explores an expanded set of contexts in which recorded poetry is seen to operate. Foregrounding questions of methodology, and keeping open the problem of where (not just what) recorded poetry means, this book also rejects the familiar cultural studies move of disciplining our never-quite-defeated formalism by minimizing the literary object, thereby pushing us (supposedly) into the domain of the social. Rather, I seek to dive in more intensely to the aesthetic dimension of poetry recording, only to discover—right there—the outside social and historical world.

"Genuine interpretation directs the attention back to history itself, and to the historical situation of the commentator as well as of the work," says Jameson in his early essay "Metacommentary."[15] In *Narrowcast*, recording *literalizes* this process of metacommentary, embedding within itself (often unintentionally or as a distracting "mistake") information about both "history itself" and "the historical situation of the commentator": the hum of his car engine or the squeal of his tires on the highway; the creaking of furniture or the buzz of a refrigerator, which might swoop up periodically and swamp the enunciation of words, presenting problems both for the poet himself and for his listeners from the Bureau and the Agency. This artifactual narrowcasting, which transcends the intentionality associated with spatial and temporal modes, nominates tape as a special object of historical study, wherein the "problems" associated with the audio work are also openings to the social world beyond it, next to it, or, in a sense, *inside* it.

The four chapters that follow present experimental case studies in framing or situating poets' recordings, one of which begins or organizes the process in each case: the Uher reel-to-reel tape Allen Ginsberg generated, driving across the country in a VW van in 1965 and 1966 for his book *The Fall of America*; the Nagra reel-to-reel recording Barry Miles made in 1969 of Charles Olson in the latter's apartment in Gloucester, Massachusetts, which would, after editing, become the Folkways LP *Charles Olson Reads from the Maximus Poems IV, V, VI* (released in 1975); the stereo recording made by Amiri Baraka and several musicians in Harlem in 1972 that would become, that same year, the LP *It's Nation Time*; and the cassette tape of Larry Eigner recorded by the German S Press in 1974 and released the following year as *around new / sound daily / means*. But to describe or contextualize these literal recordings, to place them, first, merely within these poets' oeuvres, I had to expand my context to include not only other recordings made by or of the poets but also the negative datum against which these recordings were conceptualized: radio for Ginsberg and Eigner; mainstream poetry and music LPs for Olson and Baraka, but equally air-raid sirens, Broadway musicals, and other radio and film productions associated with the Office of War Information (OWI). Yet these poet audio recordings, as I try to demonstrate, could also be heard as evidence within a range of larger contexts: from state surveillance and defense infrastructure, on the one hand, to New Left critiques of both, on the other.

Underneath the question of what kind of evidence recorded poetry might provide is the larger question of *where*, in what context, we might hear these recordings proving their points. Again, I linger on these problems not because I think they should or can be settled definitively but because, at this early moment in our inundation in recorded poetry, it may be worth pressing pause for a moment to conceptualize just how we hope to navigate this new landscape. Unlike the single printed poem, which has had (until recently) a long life at the center of literary study, the poetry recording is not encrusted, as Jameson would have it, with layer upon layer of critical methodology. Yet its comparative "newness" as an object of study, its inability to provide a geological cross section of our discipline's methods, should not fool us into hearing it as self-evident.

The collection that has arguably done the most to turn attention to the interpretation of poets' recordings is the 1998 *Close Listening: Poetry and the Performed Word*, edited by Charles Bernstein. In the introduction, Bernstein proposes a number of frames and terms that might still organize further work on audio archives. Pointing to the poetry reading as a public staging of invented rather than established poetic forms, Bernstein proposes that because poets use "sound patterns" that are "*made up . . . the poetry reading is a public tuning.*"[16] He does not elaborate on the social or philosophical dimensions of this operation, but presumably it involves not simply the poet testing and adjusting her forms to meet an acceptable frequency but rather a set of reciprocal moves from audience to poet, and vice versa. In any case, this process by which a poet and a social formation adjust to one another suggests a link to Émile Benveniste's concept of "rhythm," a term whose history evokes the social dimensions of temporal measure at the heart of this book. In a remarkable article, Benveniste calls rhythm the "vast unification of man and nature under time, with its intervals and repetitions," before using a vertiginous etymological path to trace the term back, before its naturalization via Plato as the regularized movements of dance and music, to its pre-Socratic, atomist meaning of "form as improvised, momentary, changeable."[17] Only after Plato's transformation of the term was it "determined by a 'measure' and numerically regulated."[18] Benveniste's excavation of a singularity lurking in the would-be regularity that goes by the name of rhythm was claimed by the poststructuralists. It serves equally to focalize a key feature of the Language writers' turn to performance. "To speak of the poem in performance is," Bernstein argues, "to overthrow the idea of the poem as a fixed, stable, finite linguistic object; it is to deny the poem its self-presence and its unity." To pursue this unsettling of self-presence and unity, Bernstein enlists Jerome McGann's textual condition for performance, characterizing the reading as "a space of authorial resistance to textual authority."[19] Here, then, is how Bernstein puts this basic paradox of the reading:

> For in realizing, by supplementing, the semantic possibilities of the poem in a reading, the poet encourages readers to perform the poem on their own, a performance that is allowed greater latitude depending on how reading-centered the poem is— that is, how much the poem allows for the active-participation of the reader (in both senses) in the constitution of the poem's meaning.[20]

For those familiar with the Barthian model of the reader's coproduction of meaning by which some members the group framed their early practice, this might seem like the representative critical gesture of Language writing—now extended to the live scene of the reading.[21] As such, the poem in performance gets understood "not as a secondary extension of 'prior' written texts but as its own medium" in which "sound registers the sheer physicality of language." What listeners do, then, at poetry readings is "find the sound in the words, not in any extrinsic scenario or supplemental accompaniment." This "rematerializes language, [returning] it from 'speech' back to 'sound.'" In its foregrounding of sound and not speech, the poetry reading can touch "on the essence of the medium."[22] Whatever one makes of Bernstein's somewhat high-modernist suggestion that a medium like poetry might have a singular essence, his proposition that "sound, like poetry 'itself,' can never be completely recuperated as ideas, as content, as narrative, as extralexical meaning" remains one of the central challenges for anyone writing about sound in poetry.[23] The question for me is what one makes of this excess, this nonidentity.

While the excessive and disruptive dimensions of sound are a concern throughout, they do not—contra Bernstein—serve as an organizing goal, an experience of the essence of the medium, or even primarily as a way to undo textual authority. In offering instead four experimental case studies that all in different ways concern how poetry's recorded sound exceeds its more established semantic terrains, I suggest, perhaps paradoxically, that it is the impossibility of cleaning sound up into a pure registration of speech, into a frictionless idea, that allows tape recording to engage with dominant media's regimes of space and time. The poets I study, too, might often have associated this dimension of recorded speech with "artifactual" distortions. However, these could not simply be set aside from the presentation of corporality, intimate space, and ongoingness central to their recordings. By proposing that avant-garde poetry offered alternate modes of spatial and temporal measure, I am pushing back against a long-standing tendency to understand such writing primarily in terms of its negations: of linguistic transparency, of centered subjectivity, of identity. Certainly such negations have been crucial to avant-garde poetry over the course of the twentieth century. But the proposition that poetry exhausts itself in these powerful gestures of undoing seems increasingly unsatisfying and incomplete as an account of poetry's actual intellectual and social functions. And it is for this reason that I emphasize the spatial and temporal modes of contestation associated with postwar poetry, with its intimate scale, on the one hand, and its cultivation of ongoingness, on the other.

In one sense, attention to ongoingness represents a turn to genre against history—to take an opposition between two art historical modes of representation.[24] In traditional art historical discourse, genre paintings are often taken to represent mere empirical observation of readily available objects, while history paintings, if open to the charge of invention and fantasy, nonetheless show us grand subject matter, singular occurrences to which we are still indebted. But underneath this familiar opposition is the possibility that genre painting, like what we might call genre poetry, is actually concerned with the underlying conditions of our access to temporal experience, the groundwork for what we (most often mistakenly) think of as discrete events. Attention to this underlying continuum extends at least back to the work of Jacob Burckhardt, who turned away from "all mere 'events' in the past" to a synchronic mode of cultural history.[25] Such an orientation keyed itself more directly to daily life, however, in the twentieth century in the works of the French Annales school, especially in the writings of Fernand Braudel, who, at roughly the same moment as the poets in this study, turned to the longue durée and daily life as ways to contest the naturalized understanding of history as a matter of discrete events, especially wars and treaties. So a genre poetry worth taking seriously would not be simply about quaint verbal sketches of floral arrangements or piles of dead game but about, again, the conditions of our access to temporal experience, to a nonmonumental temporality. While fully elaborating a model of genre poetry is beyond my scope here, the possibility that genre might represent a critique of normative history, not merely a capitulation to less ambitious, always available subject matter, will, nonetheless, help me at crucial points account for the status of historical thinking in the poets in *Narrowcast*—especially among poets who might seem firmly committed to "history" *as opposed to genre.*

Indeed, this model of genre poetry as a cultivation of ongoingness might seem to explain Larry Eigner best but leave questions for the other, more explicitly activist New Left poets who would all in various ways seem to be engaged with a historical poetics committed to discrete countercultural events: marches, teach-ins, demonstrations, debates, and outright revolutions. And yet, despite interest in the transformative event, we hear in these writers' audio works sustained imaginative involvements with underlying conditions of experience and models of ongoingness that complicate the simple elevation of the event as the preferred state. With Olson, for instance, one needs the qualification that his avowedly "historical" poetics itself, his pursuit of alternative genealogies through experimental research, was, as we will hear, approached as a *real-time* research activity to be documented textually and, indeed, aurally in his recordings. As it slowed down into an extended time of process, historical thinking became for Olson a kind of genre activity, documented in durational form. Similarly, for all the Ginsberg lore generated by his being declared "King of May" in 1965 in Prague by students critical of the Czechoslovakian state, his focalizing presence at the anti–Vietnam War protests in Berkeley that October or his close collaboration with the Yippies during the Democratic Convention in Chicago in 1968, Chapter 1 uncovers how his presence at events (including his eventlike readings) was designed less to catalyze actions than to demilitarize would-be actors, to return them to a pre-event time of the body before it has been galvanized into a violent tool: indeed, at all three of these events the chanting of Indian mantras was central to Ginsberg's "intervention." The rub might seem to be Baraka: while it's indisputable that Baraka is interested in "historical" events of the first order—a Black Nationalist revolution that involves property changing hands—what I uncover in his audio archive is, nevertheless, a tension between the discrete cut of history and the ongoing sense of lived existence. We find the latter, perhaps surprisingly, in Baraka's understanding of John Coltrane, who forms the basis for his Black Nationalist audio aesthetics. The Coltrane of ongoingness points to a whole, continuous mode of life, not merely a discrete revolutionary event; this is also associated with "genre" music—the fallen, middle-class domain of "My Favorite Things" before it's been appropriated, the "rococo cocktail music" that will become the occasion for Coltrane's bravura intervention.[26] Even in arguing for historical events, Baraka grounded his claims in a surprising and largely unrecognized world of ongoing conditions.

The very fact that poets' recordings lack long critical histories, agreed-upon evidentiary status and sedimented levels of methodology suggests that the scene of description, the basic operation of characterization and subsequent contextualization, remains primary. It was in part this very problem that drew me to poets' recordings: one must describe them (and develop arguments from these descriptions) without layer upon layer of precedents. Perhaps tape recordings are, in this sense, a testing ground for method. This intuition buttressed my sense that narrowcasting was a methodological concern as well as a thematic one. But if problems of description meet us the moment we begin to make arguments about tape recording, seen in relation to texts, this is finally a matter of degree, not kind. Indeed, description in literary studies more broadly cannot ever quite be banished from argumentation, even among those critics operating at vast scales or on abstract, conceptual problems. Still, the more we narrow down to individual texts, the more inescapable this problem appears. There, at the level of the single text, description remains most immediately visible as a methodological question, since it provides the primary ground of appropriation and recoding, the most granular level at which the literary work will be understood as a series of features and patterns that allow for the larger scale of context making, theoretical reframing. To build a context for a work of literature, then, is not merely

to appeal to some rhetoric of immanence by which the latent story of its participation in history is rendered explicit. It is rather—as the metahistorians
have long insisted—to select some (and not others) of its features so that the
newly described work can be placed within one of many possible narratives in
which it might serve as an example or an event: "The same event can serve as a
different kind of element of many different historical stories," Hayden White
reminds us, "depending on the role it is assigned in a specific motific characterization of the set to which it belongs."[27] But while we have had a (surprisingly widely ignored) discourse on the contingency of historical narratives
since at least Hayden White, if not since Carl Becker and Friedrich Nietzsche,
perhaps the new surplus of historical evidence that has come with digitization
will finally force us to confront this underlying methodological problem more
directly.

Even twenty-five years ago research was a fundamentally different enterprise. When I began working on Frank O'Hara in the early 1990s, for instance,
I pursued his thicket of referentiality mostly by reading period books, magazines, and letters—archival and printed. I consulted a few reference works and
sometimes spoke to people who had been in or near O'Hara's scene. While in
the later phases I began to use the Internet, the intellectual terrain of the study
had by then been established, and, moreover, the web resources to which I had
access then were far less robust and various than they are now. Somewhat out-
landish comparisons and contextualizations could still emerge in that leaner
climate of evidence, but they were fewer and farther between, and deciding
on one represented more of a commitment, since following it through to the
point at which it might become persuasive would simply involve more work.
If the threshold of persuasiveness remains daunting in our current moment,
this is for slightly different reasons: while the evidence itself will be comparatively easier to assemble, this very fact itself will now—or should now, I'm
arguing—alert us to the *number* of possible narratives that *might* have been
assembled and therefore to the question of why *this* narrative, of all those
available, was selected and pursued. It is thus surprising and disheartening
how frequently one still hears the old justification that an article or book has
been undertaken simply because the story it presents hasn't yet been told.
Whether the new narratives reframe known cultural entities by appealing to
unexpected contexts, redress questionable omissions by bringing off-screen
characters or events into focus, participate in the historiographic revolution

whereby concepts that had traditionally been held as timeless can be shown to have surprisingly concrete histories or perform some other intellectual operation altogether, the surplus of historical evidence with which we are now deluged calls on us, more than before, to articulate the values and theoretical implications of the necessarily contingent critical narrative we have selected. The alternative is that bad infinity of pluralism that masquerades everywhere as freedom.

Accordingly, let me announce at the outset that *Narrowcast* narrates but one of many possible histories of the analog precursors to our generalized digital surveillance culture—here, a history told through a small collection of detailed case studies centered on tape recording's stranger roles in postwar American poetry and society. While there are thousands of other recordings I might have selected, I have opted for depth over comprehensiveness, theory and method over documentary history, in order to draw out a series of problems I found myself gravitating toward in the course of researching the book: those of tape's status as evidence, its position within competing regimes of research, its relation to empirical spaces, its odd tendency to level humans with the environments it registers. My hope is that my specific attention to these theoretical and historiographic problems will be more generative than a wider documentary history of tape recording within poetry.

But a characterization like this one suggests that my method and objects of study were planned in advance and remained consistent throughout, when that is not the case. In fact, while listening to these poets' recordings, tracking them in relation to print, and following both audio and text into an array of sites within postwar American culture and politics, I allowed myself to be "distracted" by the fact that Allen Ginsberg had also been an *object* of tape recording, that he and his friends in the New Left had been under surveillance. This brought me to the work of James Jesus Angleton, Henry Kissinger, Sherman Kent, and William Johnson. State surveillance seemed worth pursuing at first because it offered an odd and unfamiliar counterweight to the would-be heroic narrative of countercultural audio works. But it soon became clear that the state (as a defense and war infrastructure, as a publisher, as a spying machine) was not simply a counterweight: Olson and Baraka, for instance, *worked* for the Office of War Information and Strategic Air Command (SAC), respectively; in deciphering tape recordings, the state's researchers confronted the same artifactual problems poets did; and perhaps most important of all, the problems state literary critics confronted in organizing and narrativizing their research were, finally, also problems of literary historiography, of method and theory. Before long, I found the state's theorists of method speaking both to the canon of reflexive historiography (Hayden White, Fredric Jameson, and others) and to the methodological questions *that were driving my own book.*

As Hoover and Kissinger, for instance, generated vast archives of compromising audio evidence, they parted ways with a more traditional model of scholarship wherein hypotheses (ultimately about a critical narrative that might be told) lead to research designed to substantiate those hypotheses—a model we see manifested, in Chapter 1, in the historiographic writings of CIA operative and Yale history professor Sherman Kent. For Kissinger and Hoover, unlike Kent, any number of narratives might occur involving the accumulation of power by a figure considered a threat or the shift of friend to foe; the point was to be prepared for these contingencies by having a preexisting audio archive that might be mobilized to pacify, threaten, or take down a new adversary. Obviously this research was used for unethical ends; yet the narratological shift it embodies (from a hypothesis and substantiation model to an allover evidence collection model that awaits its final narrative form) should not be simply dismissed because of this. Indeed, sophisticated scholars the world over will know this latter model from their own research. They will know that, as Carl Becker said in the 1930s, historical facts come to life only when they have been situated within a narrative frame.[28] And thus it was a particularly traumatic moment in the history of audio research when the Nixon administration's own archive of compromising facts (including self-compromising ones) was rendered public, narrativized, that is, against its keepers. It was, then, in coming to see Nixon, Hoover, Angleton, and Kissinger as audio researchers and keepers of archives that I began to understand their relation to the poets on whom they spied as more than that of an inert, though hostile, backdrop.

So I began to think these scales, contexts, and politics of audio research in relation to one another: the US state and the New Left poets. Rather than present the state's audio research as separate from that of poets' at the level of method and structure, *Narrowcast* explores the ways that *both* were drawn into operating in contexts below the threshold of the public: while the state could, of course, address "the public" directly or indirectly via television, film, radio, and print, Bureau and Agency researchers *needed* to separate themselves from public channels—both because what they were doing was secret and, more important, because it was often illegal. Therefore, as the poets pulled back from a wider concept of a universal or national audience, they were not simply separating themselves from the state.

One problem I confronted early on was the asymmetrical power dynamic in this relationship. I felt called upon to answer the objection that it was fine for the poets to play around with tape recorders but that what my own research suggested finally was how ironic it was that poets would see tape recording as a tool of contestation when its *real* political meaning was precisely that of their own subjection to it via state surveillance. Despite what literature's deluded makers wanted or thought—this line of objection seemed to go— the final political significance of their actions could be understood only by appealing to the larger system in which their work operates and that controls them. As much as I wanted to think totality, this was not what that operation meant for me: there were odd points of *agreement* between the state and the poets at some moments, including on some refined points of interpretation and theory, and then other moments in which the state pluralized itself into a frightening array of discrepant practices; meanwhile, poets took up a range of relationships to state power that could not simply be summarized and contained by a single model. The relationship, in short, was not entirely top down.

One strategy for bringing this strange dynamic out was to explore the state's various and semi-discrete attitudes, its discrepant methods and shifting faces: some of the agents gathering audio surveillance via tape believed that the entire counterculture was a construction of the KGB; others struggled to convince their research supervisors of the authenticity of the New Left. When *some* state operatives ran into walls with their research, they shifted modes by turning from monographic surveillance (work devoted to individual figures) to sociological scholarship designed to characterize larger swaths of the population; when *other* sections of the state's research team got frustrated by its inability to discover the audio proof of culpability they wanted, they responded by planting evidence and even carrying out the crimes that would justify the repression they hoped to enact in the first place. At times the state looks very much like James Angleton, J. Edgar Hoover, or Henry Kissinger. More surprisingly, it also looks like Charles Olson and LeRoi Jones—during their work for the OWI or the air force. At other times, however, the state recedes beyond the anonymity of blocked-out documents in the

CIA archives; it eludes biographical organization, becoming the anonymous agent who monitored the recording at such and such a location or the one who wrote up this report for distribution on this or that date. Throughout its various manifestations, the state is more than an abstract or uniform force of repression. Tracking how it acted concretely through (and as) humans, helps us, I hope, to understand the contexts of poets acting in response: not simply to audio surveillance but to the larger politics of state-supported audio recording and broadcast via radio and the way that radio managed opinion, and time more generally.

But why present the comparatively minor medium of radio as the primary negative context for the tape works I discuss when, arguably, it is far more pervasive and insidious television against which a New Left countermedia poetics would want to define itself? My answer is that I'm studying poets' relations to radio because they had *access* to it as producers (not merely consumers), and they were often linked up (made aware of one another) by radio in ways that were largely impossible with television. The argument is thus not that, during the 1960s and 1970s, radio's social significance eclipsed that of television but that if we want to understand how these poets invented new modes of temporal organization, their involvement with radio gives us a far more concrete context for doing so.

Rejecting the fake universality underlying many conceptions of "the public," the writings and recordings addressed in *Narrowcast* achieve their traction against the public domain created by dominant radio programming and commercial recording in large part by insisting on overspecificity. This is one main sense of their narrowness: Olson's recording of his furniture, bodily noises, and the real-time duration of his research; Eigner's thirty-year daily reports on audio occurrences along his block in Swampscott, Massachusetts; Baraka's sonically actualized counternation of African Americans that uncouples itself from the nation proper. And while Ginsberg might seem to present something of an exception, inasmuch as his poetry and image did circulate widely within the media, he too was capable of a similar strategy. Indeed, we consider a project—*The Fall of America*—that pits the personal recording studio of his VW van precisely against this larger media apparatus, insisting, like the other poets in *Narrowcast*, that sonic features of this immediate site, the van and the bodies in it, be used as a grounding and corporealizing resource that might trouble what Ginsberg perceives as radio's ability to produce war-ready subjects in part by separating persuasive language from the actual bodies that it comes from and finally affects.

While the works addressed in *Narrowcast* have not necessarily been identified in their reception as coterie productions, nonetheless they share a commitment to overspecificity. They may not marshal long strings of proper names or find themselves castigated by upholders of "the public." But they do display a coterie logic, a provocative narrowness, inasmuch as they dip below the radar of universality, of acceptable public discourse. A poetry of narrowcasting is thus, as I'm proposing it, rather different from the word's common association with niche marketing; it is true that audiences for Larry Eigner's writing, for instance, were and remain relatively small and that his work, and Olson's, trafficked mostly in reception networks associated with the Black Mountain wing of New American poetry, whereas Ginsberg and Baraka were eagerly read not only by the larger audience for Beat writing but also by many associated with the New Left more generally. But my interest in the word "narrowcast" is not just with the empirical size of an audience. Rather, it is a way to pinpoint something odd that happens with these poets' recordings. Narrowcast would name, then, the status of works that occur within the potentially vast reception network of recording and broadcasting but nonetheless insist on elements that specify, concretize, ground, or in some basic sense reject the generalized address that appears to be offered there. We should see both the blinking antenna and the patch of worn grass just underneath it; or, as the poets themselves tend to insist, "voice" and also body, but body not in the sense of presence or identity—body as the site of the inarticulate dimensions of speech, the clearing of throats, the rumbling of stomachs, the unsuccessful management of mucus. This insistence on the site of articulation also extends to the rooms or environments in which the poets rattle mike stands, creak their chairs, or bang their furniture. To ground, corporealize, and insist on nondramatic, real-time duration inside recording was, for these poets, not just to contest specific media "content" such as support for the Vietnam War, or even to point to radio's omissions—its ability, for instance, to allow us to forget the literal bodies that will be involved in, and dismembered during, war. Instead, these narrowcasting operations served, in various ways among these poets, to produce models of temporal measure that more fundamentally contested the content of radio's form, its parceling of the day into units of attention, frames naturalizing the relation between labor and leisure, production and consumption, while building into the listening subject a sense of participation in, and identification with, national concerns.

To trouble this normative temporal cutting effected by radio, poets insisted on concrete spaces for their recordings: Allen Ginsberg's VW van; Charles Olson's Gloucester apartment; Larry Eigner's porch in Swampscott; Baraka's Spirit House in Newark. Throughout *Narrowcast* I consider the relations between these contained research sites or ambient modules and the state archives from which orders to monitor or silence them emerge. Here I mean less vast national libraries and databases than individual document hordes within customized working spaces such as Angleton's smoky, paper-strewn den in the CIA building; Kissinger's media command control center in the Harry Truman Building; and Hoover's FBI fuselage, whose inaccessible and universally compromising files created a hush of terror and subservience among his potential adversaries at every level, up to the president of the United States. These were personal archives mobilized for high-level effects within executive settings. Guarded with the state's power, these inaccessible document vaults were at once speculative objects of fear and zero points of origin for vast chains of state action. To work as a researcher in the 1960s, especially an audio researcher, was to labor in their shadow. In a sense, *Narrowcast* is a partial history of the Cold War informational bunker, as poets and the state fought over what this key period concept might mean and be.

Narrowcast considers the politics of access to and control of information hubs like these—points on maps that, through communication networks, state bureaucracy, and military infrastructure, radiated out into, and in various ways affected or even controlled, larger territories. At one level, the book provides an account of how poets—Ginsberg in his van, Olson in his library—set themselves up as discrete and alternative sources of authority and information. At another level, *Narrowcast* traces the larger infrastructural and military defense systems through which these two sets of archives were linked, articulated, controlled: the surveillance planes and bombers that monitor Larry Eigner's Massachusetts neighborhood (the EC-121 Warning Star) and convey LeRoi Jones toward the Soviet Union as part of an atomic reprisal team (the B-36 Peacemaker); the spots at which their operations are managed, especially the Cheyenne Mountain Complex in Colorado (headquarters for NORAD, the North American Aerospace Defense Command), which we visit in Chapter 4; the communications network that articulates relations among all these elements, especially the White Alice Communications System that projects images of the northern, arctic edge of North America into these underground vaults in Colorado, where they are converted (with the help of William S. Burroughs's family's technological innovations) into a continuous, real-time picture of possible Soviet infiltration.

But *Narrowcast* traces poets' relation to military infrastructure in a perhaps more surprising way as well: many of the recordings to which I refer—not simply those produced by the CIA or the FBI—were made by means of another key element within the Cold War military infrastructure: the university language laboratory, which, with its phalanx of tape recorders, became an indispensable educational component only as the United States decided that foreign-language learning was a key to the realization of an American century. Many tapes that survive from the 1950s through the 1970s are, admittedly, either homemade or come from alternative institutions like the St. Mark's Poetry Project (which began in 1966) and Black Mountain College, magazines like *Big Table*, and radio stations like KPFA. Still, a large number of poet recordings from the period—including key ones for this book—come from university reading series like the ones at Harvard, Berkeley, University of Buffalo, University of Arizona, and San Francisco State University, and many other such series across the country whose recording equipment can be traced to the emergence of the university language laboratory.[29] In these language-learning bunkers at the hearts of Cold War university libraries, aspiring interventionists learned not only the French and German that would stand them in good stead at cosmopolitan parties but also the Persian and Vietnamese that would enable their rise in the state's overseas covert operations infrastructure. It was, indeed, as an after-hours diversion that many of the tapes that now constitute our audio records of 1960s poetry were made.

In these phonetics laboratories, through practical work in the field of linguistics, students acquired the language skills that would allow them to operate in the various literal fields of American global influence. The larger concept of "area studies" in which this operation was initially organized thus becomes a frame at certain points in the book. My interest in it here, however, is not in the vast networks or configurations of knowledge and power it established but more specifically in the way that the very technologies involved in sending operatives into the field also, during down time, were used to record some of the poetry that forms the argumentative basis of this book. From this perspective, poetry recording itself could almost be understood as an artifactual blip on the life of a Cold War technology.

But there is another sense that links these poets to the many scholars involved in area studies: Ginsberg, Eigner, Olson, and Baraka were all engaged in site-specific research. While at times this work was comprehensible in relation to formal academic disciplines (anthropology, history, musicology, media studies), at other times the field pursued was stranger, more experimental. The fieldwork that Allen Ginsberg undertakes, for example, in going on the road to write *The Fall of America* is not primarily about a scholarly discourse but about the discursive power relations produced by American radio. Media studies as we now know it, did not quite exist. Yet Ginsberg approaches this larger discursive field through a specific site, turning his VW van into a countermedia bubble. Similarly, Larry Eigner pays inordinate attention to the micro-occurrences around his Swampscott porch in part as a way to produce a kind of countertemporality that would contest the normative time pumped into his house by radio and television. While Olson, in his customized research den in Gloucester, does evoke the scholarly field of historiography as a frame, the main sites of his interventions in *Narrowcast* are the politics of the poetry world and the assumptions underlying popular recordings of poets. Finally, when I turn, in the first part of Chapter 4, to the role of Glenn Gould's sonic fieldwork in the founding of Canadian sound studies, my interest is less in its anthropological dimensions than in its relation to Cold War technologies and political struggles; these same frames are again in place when I then look at the sonic dimensions of Amiri Baraka's war work in relation to his later articulation of a kind of sonic Black Nationalism.

A note about my time frame: The novelty of tape-based composition in poetry was relatively short lived, spanning roughly from 1965, when Allen Ginsberg's portable Uher could seem like a novel, life-changing tool, to the late 1970s, by which point the device had become a mundane (and thus invisible) household appliance. Consider the case of Bernadette Mayer: In 1972 Mayer prepared an exhibition for Holly Solomon Gallery in New York in which she used thirty-six photographs per day taken during July 1971 as the point of departure for a seven-hour tape work, which would later be the basis of Mayer's 1975 book *Memory*. In this work *tape*, the medium in play along with photography, is still strange and visible. The writing butts up against it repeatedly. "You get into bed at night you whisper, you whisper into the tape another person is there he whispers he speaks he could be awake he could wake up . . . he asks you what you are doing, you answer, he doesn't wake up you whisper into the tape."[30] This same tape comes up again in Mayer's next book, published the same year, *Studying Hunger*.[31] But by 1978, when Mayer uses a tape recorder to compose her epic of daily life, *Midwinter Day* (published in 1982), the device is an unremarkable electronic appliance and does not appear in the writing at all. To the extent that we can generalize from Ginsberg's and Mayer's examples, tape seems to burst audibly into poetry in the mid-1960s before fading into the background just over a decade later. Tape-based composition certainly persists after 1978. But the fact that it could become invisible suggests a plausible end point for my study. The four overlapping case studies that follow accordingly focus on tape from the mid-1960s through the late 1970s, though to frame them, I need to trace several strands of media and institutional history back into the 1940s.

Chapter 1, "Third Personism: The FBI's Poetics of Immediacy in the 1960s," uses the reel-to-reel tape recordings Allen Ginsberg made in his VW van on a cross-country trip in 1965 and 1966 (in preparation for the book *The Fall of America*) to focalize the contested status of audio research as it was fought over by the New Left and the US state during the 1960s. Reframing Frank O'Hara's famous suggestion in "Personism" that greater immediacy with his friends "Allen" (Ginsberg) and "Roi" (LeRoi Jones) might be achieved by simply calling them on the phone, the chapter considers what it means for postwar poetics that both of these soon-to-be-infamous New Left poets were often under state audio surveillance and thus that O'Hara's phone calls would likely have involved the silent participation of Lance or Earl from the FBI as well. Giving new meaning to J. S. Mill's famous claim that poetry is overheard rather than heard, O'Hara's immediate "Personism" becomes, in the hands of the State, "Third Personism."

Offering an account of the hypotheses, guiding assumptions, and pitfalls associated with the CIA and FBI's often Yale-trained literary critics— from James Angleton and Sherman Kent to William Johnson and William Sullivan—the chapter characterizes this intimate state audio research as more than the ham-fisted misunderstanding of experimental poetry one might expect from communism-obsessed Cold Warriors. First, I demonstrate how, in using tape recording, state researchers and poets confronted the same problems: in particular, the bleeding of voice into sonic environments that overwhelm articulation with their ambient noises. Comparing Ginsberg's preliminary tapes to *The Fall of America*'s manifestation in print, I demonstrate how the poet at once advertised the work as the pure product of a new technology but at the same time turned away from that technology's actual (voice-relativizing) effects by transcribing his audiotapes into text. I then compare this process to the FBI's confrontation with the diminished quality (and centrality) of voice in their own audio recordings, explaining how their solution, with COINTELPRO, was simply creating and planting more robust evidence themselves or acting as agent provocateurs to ensure adequate proof of the acts they sought to repress. Second, in characterizing Angleton and Hoover in particular as Agency and Bureau dissertation directors, I suggest how their communism-above-all theories (which came under increased fire as the New Left seemed to pluralize political issues) can be usefully compared to still-generative models in literary studies, including those of Fredric Jameson. By bringing poets and the state into unexpected proximity, the chapter demonstrates the oddly entangled ways both understood tape recording's possible roles as documentary tool and means of persuasion: its function in selling (or unselling) the Vietnam War to American radio listeners, its use in monitoring political adversaries, and its larger use as legal and historical evidence.

Chapter 2, "The Eigner Sanction: Keeping Time from the American Century," explores Larry Eigner's development of a countertemporality in relation both to his dominant reception and to the domestic mediascape he daily negotiated. Considering Beat, Black Mountain, and Language readings of Eigner, I demonstrate both how each translates Eigner into its own terms (rapid, spontaneous thoughts; an open field poetics; and resistance to the paradigm of speech, respectively) and how this translation was possible because of a shared but not fully articulated commitment among these groups to alternate models of temporality. To draw out how this temporal project of the New American poetry and its heirs was most powerfully articulated by Eigner, I reframe the models of ongoingness developed in his writing in relation to the parceling of time achieved by radio and print media. Thus, Eigner is presented not as a shut-in who receives word of poetry from Cid Corman's radio show and pursues a private practice but rather as the fabricator of a writing mode comparable to an alternative, real-time radio station keyed to the daily sonic and visual developments in his neighborhood and linked to the poetry world through networks of correspondence, publication, film, and recording.

The chapter then compares Eigner's reflexive daily neighborhood sound and sight monitoring to surrounding infrastructures of Cold War defense (like the EC-121 Warning Star surveillance plane assigned endlessly to circle his region in search of foreign threats) and domestic media (his parents' indiscriminate television and radio consumption that pulses through his walls, at times disrupting his attention and writerly production). Indeed, military surveillance flights, commercial airline crashes, and threatened nuclear explosions as well as network TV and mainstream radio all periodically course through Eigner's airspace, where their eventful urgency gets recast by the poet's horizontal model of time. Eigner's role as an alternate broadcasting system then gets drawn out through an analysis of the ways that the Henry Luce media (also referenced by Eigner) took on the role of organizing national time at the level of the week, month, year, and even century. Yet, as suggested by my reading of his cassette tape *around new / sound daily / means*, Eigner's media intervention proceeds not through the familiar development of a smooth FM voice but, paradoxically, through an attempt to link actual vocalizations of his work more directly to their textual bases, a process I demonstrate in Eigner's critiques of recordings of his work made by himself, David Gitin, and Allen Ginsberg.

In Chapter 3, "Olson's Sonic Walls: Citizenship and Surveillance from the OWI to the Nixon Tapes," I position Charles Olson's work for the OWI (where he monitored and addressed foreign-language speakers within the United States in the attempt to win them over to the war effort) in relation both to the postwar emergence of area studies and to the models of research and network building he develops later in his career, as focalized through two recordings: his 1965 reading at Berkeley and the recording made of him in 1969 that was posthumously released as a 1975 Folkways LP, *Charles Olson Reads from Maximus Poems IV, V, VI.* Situating Olson's OWI pamphlet, *Spanish Speaking Americans in the War*, within the larger World War II weaponization of sound in anthropology and music, I offer an account of the drive for alternative models of social affiliation that causes Olson, in his later sonic research, to shrink his model of audience/community from nation, to city, to virtual network, and finally to the body of the researcher at work. Drawing out unexpected relations to the sound and performance art of Robert Morris and Vito Acconci, I suggest that Olson's attention in his recordings to process, to the real time of thinking, becomes a more symptomatic real time of poetry community roll call and hierarchy building in his readings and performances.

I then frame Olson's state-sponsored work in foreign languages in relation to the linguistic underpinnings of Cold War area studies, or the practical administration of the American Century. Here I use fellow Harvard student and avid audiotaping enthusiast Henry Kissinger's commissioned work from Paul de Man (both instruction in French and summaries and translations for Kissinger's magazine, *Confluence*) as a case study to explore the ways in which language learning and area studies were interwoven. In particular, I suggest that tape-recording in language learning may have provided a precedent for Kissinger's extremely widespread use of tape later in surveillance of domestic and foreign associates. In sketching how state audio surveillance came apart at the seams with Kissinger and the Nixon administration in the early 1970s, I suggest how Kissinger's model of research, in which documentation precedes (or transcends) a driving hypothesis, operates as an "avant-garde" form of surveillance in relation to the more classic evidentiary models I describe in Chapter 1. I test this assertion by situating Kissinger's work in relation to a 1972 court case won by historian Hayden White in which the latter sued the Los Angeles Police Department (LAPD) for sending an officer pretending to be a student into his historiography class at University of California, Los Angeles (UCLA). Here I demonstrate the shared structural features that, despite the obviously different goals and political orientations, link modes of research undertaken by the LAPD, Kissinger, White himself, and Olson. But rather than chide poets and historians for practicing a form of experimental research comparable to that of the state, the chapter concludes by suggesting how, as Olson's recordings make clear, it was precisely this real-time, plot-suspending research that allowed his audience, paradoxically, to avoid the conscription that awaited them in empirical encounters with Olson the performing pedagogue.

Chapter 4, "The Strategic Idea of North: Glenn Gould, Sergeant Jones and White Alice," begins with an account of sound studies that stresses its site-specific, Canadian origins, as manifest in the explorations of Canadian space undertaken by R. Murray Schafer and Glenn Gould in their field trips across the country and toward the north. The chapter describes their related attempts to construct the Canadian audio subject as a listener attentive to, and beginning to control, his audio horizon: from broadcast radio to the widely differing accents and tones of voice of Canadian subjects; from the movements of wind and water in the enormous Canadian landscape to the noontime air-raid sirens in Vancouver. However, I then outline the American Cold War technological infrastructure that preceded and underlay these musicians' movements into Canadian space, especially the three lines of radar stations erected to monitor Soviet incursions into the North American continent, which communicated to American missile defense systems stationed in Colorado via the White Alice Communications System.

The mechanics of this system then come into focus through an individual case study of one of its functionaries, Sergeant LeRoi Jones, who spent his time at Ramey Air Force Base in Puerto Rico practicing missions of atomic reprisal aboard a B-36 Peacemaker in anticipation of a real call from White Alice. Finally, I follow this atomic target study—via Jones's account of its oppressive sonic dimensions—into the poet and music critic's later work, as Amiri Baraka, fashioning a series of exemplary or prototypical sounds that would embody Black Nationalism, especially those on his 1972 LP *It's Nation Time*, and in his understanding of John Coltrane's recoding of Rodgers and Hammerstein's "My Favorite Things." Here my argument is that, as much as we associate Baraka with the desire for decisive historical events, in fact his attention to would-be exemplary revolutionary acts is undergirded by a commitment to ongoingness, and to genre, that he located through the temporal complexities of *It's Nation Time* and the genre underpinnings, the rococo cocktail music, recoded by Coltrane in his "My Favorite Things." Rather than understand this as a contradiction or a lapse in taste, however, I argue that for Baraka the problem of a revolutionary culture is not simply the eventlike cut that brings it into being but also its sustained ongoingness. While one might expect Baraka to engineer a series of untainted Black Nationalist sounds as the basis for the movement's new modes of subjectivity, it is precisely the turn to, and the recoding of, compromised sounds—air sirens, kitschy Broadway jingles—that helps the Black Nationalist subject focalize the marginal position in which he finds himself and thus the continued need for an immanent recoding of the social and cultural materials at hand.

Each of these chapters is structured around a scalar mismatch in which the human-sized domain of personal research encounters or gets framed in relation to vast, impersonal infrastructures of defense or surveillance scaled nationally or internationally: Glenn Gould's car, as it travels along the northern edge of the Great Lakes, and the US national nuclear defense system (from White Alice and NORAD, to the range of the Peacemaker, and the paths of Soviet intercontinental ballistic missiles [ICBMs]); Larry Eigner's Swampscott porch and the temporal management undertaken by the entire Luce media; Allen Ginsberg's van, as he is conducted from San Francisco to New York, and the frighteningly extensive networks of Bureau and Agency audio surveillance directed by J. Edgar Hoover and James Jesus Angleton; Charles Olson's dining room table in Gloucester and the internationally reticulated infrastructures of the OWI and postwar area studies.

As a whole, *Narrowcast* presents four case studies in the poetics of recorded research, which in turn are organized around four senses of narrowcasting: spatial, temporal, artifactual, and methodological. In considering spatial and temporal narrowcasting, the book demonstrates how poets turned to recording to contest American radio and television's support for the Vietnam War and its larger parceling of the temporal continuum into a series of useful, productive units of attention and labor. Taking up what I term "artifactual narrowcasting," however, the book also explores how both poet audio researchers and FBI and CIA scholars confronted many of the same problems: isolating a human voice from within an ambient environment and presenting that voice as evidence in relation to a range of larger-scale hypotheses. While recording is typically seen to project auditory effects beyond speaking bodies and broadcast poetry's "I" across space, *Narrowcast* instead brings into relief recording's site-specific dimensions; it charts how poets' recording tends to ground voice in nonintentional, often nonhuman audio environments, merging the expressive and the nonintentional, the prepared "text" and the unpredictable audio site of its emergence. Finally, in taking the interpretive and evidentiary dilemmas generated by tape recording as an unavoidably shared ground for poets, the state, and later critics like myself, I have also pursued what I term "methodological narrowcasting," or lowercase theory. This has meant that poets generate rather than just instantiate interpretive models, that these same poets converse with the state in surprising ways, and that my own research itinerary has been transformed by unanticipated encounters and shifts in direction along the way. Chapter 1 walks the reader through perhaps the most surprising of these shifts.

Third Personism
The FBI's Poetics of Immediacy in the 1960s

To think of you alone
Suffering the poem of these states!

—Ted Berrigan, *The Sonnets*, 1964

In 1965 Bob Dylan gave Allen Ginsberg six hundred dollars to buy what was at that time an exotic technological device: a state-of-the-art portable Uher tape recorder, which Ginsberg then used on his December 1965 through March 1966 trip from San Francisco to Los Angeles, Wichita, Kansas City, St. Louis, Bloomington, and Bayonne, writing the poems that would make up the first part of *The Fall of America: Poems of These States, 1965–1971* (1972).[1] Driven by Peter Orlovsky through a range of shifting American environments in his white Volkswagen camper, Ginsberg could capture his own voice, and make almost instantaneous notations, without having to scrawl in a notebook or type on a typewriter.[2] Dylan's gift seemed to buy Ginsberg a new form of immediacy on the road. And the effect of this tape recorder's entrance into Ginsberg's practice is what nominates this event as my point of departure for this chapter: it is an early moment in which the technologies of popular music inform and literally restructure the writing of poetry.[3] Over the course of the 1960s, the construction of the rock star and the social possibilities of the rock concert would continue to affect poetry, with Ginsberg himself, who would hire his own booking manager at the end of 1966, becoming the prime example of a crossover performer.[4] My interest, however, is not merely in the cultural space sometimes shared between these disciplines but also in the ways that poets made use of the technological underpinnings of rock music. In Ginsberg's case, for instance, portable tape recording helped him revisit critically the Beat romance of the road. Dean Moriarty had, in Kerouac's *On the Road*, exhorted his friends in the car at the beginning of one of their cross-country trips to "admit that everything is fine and there's no need in the world to worry" while he drummed "on the dashboard till a great sag developed in it."[5] For Ginsberg a decade later, however, the rhythmic pulse of the car radio is no longer an incantatory magnet that pulls one through a secret America of infinite potentiality. Now the unconscious actions generated by the radio (support for the war in Vietnam, consumerism, participation in fake emotions) are exactly what Ginsberg has gone on the road to inventory, literally record with his new reel-to-reel, and bring into the open in order to generate effective resistance to them. The "heavenly echo of Dylan's despair" might provide an occasional break. But even this was a "mass machine-made folksong" within a largely martial radio space where Barry Sadler's "Ballad of the Green Beret" was then the most popular song in the country.[6]

Dashboard pounding was now a matter of frustration, not timekeeping, since nothing was fine and there was very much a need to worry. So *The Fall of America* offers itself as a real-time document of Ginsberg's resistance to radio's false allure, the disillusioned poet rolling in his camper through one heartland city after another, each displaying new symptoms of a United States whose malignant effects were stretching across the globe, especially to Vietnam.[7] Floating in his shifting micro-media bubble, the mobile bard enlists his Uher reel-to-reel to register spontaneous countermedia poems as the nation off-gases toxic media around him.

To this perhaps somewhat familiar construal of the counterculture interpreting and critically engaging the dominant culture, let me add another less familiar element. As Ginsberg transformed himself from a beatnik poet of alienation to an activist poet of the New Left, as he shifted the emphasis of his writing's imagined context from the tortured bohemian interior to the torturing anti-bohemian state, and went about tracking that state's implications internationally, the state—with its CIA scholars and FBI researchers—in turn became curious about Ginsberg. Enter the other massively significant new role for tape recording. Like Amiri Baraka, William S. Burroughs, Ed Sanders, his Yippie friends Abbie Hoffman and Jerry Rubin, and many other writers associated with New Left, Allen Ginsberg was an object of extensive textual and audio surveillance. The FBI developed enormous numbers of detailed files on these poets and activists, files that suggest a perhaps surprising level of cultural knowledge and interpretive skill, including a close familiarity with canonical texts in the history of literary criticism.[8] In what follows I want to take the state's readers and listeners seriously, drawing out the implications of their work, situating it in relation to professional discourses of literature and history and to the poetics of research more generally. While we will be forced to navigate important gaps in the record (for the most part we cannot, for instance, listen to the Bureau or the Agency listening, since both seem to have considered tape merely a mechanism for the generation of textual records), we can nonetheless learn a perhaps surprising amount about how the state read and listened, including the literary and philosophical precedents called on to frame and justify Bureau and Agency methods. At this point, the real infringements of civil liberties have been well documented. So my goal is not so much to restore, say, eighteen and a half minutes of missing recording to mount a new case against Nixon, the Bureau, or the Agency. Rather, I put parts of the state's audio surveillance archives, along with their methodological writings, into dialogue with key moments in the tape-based research conducted by avant-garde poets during the Cold War, themselves often objects of state surveillance. Focusing on shared problems of what constitutes persuasive audio evidence and its relation to guiding research hypotheses, on what became often the difficulty of extracting the human voice from its immediate audio ambience, this chapter, like the ones to follow, explores new ways to conceptualize poetry's oddly central role within the social life of tape recording in the 1960s. In putting Ginsberg's tape-based inquiry into the American mediascape into dialogue with both FBI and CIA audio research on Ginsberg and others within the counterculture, I hope not merely to draw out the full political spectrum of sonic fieldwork (and thus question claims, like Ginsberg's, for tape's inherently liberatory dimensions) but also to suggest how sonic research's registration of sites and not merely voices, its indiscriminate and nonanthropocentric dimension, presented problems that caused its users to retreat and recoil, to compensate for this excess, which was often perceived as a lack of human control.

But my goal is not the hallowed critical one of revealing a writer's mystification by documenting the oppressive functions his uncritically accepted device actually performed. Tape may coil in conflicting ethical directions. Such dilemmas often provide the occasion for the middlebrow academic theater of problem worrying, that public hand-wringing whose function, paradoxically, is to keep these same critical hands clean, because distant from the cultural objects that would make difficult demands on them. As troubling as 1960s tape could actually be, my method here—perhaps in the spirit of sound—is immersion, an experimental process of building out from a series of recordings toward the political, cultural, philosophical landscapes they seem variously to organize or encode. This process will involve a discontinuous, often path-changing attempt to describe, contextualize, correlate, and finally theorize tape's oddly discrepant functions.

John Stuart Mill famously defined poetry as an utterance overheard rather than heard, the heard utterance being a mere matter of elocution.[9] In fact, the original version of his famous essay "What Is Poetry?" makes an explicit link between poetry and surveillance. Quoting Robert Burns's "My Heart's in the Highlands," Mill remarks: "That song has always seemed to us like the lament of a prisoner in a solitary cell, ourselves listening, unseen, in the next."[10] Following Mill, Agency and Bureau poetry enthusiasts also thought of the ideal utterance both as overhead and as bearing an intimate relation to surveillance and incarceration. They preferred poetry to elocution also because whereas the latter was designed for an audience—composed and edited, that is, in relation to future, potentially critical auditors—the former was poured out unfiltered and thus far more likely to compromise its speaker.

But the advent of mechanical recording—toward the end of Mill's life—produced another fold in poetry's relation to eloquence. Those government listeners who used tape to document the lyric poetry of unwitting criminal confession quickly discovered something else: Inasmuch as poetry was spontaneous sound innocent of intention and strategic framing, conspirators or confessing criminals were ultimately not the only poets in a bugged room. There was a "poetry" of the refrigerator and the air conditioner; of the television and the droning radio in the next room; of clothing in movement and steps on stairs; of the gastric system and the throat; of pot and pan clang and shuffling papers. So much poetry could drive one in search of a little eloquence—especially when this kind often tended to occlude speech.

With recorded poetry, beginning in the 1870s, a newly spatialized utterance began to bleed into a range of contexts and operate in literal exterior rather than psychological interior time; taking poetry recording out of the studio, as happened in the 1960s, and using recoding now as a mode of composition only amplified and extended these problems, and poetry criticism is only gradually catching up. It has so far not even addressed what happened when the state then began to listen, intimately, to poets at home in that same decade. We could note first that many poets turning to a new quotidian poetics (which drew on supposedly nonpoetic materials like phone calls and letters in an attempt to thematize and enact close-knit social formations whose movements occurred outside monumental national time) now began to speak intimately and, for a time, unconsciously to that very same silently auditing state. With The Man's ear trained to this daily register and *record* pressed on the reel-to-reel, Bureau and Agency listeners became coterie spies—informed critics with perhaps unprecedented access to new documentary materials.

When Charles Olson suggested in 1950 that, in a field poetics of projective verse, the printed page could become an archive of time, this time was always latent, interior.[11] In recording, this temporality, and indeed some sense of corresponding spatiality, became literal. With the move from print to recording we have, already, the motivation of a whole range of semantic features unavailable in print: stress, intonation, accent, timing, and frequently encoded information about the physical and social environment of the performance. But with the move from studio tape to ambient outdoor tape, we get an even more expanded semantic field in which poetry becomes one element within a wider array of audio effects, registrations of the exterior sonic domain. This was partly what drew Ginsberg right away to his portable Uher. As Michael Schumacher, one of Ginsberg's biographers, put it,

> Delighted, Allen immediately went to work to learn how to make the best use of the recorder. He took the portable machine with him everywhere, recording his impressions of what he saw on his walks in the woods or drives along the highway . . . recording his mantra chanting with the sounds of the sea as a backdrop. . . . In essence, he was carrying the concept of verbal sketching a step beyond Kerouac.[12]

Despite what it might sound like, Kerouacian sketching is not just improvisatory description: it is *situated* description whose improvisation is a response to the real-time sounds and effects of that location. As Kerouac puts it, "Everything activates in front of you in myriad profusion, you just have to purify your mind and let it pour the words."[13] With tape, this pouring in of location's myriad profusion wasn't limited to words and didn't require heroic purity of mind. As I've suggested, audio sampling from ambient locations might be thought to muddy this very distinction between mind and site. We hear, on Ginsberg's cross-country tapes, for instance, not just the jangling pop tunes and sonorous radio announcers' sentences but also a wide range of Ginsberg's tones—exhorting to tentative, poised declamations to circular mumbles, caught somewhere in his throat and not quite released. This against the whir of the VW itself, of other cars on the road, and of environments he enters—Wichita crowds, Reno slot machines. For Ginsberg recording in his van, the road isn't just a theme but a continuous rumble that shares sonic space with his voice. Tape, in other words, registers environments and not merely voices; spatial situations and not merely oracular utterances.

That Ginsberg's actual tape, which generated the first part of *The Fall of America* and which has also been the basis for subsequent recordings, might in fact *be* the work itself rather than an inaudible pretext (a private sound reservoir that can become part of the work only once it has been transcribed into print), seems not to have occurred to him.[14] But when one compares Ginsberg's actual tapes to both the book and to the later studio recordings his initial fieldwork seems to have inspired, this first cross-country tape argues perhaps for a more crucial status within the complex of documents associated with *The Fall of America* and the poem "Wichita Vortex Sutra." In the 2004 CD version of the poem, for instance, which is based on a recording done at St. Mark's Poetry Project ten years earlier, Ginsberg's performance conveys the familiar effect of an amplified voice speaking on a stage—a clear vocal signal that separates itself from the musical frames and backgrounds offered by Christian Marclay, Philip Glass, Lee Ranaldo, Steve Shelley, and others. Even when these musical sections deploy what we might think of as noise, as they frequently do, Ginsberg's voice always rises above and separates itself. On the 1966 tape, however, this separation never occurs: the voice is emphatically part of its immediate physical and spatial environment, the VW camper—the constructed media module, the shifting soundscape, in relation to which the poet will compose, or better, as a function of which his utterances will be composed. Whereas references to music appear in the text through proper names and descriptions ("negro voices rejoice over radio" or "radio crawling with Rockmusic youngsters" or simply the names of famous musicians like Dylan, Nelson Eddy, Nancy Sinatra, the Kinks, John Lennon, and Paul McCartney),[15] in the initial reel-to-reel, often songs *themselves* become audible. Rather than intertextual nods, the songs are literal sonic environments. We hear the cuts of Ginsberg turning on and clicking off the tape machine. And each time this happens, we discern a vocal signal attempting to differentiate itself from the physical environment of car noise. Part of this noise, meanwhile, is the hiss of the open window, which marks not only the ambient sound of a moving vehicle but more specifically a way of understanding the bleed or failure of containment between poetry's space of enunciation and the world beyond.

Inasmuch as it consistently framed this relationship between a speaker and his site, a speech act and at least one possible frame beyond the speaker, field-based tape recording like Ginsberg's would seem formally to contain within it something close to a dialectics of utterance and context.

All of this should suggest the extent to which Ginsberg's van-based audio research is not quite subsumable within the poet's better-known involvement with recording and pop music more generally. Ginsberg, to repeat, was already a pop star by the mid-1960s: his performances with Dylan, Paul McCartney, and Phil Ochs all contributed to this sense—as did his reading at Royal Albert Hall in London on June 11, 1965. When Ed Sanders writes, for instance, to Charles Olson on November 9, 1965, that "Ginzap," as he calls him, "was on a couple of concerts with" the Fugs, Olson is not to be surprised with the claim that "the Zap is now billed as folk rock mantra-ist."[16] This billing would be updated throughout his career as Ginsberg involved himself with several generations of musicians: from Philip Glass to Bono; from the Clash and Patti Smith to Sonic Youth. The issue here, in other words, is not merely poetry's coming to share cultural terrain with the emerging world of 1960s pop music and then with its various afterlives.[17] Rather, in returning to the tapes Ginsberg made for *The Fall of America*, we can listen instead to a model of field-based audio research, a site-specific media monitoring, that is mixed out of the City Lights paperback.[18]

But if Ginsberg's speaking subjectivity merged sonically with its physical environment, this interpenetration tended not to occur socially. And this is worth noting about his fieldwork. Unlike the Beat romances of the road a decade earlier, *The Fall of America* is far less about picaresque adventures and the joys of spontaneous encounters with people along the journey than about the horrors of prescripted media subject production. What moves around the country is less a car full of carefree beatniks than a carefully engineered media-recording module that will house and even conceal the famous poet as he composes in relation to different radio frequencies and views of the country caught from his anonymous camper. Yet this composition was not simply a record of Ginsberg's real-time, spontaneous encounters as he put himself into contact with a series of new environments—the building up, say, of a series of insights based on his American audio fieldwork and the gradual organization of these insights into a hypothesis about the relation between the interior of America in places like Wichita, Kansas, and Vietnam. Instead,

Ginsberg seems to have gone on the road to collect evidence of a relationship that he already intuited. He says as much explicitly in an interview with Tom Clark in Cambridge, England, in mid-May 1965—eight months prior to his trip: "The interior of America is not bad, at least for me, though it might be bad for a spade, not too bad, creepy, but it's not impossible. But traveling in countries like Cuba and Viet Nam I realize that the people that get the real evil side effects of America are there—in other words, it really is like imperialism, in that sense."[19] It seems that Ginsberg takes to his camper to record precisely the origin points for these effects within the "interior of America." Tuning in to this guiding frequency long before he sets off in his van, Ginsberg will now survey the quiet, comparatively mild launch sites for this radiating American oppression that gathers force as it projects beyond the space of the nation itself.[20]

So we might do better to think about Ginsberg in his VW not as an open-eared sound collector, an audio ethnographer seeking to form new hypotheses about the culture he studies. Instead, Ginsberg hits the road to collect concrete instances of what he has already decided is radio's sinister work, immersing himself in its repressive signals and taking notes. "Radio the soul of the nation," Ginsberg proposes in the first poem. Tuning in coast to coast on discrete episodes of this soul making, Ginsberg will, he believes, have an immediate experience of how US citizens think: "Hypnosis of airwaves / In the house you can't break it / unless you turn off yr set." Central to Ginsberg's listening, however, is the "Martial music" that is "filling airwaves": "drum taps drum beats trumpets / pulsing thru radiostations." In addition to fostering an immediate war climate, the radio is a problem because it allows "false emotions" to be "broadcast thru the land." The result is "natural voices made synthetic, / pflegm obliterated"—a con Ginsberg attributes to Frank Sinatra, his daughter, Nancy, and the Beach Boys. Beyond the war and the rendering saccharine of emotional life, the problem is consumption: "Factories building, airwaves pushing" this effect being to "drive yr mind down Supermarket aisles."[21]

But in what sense then does Ginsberg's critical listening offer a critical hearing or unscripted response? He suggests one way in "A Vow," which opens: "I will haunt these States / with beard bald head / eyes staring out plane window / hair hanging in Greyhound bus midnight / leaning over taxicab seat to admonish."[22] Despite the centrality of radio in the framing of this project,

Ginsberg's response, his haunting, will occur first over a longer time span than that involved in his van trip (since he also references planes, buses, and cabs), and second, perhaps more important, he will haunt the United States *by way of an image*. In one sense this makes perfect sense: Allen Ginsberg was already a cultural *icon* by 1966, so his merely being seen at a string of towns across the country had an effect: his image did indeed serve as a rallying point for the counterculture—and this accounts for the popularity of Allen Ginsberg posters at the time (especially one of the poet in a thick beard wearing an American flag hat with his arms above his head in a massive peace sign). While this image circulated in a number of formats, its primary existence was as an *ad* for *Evergreen*, an enticement to "join the underground generation" in an act of consumption that encourages the hip, rebellious buyer of books and magazines to "holler for Evergreen at [his] newsstand."

Ginsberg's iconic status and galvanizing force are worth pausing on in light of my description of the fieldwork component of his trip. The poet's arrival in each of the towns on his 1965–66 trip is itself an important event, often commented on in the press, which in turn is remarked by the poet on the tape, which in turn is transcribed into the text. This at times dramatic effect on the cities he sought to study does not in itself so much separate him from professional anthropologists working in remote locations in the early part of the twentieth century inasmuch as their entrances, too, tended to be rippling, widely important events that affected the societies they studied, and thus the materials they gathered.[23] What Ginsberg's celebrity status at various university towns suggests, however, is that he had to switch roles from anonymous recorder of the mediascape to famous media celebrity whose oracular readings tended to be recorded. Moreover, when Ginsberg took on this latter role, his appearance in the local paper and his reading at the university often immediately *produced* the very swelling up of countercultural energies his radio study was designed to generate—down the road, through print.

Even if one thinks of *The Fall of America* as resolving this tension by operating in sequence (first the galvanizing events, then the critical book that emerges from them), there remains a question about the medium specificity of a project designed to break the "hypnosis of the airwaves." How, in other words, does Ginsberg's visual haunting, followed by his public reading, relate to the resistant listening evoked in but displaced from his final text? Like his visual haunting in a project ostensibly about radio, Ginsberg's exemplary

FIGURE 1. Allen Ginsberg, poster: "Come Alive! Join the Underground Generation" (New York: Evergreen, 1966). Courtesy the estate of Allen Ginsberg.

act of critical hearing is offered back to the country's mesmerized listeners through a displacement of media—through print. Ginsberg's shifting radio environments can, in this sense, be evoked only textually and diagrammatically. Tape recording's promised indexical relation to sound sources, we might say, operates as an enabling condition of possibility for Ginsberg's project, which his subsequent texts and recordings strangely elide.

Ginsberg's ambivalence about technology here can be partly understood within Michael Davidson's argument about the ambiguous status of media within the New American poetry, where claims about breath, corporality, and immediate presence do not square easily with the mediating devices that undergird this new writing. The "new oralism" of writers like Olson, Kerouac, Ginsberg, and others was, notes Davidson, "made possible by technological advances in typography, offset printing, and . . . magnetic recording that would seem the very antithesis to any poetics of unmediated presence."[24] This dynamic gets complicated further in the case of the tapes that underlie *The Fall of America*. If Ginsberg does seem at times to have used the Uher as a mediating device for registering his would-be unmediated presence in the Volkswagen, speaking directly into the portable recording device as impressions of the land- and mediascape registered to him, just as often Ginsberg composed by pen in his notebooks, revised extensively, shifted passages, revised more, and then recorded the more refined versions into the Uher. Indeed, Ginsberg's travel notebooks from the trip tell the story of this verbal mediation and editing.[25]

In the draft, a preliminary title, "Face the Nation," is crossed out, with the title noted just as "Vortex Sutra." All the pages in the notebook show cross outs, revisions, and/or line movements. Some reduce into a tangle of editorial scrawls. This would of course not be particularly remarkable were it not for this poem's mythic status as spontaneously generated and for tape's supposed role as the basis for that generation. What the notebooks suggest, however, is that the tape recorder is not the improvisatory core of the entire book, the hands-free device that enables Ginsberg's liberation from the physical dimensions of pens, notebooks, typewriters, allowing him to be a floating consciousness enunciating itself. Instead, the Uher seems to operate as *one tool* in a much more complex process of thinking, listening to the radio, writing, revising, recording, listening to tape, transcribing tape, and revising further. Such a process was more difficult to reduce to the press-release prose Ginsberg used for his book covers.[26] Ginsberg seems, in one way, to want to cash in on the technological currency of tape and even to present it as an enabling condition of possibility that it never actually had in his process; at the same time, however, the poet feels the need to keep the literal sonic effects of tape from entering his work—in part, perhaps, because they threaten to swamp his centrality and control. This tense technological dynamic might be fleshed out by a wider-angle shot of the social life of tape recording at the time.

Just what kind of a tool was tape in 1966? It may help to recall a now partly lost sense of the word that emerged with early computing. Consider, for

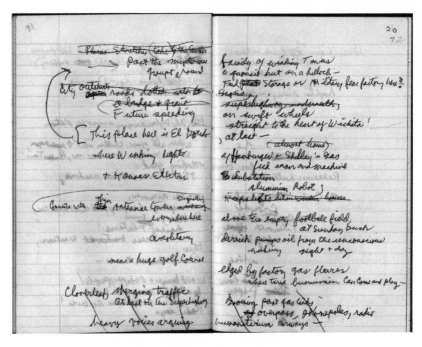

FIGURE 2. Allen Ginsberg, 1966 notebook draft of "Wichita Vortex Sutra," Stanford University Library. Courtesy the estate of Allen Ginsberg and Stanford University.

instance, Norbert Wiener's description of the emergence of "high-speed electrical computing machines" in his classic 1950 book *The Human Use of Human Beings: Cybernetics and Society*:[27]

> The determination of the mode of conduct of these machines is given through a special sort of input, which frequently consists of punched cards or tapes . . . which determines the way in which the machine is going to act. . . . Because of the frequent use of punched or magnetic tape in the control, the data which are fed in, and which indicate the mode of operation of one of these machines for combining information, are called the *taping*.[28]

Understood in this sense, it was "tapes" that controlled not only the behavior and functioning of the early computers with which Wiener was involved at his home institution, MIT, but also those that MIT developed just a few years later as the center of the US strategic defense system for responding to the possibility of a Soviet attack, Semi-Automatic Ground Environment (SAGE), discussed later.[29] In the mid-1960s, tape was the basis of what was perceived, at once, as the inhuman domain of computing, with its extension into the central infrastructure of missile defense, and as the countercultural challenge to this world of computing and national defense mounted by musicians and activists using increasingly portable recording devices.

There were, then, some hard-to-unravel tangles in 1960s tape. Was it personal, subjectively scaled, or was it infrastructural and essentially inhuman? Even if one could wrest it, conceptually, from its IBM reels at the inaccessible center of government vaults and resituate it on portable Uher players, still there were further folds: Was it merely a registration device that aided the emergence of a new, more immediate poetic oralism, or a mode of technological mediation that baldly undermined the pretenses to such an expressive, breath-based poetics? Then, as 1960s reel-to-reels spun into more common use, their conceptual and political tangle got knottier: whatever one might have felt about the degree of direct presence one might accord to a poet's speech and breath on tape, however much one believed in immediacy and spontaneity, what became clear later in the decade was that tape was also, increasingly, an invisible tool trained by The Man directly on poets' breathing and speaking bodies. Portable tape recording became a widespread method of surveillance—and poets were not incidental to this program.

The first sentence of Frank O'Hara's famous manifesto "Personism" mentions Allen Ginsberg, who comes up again, as do other poets who would soon be associated with the New Left: Personism "was founded by me after lunch with LeRoi Jones on August 27, 1959, a day in which I was in love with someone (not Roi, by the way, a blond). I went back to work and wrote a poem for this person. While I was writing it I was realizing that if I wanted to I could use the telephone instead of writing the poem, and so Personism was born."[30] Did O'Hara also perhaps call Roi to arrange their lunch? If so, this cozy phone immediacy with dangerous figures like Allen and Roi would, very soon after if not already in 1959, frequently also have involved the silent participation of Lance, or Bob, or Earl from the FBI as well. And thus the Bureau's own poetics, which we might call Third Personism, was born.

By 1959 "Roi" was already a person of interest to the Bureau because of (false) suspicions about his ties to communism that had emerged during his time in the air force.[31] There was, it seems, some tension between the claims of his 1954 loyalty oath—mandatory on joining the air force—and the testimony that was extracted from him after rumors about his political leanings began to circulate; he was questioned and admitted reading Marx and Lenin and attending meetings of groups associated with communism.[32]

> OSI records reflect subject executed signed sworn statement 7/30/56 at Ramey AFB, Puerto Rico, admitting past membership or affiliation in the AYD, CRC, and National Negro Congress. He admitted attending CP meetings and lectures by CP members. He also admitted subscribing to "The Worker" along with reading the "Daily Worker" and literature concerning Communism and Marxism. He had certified on Loyalty Form DD 98 dated 10/6/54 that he had not been associated in any manner with above organizations.[33]

By April 1958 Roi was still new enough to town that he had not yet come to the attention of the Bureau's "confidential informants in New York City," who had, however, already questioned the owners of a grocery store in Newark where Jones worked when he was a high school student.[34] As in most FBI releases, whole paragraphs and pages are blocked out, so it's extremely likely—virtually certain—that both bugs and wiretaps were used for Baraka.[35] We know absolutely that the FBI used informants to smuggle in recording devices at many of his readings and that Bureau interpreters later pored over these recordings, as they did his printed works.[36] We also know that Baraka was aware of interference from both local police and the FBI as early as 1962, probably earlier. He writes, for instance, to Ed Dorn, about police agents showing up at his apartment on Cooper Square, producing a flier he'd helped draft about an action in Times Square (which did not include his name), and explaining to him that he'd be arrested if he even showed up at the action.[37] Moreover, he notes in the same letter that this action appears to be linked to the FBI and mentions hearing on the radio a claim (which was in fact true) that about one-fifth of the Communist Party was at that point made up of FBI agents, linking this to the thwarting of his planned action in Times Square.[38] Hettie Jones, Baraka's first wife, writes of even more direct intervention:

> Roi had given the New York chapter of [the Fair Play for Cuba Committee] his name to use—he didn't actually work for them—and soon our phone broke, and I joked that it had rung itself out until one day he found some men on the roof, who'd scaled a three-story wall to repair, they said, the line. Said Joel [Oppenheimer],

whenever he heard any extra sizzle and couldn't get through: "You bastards could at least take a message."[39]

At several other moments in his correspondence Baraka registers a suspicion that FBI agents are opening his mail; at one point—in a December 19, 1962, letter to Dorn—he simply addresses the presumably snooping FBI directly, treating them as characters in William S. Burroughs's *Naked Lunch*: "I suspect the FBI or somebody is opening all my mail, in and out, so I want to say right here I think the FBI eats shit especially JEdgarHoover alias AJ of Islam Inc. alias Dr. Benway, alias Hassan O'Leary the afterbirth tycoon."[40] All this to say that by the late 1950s and early 1960s, Baraka-to-be was, already, the kind of person whose phone calls to a curator like O'Hara, working in the International Program of the Museum of Modern Art and thus instituting a key cultural component of the Marshall Plan, were of significant interest to both the Bureau and the Agency, whether or not they heard this particular exchange.

Thanks to the recent work of William Maxwell, we now know quite a bit about how the FBI monitored, or as he puts it, "ghostread," African American writers, including Baraka. And while Maxwell's account is primarily about reading, not listening, it is nonetheless useful in helping establish some of the larger contours of literary surveillance in the United States across the twentieth century. Maxwell demonstrates, to begin with, that the FBI's coverage of writers deemed threats was not casual or perfunctory. Rather, it was surprisingly scholarly. Noting the "similarities between ghostreaders and academic literary critics," Maxwell also documents the remarkable *volume* of FBI literary criticism on African American literature: between 1919 and 1972, the Bureau produced 13,892 pages of its own literary analysis, or the equivalent of roughly forty-six 300-page PhD theses.[41] Thus, in its close and careful reception of African American literature, the FBI outpaced all of the leading research universities combined, not to mention private scholars and writers themselves.[42]

Meanwhile, Hoover produced or oversaw a series of polemical and methodological works eagerly read both by his students and by the general public: from *Radicalism and Sedition among the Negroes as Reflected in Their Publications* (1919) to *Persons in Hiding* (1938), *Masters of Deceit: The Story of Communism in America and How to Fight It* (1958), and *A Study of Communism* (1962).[43] These books not only naturalized domestic surveillance by romanticizing the G-Men but also taught the public to associate very basic features of democracy (activism, strikes) with communism.[44] As one call-in crank from Missouri puts it in *The Fall of America:* "causes and agitations, then, then they're doing the work of the communists as J. Edgar Hoover says." Similarly, by calling Martin Luther King Jr. "the most notorious liar in the country," Hoover was urging the would-be law-abiding general public to distrust the civil rights movement—a stance also registered in Ginsberg's text by another call-in ranter: "God created all the races . . . and it is only men who tried to mix em up, and when they mix em up that's when the trouble starts."[45] Hoover (who makes a cameo in "Wichita Vortex Sutra" as the FBI's "little prince, unmarried all these years") was thus not just a surveillance mastermind operating behind the scenes but equally, through his books and public statements, an active force in the toxic mediascape to which Ginsberg was subjecting himself.

In tracing the phases in Hoover's attempt to situate the FBI within a series of public discourses, Maxwell also underlines a perhaps surprising feature of this narrative: a steep rise in funding for the FBI does *not* correspond to the Cold War but precedes it.[46] "Under FDR and the coming of World War II—not McCarthyite Republicanism and Cold War panic—most practical limits on Hoover's surveillance of presumed enemies were broken in plain sight. Wiretapping, 'trash covers' (garbage-can inspection), 'mail covers' (mail monitoring), and 'black bag jobs' (authorized break-ins) became visible within the Bureau's tool kit."[47]

Even if such tactics were not new to the FBI in the late 1950s and early 1960s, the scope of its programs would, at that point, radically expand. Within the COINTELPRO alone—a secret and highly illegal FBI program—the Bureau performed 2,218 activities between 1956 and 1971, including 2,305 phone taps and 697 admitted bugs (*JA*, 240). This generated almost sixty thousand pieces of correspondence. If O'Hara was indeed overheard by the FBI, he would join the company of Baraka and Ginsberg, Ed Sanders, the Yippies, and probably hundreds of other writers and activists. Baraka's FBI file is more than seven hundred pages long, and he is also mentioned in FBI operations against Black Nationalist operations. Sanders's file, which he was able to request, reveals that his apartment on Avenue A was bugged by the FBI.[48] It's very likely that Ginsberg's apartment was also bugged.[49] Some of his phone calls to US government officials—including one to Henry Kissinger, then secretary of state—were in fact recorded.

When FBI listeners had trained their ears on the interior of Sanders's house, or on the operations of Baraka's Spirit House in Newark, what exactly had they expected to hear? This depended, of course, on the presuppositions and goals that led their research. Ginsberg, for instance, had come to the Bureau's attention first because of his involvement with Cuba—and despite some notes about his support for the decriminalization of marijuana (a term that is interchangeable with "narcotics" in his dossier) it was a connection to communism that was the Bureau's main concern.[50] Later, anti–Vietnam War work would be of interest to the Bureau—but, this too, oddly enough, was understood primarily within a communist framework, since Johnson, Nixon, and Hoover all continued to believe, into the 1970s, that the antiwar movement was in fact organized by Soviet agents.[51] Nor could Ginsberg's open homosexuality and support for LGBT rights be seen as part of an emergent new social movement; rather, the FBI persisted in understanding this as a mere character flaw—associated with his general "instability" (measured more by his failure to keep regular employment and a fixed abode than by the actual time he'd spent in a mental institution). Indeed, the FBI seems to have held on to a photograph of him "in an indecent pose" and labeled it "for possible future use."[52] The FBI thus cherished a supposedly "compromising" photograph of Ginsberg himself—as if its publication might ruin his reputation. Despite Ginsberg's explicit critiques of Fidel Castro's crackdown on gay men in Cuba, the fact that he'd had any interest in debates about Cuba red-flagged him, rendering Ginsberg, in the FBI's eyes, a danger to the president.

It's easy enough to ironize the quaint interpretive paradigms of the FBI and the CIA. So much so that rather than distance us from them, I'd like, instead, to bring them just a bit closer. William C. Sullivan, third in command at the FBI behind Hoover and Clyde Tolson, commented directly on the scholarly nature of intelligence work, separating it from the, in Sullivan's estimation, less intellectually demanding criminal wing of the Bureau:

> The man who excels at criminal investigation would be lost in intelligence. Instead of having clear-cut black-and-white issues, intelligence is full of gray areas. In intelligence, a man can investigate for years without getting any real results. A man who enjoys solving tantalizing and complex problems, who likes to experiment, would be bored stiff catching bank robbers and belongs in intelligence.[53]

The intelligence research Sullivan here sketches would have encompassed almost all of that conducted on the New Left (which committed few crimes in proportion to the amount of government surveillance lavished on it), including that structured around the suspicion of Soviet influence. From our current perspective, the tenacious pursuit of this suspicion itself, especially in the face of so much counterevidence, shows Bureau scholars as inept and bumbling. While this may have been true in many instances, US government research into Soviet infiltration was not quite as coarse as we might now imagine, especially if we shift our frame momentarily to the CIA, and from intelligence generally to counterintelligence specifically: the pursuit of moles within the Agency. CIA operatives focused on communist infiltration of their organization not because they were paranoid monomaniacal Cold Warriors but rather because, seeking high-grade information, they themselves worked constantly to infiltrate the KGB and reasonably assumed that Soviet agents did the same in relation to the CIA, and in the United States more broadly—including within the antiwar effort.[54] However, by the late 1960s and early 1970s, both Bureau and Agency researchers were beginning to notice that their communism-above-all interpretive paradigm was not making sense of a wide range of social practices. Sullivan was one of those pushing for (and secretly supporting) new kinds of Bureau research, while also having to answer to Hoover, at once dean and dissertation adviser in the Bureau.[55] Hoover was therefore under pressure from Sullivan and others to disaggregate his concept of evil—to approve, we might say, new kinds of dissertations and the surveillance fieldwork that would actualize them. But if this bottom-up pressure was rising, so too—more powerfully—was the top-down pressure from Johnson and Nixon. So Bureau field agents continued, longer than one might have expected, to organize their research around the hypothesis of communist influence.

When FBI agents took to the field to gather evidence to support their suspicions about writers like Ginsberg, they performed a kind of interpretation unique within his (as it was within others') reception history. The fieldwork necessary was long and tedious and depended on the new modes of evidence collection I've described so far. But the rewards for successful FBI scholarship were extremely high—and indeed altogether novel. If an FBI scholar located decisive proof of his hypotheses, he didn't, like his colleagues in literature, merely publish a monograph whose ultimate aim was, as we say, to intervene decisively in the poet's critical reception, the afterlife of his writing. Successful FBI scholars intervened decisively in the poet's immediate production and life. Bureau scholarship intervened by incarcerating its subject and halting his publication. This was the James Russell Lowell Prize of FBI scholarship.[56]

Though Bureau and Agency Ginsberg scholars did not attain these summits and much of their research remains inaccessible, it does seem possible nonetheless to reverse-engineer certain key theoretical propositions out of documents in their orbit.[57] This is the case, for instance, with a book on historiography by Yale historian and CIA operative Sherman Kent (1903–86); in 1941 he published the introduction to the discipline of history, especially historical research, *Writing History*. While the book may have been designed for undergraduates, it seems plausible to hear many of its suggestions as governing the construction of Agency case files as well. Noting, for instance, that, "much like research in the natural sciences," historical research "consists of gathering facts—old and well-known ones at first, and later, with the help of deeper knowledge of bibliography, new ones," Kent proposes that, in the gradual movement from the domain of established references to the production of new knowledge, (case) history writing involves both the classical operation of "forming hypotheses on the basis of these facts" and the critical, corrective, and proleptical process of "testing these hypotheses for traces of one's own ignorance or bias."[58] While all this may seem commonsensical, the result, for Kent, is not simply the production of historical truth but the building of "better hypotheses than already exist," which are not offered as final or correct in themselves but as "relatively more true" inasmuch, especially, as they add detail, revealing "a sharper picture of what happened."[59] Though still committed to some idea of progress, there are faint echoes of the interwar historical relativism of Carl Becker and Charles Beard here, which emerge again soon after, when Kent pauses "to exorcise once and for all any mystery attached to a 'hypothesis'":

> The word is admittedly formidable, but the thing it names is one of the commonest in life. Every time the mind perceives a relationship between two things it creates a hypothesis. The sight of a running man creates the hypothesis "hurry"; the sound of a howling child creates the hypothesis "unhappiness." This habit of jumping at conclusions is one of the mind's most irrepressible activities, and without this perpetual and involuntary spark the mind would be no mind at all. A student who submits his intelligence to a set of data will find that whether he likes it or not the intelligence starts arranging the data into a pattern.[60]

The straw man here for this CIA theorist is a kind of uber positivism wherein the "unbiased" and "objective" historian neither jumps to conclusions nor "interprets" history but lets the facts, once painstakingly assembled, speak for themselves. Kent proposes instead that the historian not pretend to check his natural inclination to make connections but only that he test these as more "data" emerge. While such a formulation avoids the extreme positivism I've just sketched, it also naturalizes the writing of history as a matter of increasingly sophisticated hypotheses—understood both as organizing questions and as tentative answers to these questions—as these emerge spontaneously out of the novice history writer's (or seasoned Agency operative's) contact with historical evidence. Inasmuch as Kent's position describes a historiographic method within the Agency—and we look at several cases that seem to align closely with his ideas—we will consider it in relation to other, less classical models of evidence generation and argument production both within state surveillance and within academic scholarship. Thus, what is surprising here is not so much that Kent's historiographic manual might hold implications for CIA and state scholarship more generally but that if we want to designate Kent as a kind of normative position, critiques of that position emerge from both academic historiography and state practice. There was a surveillance avant-garde.

While the more typical problem is this one of extracting theoretical principles either from texts like Kent's not explicitly about Agency work or from the CIA's fieldwork itself, there are a few public CIA theorists, such as William R. Johnson (a published poet, trained in literature at Yale), who write more directly about the audio dimensions of state dossier building. Whether as a function of the atmosphere generated by the technology or because of the threat of surveillance, a Bureau listener himself proposes (somewhat remarkably) that phone conversations pressure speakers into inevitable slips: "There is something intimate and insidious about a telephone call that has me making bloopers even when I know that my phone is tapped," says Johnson in his treatise *Thwarting Enemies at Home and Abroad: How to Be a Counterintelligence Officer.* "I mention," he continues, "the real destination of a forthcoming trip or the real name of a contact that I am supposed to keep secret." Even an inkling of this potential problem, or a stance generated to combat it, becomes an audible sign: "If I am obviously careful, I gave away the fact that I suspect I am being watched."[61]

While a hidden microphone or bug reduces some of these problems, it introduces others: "If you collect oral history by recording interviews,"

Johnson casually notes about the audio aesthetics of his interrogation sessions, "you have noticed that your machine picks up and amplifies the rustling of paper, the striking of a match, the sound of an aircraft overhead, which the conversers do not notice. Yet the microphone will fail to get muttered phrases that the conversers understand clearly."[62] Because a microphone, unlike the human mind, "cannot filter out irrelevant sound nor supply meaning through rational interpretation, monitoring and transcribing the take from a bug are therefore demanding chores":

> The monitor must strain to hear the words, playing portions over and over. He or she must speculate continuously about what communication is going on unheard— gestures, facial expressions, scribbled notes passed back and forth. The monitor must fight boredom and fatigue as hours go by without a word being uttered. Finally, the monitor must keep the kind of log that can be understood by an analyst and that can be easily collated with information from other sources.[63]

As Johnson notes, bugs are indiscriminate: they catch not only the moments at which suspects confess their revolutionary plots to their assembled conspirators, who assent audibly, but also the moments suspects flush their toilets, dry their hair, rattle their dishes, or remain silent for several hours between periods of terse, nonrevelatory conversation. Worse, bugs don't separate this ambient sound from speech, lumping airplane hiss, match striking, paper shuffling right along with the Bureau's preferred domain of self-compromising sentences in the truly confessional mode of lyric poetry. This loss of fidelity and entrance of ambient sound ultimately estranges conversation, all of which puts the "monitor" into the position of replaying the tape and trying to make out muttered, partly inaudible words—trying to establish a reliable lexical record—and reenacting the drama of human interaction by adding the nonlexical dimension of gesture, expression, and so on. Such an interpretive practice calls on the monitor's general scholarly skills and imagination, as well as on a specific readerly practice (in which Johnson would have been trained at Yale) that has been at the center of poetry interpretation since the invention of the "persona" in the early twentieth century: the reconstruction of a speaker's "attitude," "tone," or "situation." Here it is the perceived lack in the audio archive that calls out for this imagined completion, with the monitor acting out the various emotional stances a particular speaker might have struck upon enunciation of individual phrases.[64] Such hypothetical reenactments might have been one strategy for filling the long gaps in the audio archive, which introduce, as Johnson says, the threat of boredom.

The character of this boredom may take a moment to imagine in this era of digital searches, when audio research no longer necessarily involves the sharing of duration: listeners now, that is, can speed through the dull moments until they hit on the word or phrase they want, whereas 1960s listeners were forced to share at times seemingly interminable ongoingness with their subjects. These listeners from an older technological regime, that is, shared downtime with those on whom they spied; they shared the time between events—the lulls, gaps, and digressions of everyday life. If wiretaps tended to condense the experience of surveillance into content-rich epiphany-poem-like exchanges, bugs flattened what the Bureau knew as content into a temporally extended and not always human-centric field—an "allover" surveillance work very much like the Black Mountain poets and other modernist open field poets were beginning to create in the 1950s. Bureau spies who wanted the crisp confession of guilt one hears in "My Last Duchess" were confronted instead with the uncontainable ongoingness of *The Maximus Poems* in a frightening array of bugged hippie crash pads. Where exactly to direct one's attention?

Ginsberg seems to have shared the CIA's frustration: he too confronted the difficulty of making out words in ambient settings subject to background noise—like his VW camper. "Quietness, quietness / over this countryside / except for unmistakable signals on radio."[65] If radio was unmistakable, his own voice in the VW was not. "It's not the vast plains mute our mouths."[66] In an environment of road noise, radio drone, and open-window hiss, the logos of poetry was subject to qualification; lifting one's voice aloud to declare the end of the war was also a matter of distinguishing that voice from the non-semantic symphonies that threatened to envelop and neutralize it: air and radio hiss of the inner environment, snatches of conversation, as well as ongoing nonintentional corporeal sounds—coughs, stomach rumbles, displaced mucus. Here, the "pflegm" Ginsberg missed in the Sinatras came back with a vengeance.

While this dimension of the project is now perhaps its most compelling part, at the time it appears that Ginsberg saw his Uher merely as a voice-registration machine or as a text-to-be registration machine. And, indeed, its very status *as* a machine was somewhat tricky, given Ginsberg's continuous evocation not merely of unmediated presence and breath but of an antinomy between this value and its would-be self-evident opposite in the world of technics: television, radio, mechanized war—"all this black language / writ by machine!"[67] Machinic language supported the war. While the poet's own statements about his trip did acknowledge and even advertise the use of the Uher, this technological interface could perhaps be managed by keeping its actual effects, its overlapping of sonic regimes, and its courting of site-specific audio effects and of the nonsemantically corporeal away from our ears.

Had Ginsberg wanted to, he, unlike most poets, could probably have brought out *The Fall of America* or even just the poem "Wichita Vortex Sutra" as an LP in 1966. Ginsberg, the former ad man, was indeed extremely savvy about situating his work.[68] Encountering enormously positive feedback at his readings of the poem, Ginsberg decided not to wait for *The Fall of America* (which would not be completed until 1972) but instead to publish "Wichita Vortex Sutra" immediately—first in *The Village Voice* (April 28, 1966), then in the magazine *Ramparts* (November 1966), and finally in the book *Planet News* (1968). The poem was devoured in its paper and magazine publications: in *The Village Voice* by New York counterculture; in *Ramparts* by a much wider and more geographically dispersed New Left readership. *Ramparts*, in 1966, was in fact the most influential Left periodical in the United States.[69] This was so for a number of reasons, but the most important was its revelation, in the April 1966 issue, that the CIA had secretly used Michigan State University to train Saigon police.[70] The CIA had known that this revelation was coming and already begun hostile research on the magazine's editors, contributors, and funding sources. Despite looking into it, the Agency had not found a way to shut down *Ramparts*, so the article was published.

By November 1966, when Ginsberg's poem was printed in *Ramparts*, the CIA was even more interested in the magazine than they had been the previous spring because the CIA had learned of its plans to do an even larger piece on the Agency's underwriting of both the National Student Association and the Congress for Cultural Freedom. It was in this context that Ginsberg's poem would have come to the attention of William Johnson's boss at the Agency—James Jesus Angleton (1917–87), a CIA critic whose close relation to literature was evident throughout his career—so much so that Angleton's famous description of counterespionage work as a "wilderness of mirrors" is a quote from T. S. Eliot's "Gerontion." "It is no accident," Johnson writes with Angleton in mind, "that some of the most effective British and American CI [counterintelligence] officers in World War II were drafted into that war from their positions as critics of English literature," as were both Johnson and Angleton—classmates at Yale.[71] In Angleton's case, this drafting happened at the hands of one of his professors at Yale, Norman Holmes Pearson, a well-known anthologist and archive builder among high modernists, who, in 1943, secured Angleton a position in London at the Office for Special Services (OSS), the forerunner to the CIA. Pearson, Angleton, Johnson, and other Yale-educated CIA agents saw literary study, and New Critical method in particular, as powerful training for intelligence work. It was, indeed, this *other* Yale School that provided the methodological underpinnings for the CIA's research, audio and textual. Such students of English literature had been trained, Johnson continues,

> to look for multiple meanings, to examine the assumption hidden in words and phrases, and to grasp the whole structure of a poem or a play, not just the superficial plot or statement. So the multiple meanings, the hidden assumptions, and the larger pattern of CI cases were grist for their mill. I do not require my young CI officers to be able to discuss the complexities of a Shakespeare play, but if I catch them studying Brooks and Warren's *Understanding Poetry*, I do not instantly send them off to the firing range. I tell them to go read Cleanth Brooks on "the language of paradox," because CI is the act of paradox.[72]

In addition to studying with Pearson, Angleton had taken classes at Yale with Maynard Mack and William Wimsatt.[73] Beyond his immediate professors, Angleton was exposed to the larger New Critical method through the writings of I. A. Richards, Brooks and Warren, and above all William Empson, whose *Seven Types of Ambiguity* was especially influential.[74] But Angleton was also a poet and editor, and it was in this capacity that, at Yale, he began coediting (with Reed Whittemore, and later Johnson) the literary magazine *Furioso*, which ran from 1939 until 1953 and published high-modernist authors including Williams, e e cummings, Lorine Niedecker, Ezra Pound, W. H. Auden, Marianne Moore, Wallace Stevens, Henri Michaux (and perhaps surprisingly, Neruda and Brecht), as well as younger poets such as John Ashbery, Jackson Mac Low, Kenneth Koch, and Robert Lax.[75] Thus, Angleton's close involvement with the critical methods of his professors and the wider culture of Anglo-American midcentury critical thought was not limited to his undergraduate years. Providing him the opportunity to edit and correspond extensively with a range of significant critics and poets, the magazine seems to have launched Angleton in the literary world.

Angleton's access to high-modernist writers was also aided by his job during World War II, when, while working on the OSS's counterespionage team (in which the British trained Americans in espionage in exchange for war help), he was introduced to Pearson's circle: H.D., Eliot, E. M. Forster, the Sitwells, Graham Greene, Benjamin Britten, and others.[76] Ultimately H.D.'s daughter Perdita became Angleton's secretary and coined the term "Tapeworm Manor" for Bletchley Park, since the use of tape was crucial within the decryption process under way there.[77] "Angleton had first been taught close reading by American masters: Pearson's colleagues at Yale, chiefly Maynard Mack," his biographer, James Holzman, notes. "The war would teach him to read all over again. It taught him to read secrets. It also taught him to look for secrets to read" (*JA*, 50).[78]

Though we can thank Holzman for bringing out the literary implications of Angleton's work in great detail, it is also worth noting that poets in the 1960s and 1970s were aware not only of Angleton's labors for the Agency but also of his larger effect on poetics. In a remarkable piece, "T. S. Eliot Entered My Dreams," Ginsberg himself imagines confronting Eliot about offering Angleton modernist poetics as the wilderness of mirrors out of which the latter would carve a counterintelligence practice: "And yourself . . . What did you think of the domination of poetics by the CIA? After all, wasn't Angleton your friend? Didn't he tell you to revitalize the intellectual structure of the West against the so-to-speak Stalinists?" Ginsberg seems not to have been satisfied with Eliot's answer that "there are all sorts of chaps competing for dominance, political and literary . . . your Gurus for instance, and the Theosophists" and that Angleton's actual literary influence was "well meant but of no importance to Literature" since the younger poet continues to lecture Eliot for another five pages on the evils of "energy monopolies" and the Angleton-influenced "square intellectuals" that, under the umbrella of the CIA, propped them up.[79]

The American part of the career Ginsberg here laments began in Washington when Angleton brought his literary skills to the CIA's counterintelligence staff beginning in 1954.[80] One of Angleton's jobs was the illegal reading of mail to and from the Soviet Union, which both the Agency and the FBI were surreptitiously intercepting.[81] "A total of 215,820 letters would actually be opened, producing a computerized index of 2 million names."[82] Indulging

the "taste for irony . . . he had acquired at Yale," the counterintelligence officer would, in later life, respond to casual inquiries about his profession with
the suggestion that he was "a Post Office employee" (*JA*, 174). Angleton—who
we are told "would spend an hour and a half every morning going through
his office to see if it had been bugged"[83]—was also directly involved with
tape, since the main telegraph companies (which voluntarily delivered all of
their messages directly to the National Security Agency [NSA]) stored their
information on magnetic tapes.[84] Ultimately, however, the mass of information Angleton obtained through paper, tape, and electronic surveillance was
used primarily to pursue counterespionage, the rooting out of potential moles
within the Agency.

The suggestion by the would-be Soviet defector Anatoliy Golitsyn that he
might be able to help identify an already-existing mole in the Agency was
one of the reasons Angleton lavished enormous attention on his case, along
with that of Yuri Ivanovich Nosenko, about whom Angleton was far more
skeptical.[85] Were they authentic defectors or KGB plants designed to spread
misinformation? Here, Angleton's skill as a close reader, a student of ambiguity, was at its best: studying every utterance and gesture within a vast world
of possibly relevant information, Angleton eventually came up with a set of
meticulously reasoned hypotheses about their relative merits as defectors,
the authenticity of their would-be information, and their future reliability.
Over the course of his research, his CIA began to run into conflicts both in
articulating its own priorities and, with the FBI, in divvying up territory and
agreeing on methods.[86] Angleton's work on Nosenko or Golitsyn was what we
might think of as monographic CIA scholarship: a single figure, studied in
excruciating detail, organized a vast landscape of political struggles. At the
same time, however, the CIA was under pressure to produce evidence of the
KGB's funding of antiwar efforts, and this entailed casting a far wider net and
operating within a broader, more sociological or historical mode of analysis.
As it increased its bugging and wiretapping of the New Left, the CIA also put
every single member of SDS under surveillance, as it did every major peace and
protest group throughout the country (*JA*, 178–79). "Some 300,000 individuals were indexed in a CIA computer system and separate files were created
on approximately 7,200 Americans and over 100 domestic groups during the
course of CIA's Operation CHAOS (1967–1973)" (*JA*, 287). During this period,
thousands of academics began to work for the CIA, in turn generating even

more data for the Agency.[87] Rather rapidly, the volume of this surveillance fieldwork became a problem.

Given the ambition and scale of such a research project, it was difficult for CIA agents to reconcile the close study of singular Soviet masterminds like Nosenko and Golitsyn with the vast surveillance networks that were now in operation. The new methods meant not only that greater amounts of information were generated but also that new kinds of patterns began to emerge within this morass of "data."[88] With this much information, again computer tape was required to organize and sort such an archive, specifically the Interdivision Information Unity, which merged the FBI and CIA file systems. Receiving more than forty-two thousand intelligence reports a year, "IDIU computer tapes, which included 10–12,000 entries on 'numerous antiwar activists and other dissidents,' were provided to the Central Intelligence Agency in 1970" (*JA*, 247). As computerized "tape" began to organize a newly sprawling archive of surveillance subjects, the Agency's model of interpretation also transformed.

This shift could be understood as one from monographic to sociological surveillance, from extensive interpretation of singular masterminds to broader, more historicist readings of many figures considered as types or models but whose interiorities did not receive the kind of extended scrutiny accorded to the Soviet defectors or faux defectors. The problem was, however, that the close-reading techniques of the CIA's stable of Yale-trained or Yale teaching theorists (including Angleton, Johnson, Pearson, and Kent) did not quite lend themselves to a sudden historical or sociological turn. Unprepared, this *other* Yale school was in the process of transforming its reading protocols when the Agency's dirtier work began to be exposed in the early 1970s and then came under massive public scrutiny by the Church Committee.[89] By that time Angleton was fired and the Agency, more generally, was transformed. Still, a decade before New Historicism, and even before post-Althusserian Marxism had fully entered the United States, this first Yale school was struggling to turn away both from monographic criticism and from the one-cause-above-all theory of Soviet infiltration.[90] While the results of their fieldwork and evidence collection within the New Left suggested the necessity of these new interpretive paradigms, presidential pressure and perhaps long habits of thought continued to make fundamental change difficult.[91]

But if the one-enemy theory supported by Angleton, Nixon, Hoover, and others seems to do violence to the various energies that mobilized the New Left, it may be useful, before dismissing it out of hand, at least to compare some of its structural features to a theoretical model that has remained central to the humanities since its articulation only a few years after: that of Fredric Jameson's classic work, *The Political Unconscious* (1981). Recoding Northrop Frye's four levels of interpretation (literal, allegorical, moral, and anagogical) from a theological into a political register, Jameson takes aim at a pluralism that would find itself satisfied in a text's ability to generate meaning on many levels instead of taking on the more rigorous project of correlating, organizing, and finally producing a hierarchy among those discrepant levels. Within the larger context of the "critical marketplace," such a pluralist stance might advertise a text's ability to sustain psychoanalytic, structuralist, myth critical, and Marxist readings. But rather than just note a lack of critical rigor in the failure to correlate and evaluate these frames, Jameson suggests a more insidious ideological project. Since, according to him, "the mind" is in fact "not content until it puts some order in these findings and invents a hierarchical relationship among its various interpretations," the real motivation for pluralism is less a wide-eyed marveling at a text's boundless generation of effects than a negative project, an attempt "to forestall the systematic articulation and totalization of interpretive results which can only lead to embarrassing questions about the relationship between them and in particular the place of history and the ultimate ground of narrative and textual production."[92] Pluralism, then, is for Jameson a negative enterprise designed precisely to *contain* the threat of Marxism. The point to emphasize, in the context of Bureau and Agency interpretation, is that these "embarrassing questions" would pertain not merely to the other critical models listed previously but also to explicitly New Left methods: critical race studies, feminism, and ecology, for example, when seen in relation to anticapitalism and anti-imperialism.

We have, in other words, an inverse version of Angleton's one-enemy theory. To highlight this is not to critique Jameson for insensitivity or failure to recognize allies. It is rather to suggest that part of the bravura force of Jameson's book, part of what accounts for its ability to remain within critical discourse for almost forty years, comes from the way that it rethinks critical methods in relation to one another without infinite pluralization—and this necessitates subordinating some questions to others, if also recoding the relationship between these various methods.[93] While obviously Jameson's politics are an inversion of Angleton's, nonetheless Jameson claims to see *through* the various surface disruptions of the New Left to what he describes, unequivocally, as their "untranscendable horizon" (and thus their potential reconciliation) within class antagonisms endemic to capitalism.[94] Jameson's work is antipluralist (it hardly needs saying), not because of a lack of sympathy for the concerns that drive the various branches of the New Left but because a pluralism of causes is understood to stand directly in the place of, and thus render impossible, a more primary struggle against capitalism, which, in his model, gives rise to these other antagonisms as well. The subtler one-enemy theorists within the state certainly welcome pluralism and, even, in a pinch, grant its real force for many in the New Left; they simply assert that whatever the pluralist desires that may mobilize New Left activists, the very fact of their coming together (as a counterculture aligned against the Vietnam War and the daily revelations about the illegal activities of the surveillance state) both works into and is crucially aided by the main Cold War adversary of the United States. What these inverse "untranscendable horizon" arguments share is a common referent and understanding of antagonism, as well as a fundamental sense that the final significance and effects of political activists should be understood as independent of intentions.[95]

In the overall scope of things, Jameson's generative thinking is not likely to suffer by briefly entertaining the bad company of Angleton: a "theorist" who long believed that Henry Kissinger was a KGB spy and that the Black Panthers were a North Korean front operation. Despite the jaw-dropping character of some of Angleton's views, they were, as I've suggested, part of a rare commitment to understanding totality that invites the comparison. Nor am I trying to suggest that distortions (of the lumping rather than splitting sort) are an inevitable by-product of totalizing thought, Angleton's or Jameson's. Rather, I push on these odd, uneven, and perhaps uncomfortable comparisons to propose that the interpretive practices of the Agency and the Bureau (often seen as caricatures of ineptitude) are better positioned a bit closer to the world of poetry and poetics in which government spies were educated, with their ongoing struggles for currency and prestige.

Angleton found himself within such a struggle in June 1966 when he turned to the *Ramparts* case and was asked to read it within the more horizontal, sociological mode rather than within the biographical, vertical mode that was his specialty. Still on the case later that year, he would, in the November 1966 issue, have encountered "Proem to Wichita Vortex Sutra" (the first printing of part 1 of Ginsberg's two-part poem).[96] Angleton read *Ramparts* very carefully, eventually, in his thematic analysis of the magazine, suggesting that the magazine had transformed "from a New Left organ to an outlet for standard Soviet propaganda" (*JA*, 236). "He based this," Holzman explains,

> on the percentage of times certain themes appeared in the magazine's articles—how many times they said the United States was "sick," for example; how many times they said the present U.S. government was fascistic; how many times the magazine said the Catholic Church was reactionary and hierarchical; and how many times the publication said the FBI and CIA were "evil." (*JA*, 236)

One imagines that, considering Ginsberg's countercultural and antiwar profile, his poem was given the political power the Agency associated with articles in prose and read in this category. How, then, would the results have looked? Ginsberg does not speak directly of the government as "fascistic," or the United States as "sick." But his poem (like *The Fall of America* as a whole) is obviously about something very close: the country's "sins" (especially in Vietnam, mentioned explicitly), the aggression of its leaders—straight (Johnson) and closeted (Hoover)—and the media climate that sustains this aggression: "How big is the prick of the President? / How big is Cardinal Viet-Nam? / How little the prince of the F.B.I., unmarried all these years!"[97] While it sounds wrong to speak here of nuance, one wonders nonetheless whether Angleton's lexical searches could capture the slight deviation between his search terms and Ginsberg's vocabulary.

Certainly the poem presents the poet's own dramatic entrance into Kansas as a threat to government: "angry telephone calls to the University / Police dumbfounded leaning on / their radiocar hoods."[98] And yet this threat is not figured as a violent political transformation that might galvanize elements of the New Left into revolutionary actors so much as a *degalvanizing process* that might take sectors of the population out of consideration for military service at the same time as it brings them into a new relation to their own bodies. Ginsberg says directly to students in Kansas: "Make it inconvenient for them to take you, tell them you love them, tell them you slept with *me*."[99] While that specific strategy does not get mentioned explicitly in the poem, the larger attention to contact and corporality does: "Babes need the chemical touch of flesh in pink infancy, / lest they die Idiot returning to Inhuman."[100] Becoming "freer than America" will, in Ginsberg's logic, bring us all into closer contact with our "small hairy bun'd vaginas, / silver cocks, armpits and breasts."[101] What did this mean to Angleton, to whom a coworker had to explain what the word "fellatio" meant? Inasmuch as Angleton believed that the magazine was bound up with a "Soviet plot" (*JA*, 233), perhaps the threshold of the problem for him was a commitment to the antiwar movement: in this scenario, *whatever* one's reasons might have been, *all* war protesting was—as Hoover might have put it—doing the work of the Soviets. And while it is certainly plausible that the KGB was involved in supporting the antiwar movement, the attempt to make that movement a simple function of a communist plot obviously did violence to the complex realities of the New Left, including, in Ginsberg's case, civil rights, antihomophobia, the decriminalization of drug use, feminism, and ecology.[102]

There were, to be sure, some established New Left figures publishing in *Ramparts*: Frantz Fanon, Regis Debray, Eldridge Cleaver, Noam Chomsky, Tom Hayden, Cesar Chavez, Howard Zinn, Paul Krassner, John Scheer, and Studs Terkel.[103] But Angleton's argument, again, was not that the magazine was a threat *because* of its strong New Left orientation but because of its supposed shift beyond that position, "from a New Left organ to an outlet for standard Soviet propaganda."[104] Through the complex analyses offered by *Ramparts*'s writers, through the various and disparate accounts of America's political situation across a wide variety of genres, it was as if Angleton could hear only a higher or lower proportion of references to sickness, fascism, or sins: a series of lexemic keywords has overtaken a syntax of thought; a substantive-based model of equivalence has crowded out relational thinking of differences, gradations, and even singularities. Despite the temptation to distance Agency scholarship from would-be rigorous criticism in the humanities, the more fascinating and accurate path is to recognize its deep kinship to much current scholarship: Angleton, in fact, seems to anticipate current scholarship in the digital humanities. This is, moreover, a short-term side project in comparison to the work for which he is better known: his monographic, high-modernist interpretation of would-be Soviet defectors, which apparently kept the Agency free of moles and thus earned its central position within the theories developed by the first Yale school. Nor was the CIA's theoretical range contained within the opposition between author-centric monographic criticism and historicist attention to themes and keywords. Rather, the Agency's readers also pronounced more broadly on problems of evidence collection, on the nature of the hypothesis in argumentation, and on the medial conditions of (and consequent interpretive dilemmas generated by) their own surveillance equipment.

But at times practical exigencies could crowd out theoretical niceties. This seems to have been the case with the Agency's work on *Ramparts*. By the following April, after *Ramparts* had further revealed that the National Student Association and the Congress for Cultural Freedom were both CIA fronts, the CIA would have twelve agents researching more than three hundred people associated with the magazine.[105] Their interest, now, was simply in halting the publication that was churning out these exposés on the Bureau and Ginsberg's critique of American radio; "the Agency was," as Holzman tells us, "trying to find a way of shutting down the magazine that would stand up in court" (*JA*, 231).

But if "Wichita Vortex Sutra" was an experimental response to radio's role in national subject formation, Angleton would in reviewing *Ramparts*'s output for 1967 also have run across another, perhaps even more troubling model of a sonic counterpoetics: this in Gary Snyder's review of William S. Burroughs's new novel, *The Ticket That Exploded*. The article might have registered first merely because it included words and phrases Angleton likely classed within his Soviet lexicon: Western culture is "exploding in our hands," in part because of our "overreaching craving and aggression"; the novel's plot line is the "destruction and renovation of the universe." More fascinating, however, is the specific characterization of this political struggle: not so much that it "is taking place not in any obvious political arena but in the consciousness of most beings on this planet"—a common enough point of departure for ideological analysis—but that because of this, new technologies are the key to winning, especially, a new set of critical soundscapes established by "sophisticated mixing and scrambling of tapes."[106]

Burroughs had asserted this in an essay titled "The Invisible Generation" appended to the novel Snyder was reviewing. To step briefly outside Snyder's review and directly into Burroughs's essay, we note the latter's claim that "what we see is determined to a large extent by what we hear," and that "a tape recorder is an externalized section of the human nervous system."[107] This leads Burroughs to propose that studying one's own sound via tape allows one to understand "who programs you" and "who decides what tapes play back in present time."[108] Like Ginsberg in his mobile recording van subjecting himself to and pushing back against, the radio soundscape of the Vietnam War in the United States, Burroughs believes that hearing precedes and conditions sight and forms subjectivity: "Look around you   look at a control machine programmed to select the ugliest stupidest most vulgar and degraded sounds for recording and playback which provokes uglier stupider more vulgar and degraded sounds to be recorded and play back inexorable degradation."[109] Burroughs hears a cruel and cretinous American logos clicking the state's pervasive, infinitely networked tape recorder—and thus holding in thrall a vast army of abject zombies, awaiting only their marching orders. Burroughs proposes that the "only way to break the inexorable down spiral of ugly uglier ugliest recording and playback is with counterrecording and playback   the first step is to isolate and cut association lines of the control machine."[110] Burroughs then outlines an entire repertoire of counterrecording techniques: from sound gathering—"recording your boss and co-workers," or going "to the zoo [to] record the bellowing of Guy the Gorilla"; to hostile or sympathetic editing; to public, disruptive playback in order to "influence and create events," in short, to disrupt existing media/political regimes and create other ones.[111]

One of the keys to this, Snyder emphasizes, is a new kind of composite subjectivity that would emerge via the overlap of two discrete voices: "in splicing together two voices onto one tape, alternating the voices at very short intervals, and then playing back . . . one gets a remarkable breakdown of separate entities and a third, new entity emerges whose existence is in the medium of sound alone."[112] This, according to Burroughs, leads to a radical breakthrough: "The practical effect on personality, we are told, is enlightening, in that it destroys one's usual thought-and-word association habits. . . . So, Burroughs suggests, extensive tape recorder spiritual-psychological discipline will liberate you from our old controlled nervous system habits better than 'twenty years of sitting in the lotus posture.'"[113] Burroughs, however, remained concerned that his "insights" had not been correctly followed. Two years later, in another piece on tape recording, he paused to contemplate the reception of his first essay: "(I wonder if anybody but CIA agents read this article or thought of putting these techniques into actual operation.)"[114]

Certainly the CIA and the FBI *did* read *The Ticket That Exploded*, especially its appended essay on tape recording. Yet its methods would have been by then somewhat passé. As happy as the Agency and the Bureau both might have been about the pro–Vietnam War mediascape from which Ginsberg recoiled on his cross-country trip, their strategy was not merely to program listeners via sound—to send messages and wait for responses, to follow the sonic protocols Burroughs outlines. Rather, from the late 1950s onward, the FBI increasingly followed another path—one spurred by the fact, to which all of us can attest, that research-oriented scholarship is often more time-consuming, less satisfying, and less conclusive than it ought to be. It was as a response to this frustration that J. Edgar Hoover and Clyde Tolson, over a lunch of thick bloody steaks, had the brainstorm for the COINTELPRO, which made the crucial shift from gathering evidence to planting it, from passively spying to infiltrating, disrupting, and indeed acting out the imagined crimes of the New Left. In other words, the FBI now sought simply to *produce* the revolutionary acts it had initially tried to record via tape.[115]

Sonic research's registration of sites and not merely voices, its indiscriminate and nonanthropocentric dimension, presented problems that caused its users to retreat and recoil, to compensate for this excess, which was often perceived as a lack of human control and human centrality. But whereas Ginsberg, when confronted with the soundscape of his actual cross-country tape, retreated to the safe domain of print, the Bureau and Agency listeners understood the evidentiary problems of tape to point in another direction: *their* reassertion of decisive authorship among landscapes of static and inconclusive grunts took the path of parachuting their own men into the scene so that now, finally, they could hear and see the evidence of disruption they so wanted.

The Bureau did this by planting evidence—by, for instance, stealing the diary of a Progressive Labor Party member in Los Angeles, altering it to include incriminating "evidence," and then sending it to another member of the party in hopes of creating the suspicion that the first member was an informant; a Bureau memo from August 31, 1970, documents as much. Similarly, in an effort to trip up SDS, Bureau scribes assumed the roles of disgruntled former lovers and wrote parents about their daughters' supposed sexual diseases and crude behavior. One hateful Bureau ventriloquist had in 1964 assumed the voice of an African American preacher disillusioned by audiotapes of MLK's sexual escapades and urged King's suicide as the most practical way to cauterize the wound these tapes' release would produce for African American activists. Such strategies proliferated, however, as COINTELPRO expanded its operations.[116] By the late 1960s many Bureau writers were, for instance, imper-sonating rival gangs within Los Angeles, composing letters aimed at stirring up discontent against the Black Panthers, which led to actual killings.[117] Most common of all, however, were fake leaflets, designed to look like they were actually written by SDS or other related groups and of course to create confu-sion, competition, lack of trust, and eventual implosion.[118] These went hand in hand with doctored, cropped, or simply out-of-context photographs, such as one circulated by the Bureau to discredit Jerry Rubin of the Yippies, show-ing him "in compromising position with the Cincinnati Police Department" to create suspicion within the Weatherman organization that Rubin was actually working for the cops.[119] But when all else failed—when even the cre-ation of documentary evidence would not drive home the results the Bureau wanted—then it was time for operatives to head into the field and simply perform the acts about which they had fantasized—earphones on, concen-trated in listening, out of sight in their surveillance locations in the apartment next door or in the van down the street.[120] These were the acts—like lowering the flag in Grant Park during the Siege of Chicago in 1968—calculated most to outrage the public, discredit the New Left, and drive rifts among its vari-ous elements.[121] If they had been, not long before, state scholars listening and studying, "the man with the tape recorder," now they became performance artists enacting, and leading others toward, the very crimes that would justify the repressions they sought to enforce.

Not surprisingly, the Bureau does not leave a large body of theoretical writings about this aspect of its practice. But if, despite a few terse memos, the Bureau remained largely mute about this method, if it too seems to present a documentary gap in the record, the practice itself is surprisingly eloquent. It can sustain, I believe, the kind of immanent theorization offered here. It emerges, we might say, from the limitations and difficulties of generating compelling documentary evidence through on-site audio research. This was the case because tape, despite its celebrants' claims, could not be relied on to capture the kind of unequivocal evidence one seemed to need. This was not simply, or at least not only, a matter of the kind of medial ambiguities and disruptive ambient noises discussed by William Johnson; one also seemed to need gesture, presence—some mysterious supplement to compensate for the oddly inhuman domain of recording.

And this, too, is what Ginsberg recognized on his cross-country trip. That the original tapes used to generate both "Wichita Vortex Sutra" and *The Fall of America* more broadly did not themselves become an LP tells us something about media poetics in the late 1960s. Piano jazz was a fine background for Jack Kerouac's 1959 recording with Steve Allen, *Poetry for the Beat Generation*; musical accompaniment could also work when Ginsberg was singing William Blake.[122] But in such cases music was a clearly subordinate frame that set off the human voice. Ginsberg might even consciously mechanize that voice, as he did in the first release of *Howl and Other Poems*, in which he reads in a strange monotone—as if to suggest the inhuman pressure that bears down on a subject and forces its howl. But ambient radio sound, throat gurgles, open windows, and the hum of the car were, finally, a different matter. If these today might seem to secure for us the "concept" of a countermedia bubble moving across the toxic landscape, for Ginsberg they were a more fundamental threat—one that, to be contained, needed to be translated to the more human domain of print.

The Eigner Sanction
Keeping Time from the American Century

Whoever dwells everywhere, Maximus, dwells nowhere at all.

—Martial

At one point in Clint Eastwood's 1975 film *The Eiger Sanction*, his character, Dr. Hemlock, an art historian and retired government assassin who has been called back in to perform one last sanction, is summoned to a darkened room where Dragon, the light-sensitive, ex-Nazi albino mastermind of the secret government agency C2, is having a routine, though necessary, blood transfusion.[1] Before detailing the requirements of the sanction, Dragon, feeling chatty, teases Hemlock about the latter's art-buying habit, mentioning what he knows the brutal connoisseur has already set his crosshairs on: a rare Pissarro will go up for auction just when the fee from this last sanction arrives. But Hemlock won't soil his impressionism by dragging it into discussion with this embodiment of the lame, bloodless, and increasingly untrustworthy state. Indeed, the arc of *The Eiger Sanction*'s plot involves a typically mid-1970s disaffiliation with what had seemed (to many, at least, just a few years before) the given imperatives of the Cold War: Hemlock's targets are ultimately no worse than his "allies"— like his old friend Ben Bowman (played by George Kennedy), who turns out to be the double agent Hemlock was in fact supposed to rub out. By the time Hemlock learns of Bowman's treachery, the assassin has soured not as much on state-sponsored murder as on the petty and vindictive way in which the United States now selects its sanctions. So he grants Bowman amnesty.

What the tight-lipped Hemlock does *not* do, in other words, in his gesture of breaking with the US state's agenda, is leak compromising information about his secret government unit, as so many dissatisfied civil servants began to at the time—about Vietnam, about the illegal operations of the president, the FBI, and the CIA.[2] Displeased but not voluble, Hemlock would not have been a problem for the new legions of plumbers trying to fix such leaks by performing audio surveillance on civil servants.[3] Hemlock's response to misused power is a tad more old West. When he's not punching, kicking, or throwing his adversaries out windows, he is cutting them short in conversation—as he does with a cruel rhetorical question to Dragon's overtures about Pissarro: "Does your physical disability preclude you from coming to the point?"[4]

Two years earlier Leonard Henny and Jan Boon had produced a film on the American poet Larry Eigner.[5] Because Eigner's speech was affected by his cerebral palsy, the filmmakers decided to have Allen Ginsberg do most of the reading, in some cases followed by Eigner. After one poem and a brief scene-setting on Eigner by the narrator, Ginsberg offers his own framing of Eigner's work:

Ah, obviously the form of the verse is dictated by his physical condition of slow hesitancy and difficulty in maintaining his hand steady to write words. And as the words come swiftly through his mind he has to stop his whole thought process to write down a word while thoughts are going on still.

Two temporalities, then, in Ginsberg's reading—a fast time of thought and a slow time of difficult key pressing. Eigner's particular aesthetic, his version of an open field poetics, is produced by the irreconcilable conflict between them. He cannot come fully to the point because the physical labor of registering a single word is so great and the time of his thinking necessarily so much faster that his forlorn lexemes, out in their vast expanses of white page, will always remain but romantic ruins of the richer internal thought processes out of which they emerge. When the transcript of this film was later published, Eigner added a note to Ginsberg's statement, hinged on the word "obviously." "Obvious," it reads, "but not too good a guess."[6]

On September 22, 1965, Eigner, then living in his parents' house in Swampscott, Massachusetts, started one of his more than 3,070 poems, beginning with the line "those planes were loud."[7] First published in the 1980 chapbook *Flat and Round*, by Lyn Hejinian's Tuumba Press, Eigner's poem would thus travel both three thousand miles across the country to Berkeley and fifteen years into the future—from the beginning of escalation in Vietnam to the year of Reagan's election—before its odd, recalcitrant temporality would claim readers' attention.[8] References to the sonic dimension of air travel were a common feature of Eigner's poems. He lived less than ten miles from Logan airport in Boston and undoubtedly heard planes low in the sky on final approach and takeoff. We think of Eigner, perhaps, as the calmest, most minutely focused of the New American poets; the open field poet most given over to depiction of the micro-temporalities of his immediate daily life. "I haven't got such a relaxed feeling from anything in years," William Carlos Williams gushed about Eigner's first book: "There is no tension whatever, but a feeling of eternity."[9] "He gives to the humblest pebble," as Denise Levertov put it, "the same attention—and so the same value, by implication—as to, let's say, a man."[10] By the 1980s, experimental poets had begun to focus on how Eigner's language doubled back and complicated the picturing it might first seem to have evoked. "Eigner's poetry" was for Barrett Watten "an utterance in which things of the world and of the mind are named in a continually reflexive manner."[11] Both these features of his poetics—insistence on the contingent surroundings and their reflexive unfolding in language—suggest that the larger, exterior world of airports and transcontinental flight might seem impossibly extraneous to the second-to-second unfolding of perceptual effects among the trees in Swampscott. But looking a bit more directly at the "outside" of Eigner's poetry helps us better understand the dynamics of its singular inside—the world celebrated both by most of the poets quoted thus far and somewhat condescendingly hemmed in by Ginsberg.

If not quite at the pitch of the Cuban Missile Crisis of 1962, the Cold War was in 1965 nonetheless beginning again to simmer. Air and, above it, space were the domains, even the media, in which this agitation registered most clearly and visibly, and most distressingly if one was an American Cold Warrior involved in the space race. On March 18, the first person to walk in space had been the Soviet cosmonaut Alexey Leonov, whose Voskhod 2 mission had been launched from the Baikonur Cosmodrome, the world's first and largest space-launch facility. A month earlier, US bombers from aircraft carriers in the Gulf of Tonkin began Operation Flaming Dart in Vietnam; a week later President Johnson authorized Operation Rolling Thunder, an even larger-scale bombing mission; then in April the United States began dropping napalm throughout Vietnam, where the Johnson administration now—that July—sent 50,000 additional troops, increasing the total to 125,000.[12] In October, the United States would test a hydrogen bomb in the Aleutian Islands equal to eighty thousand tons of dynamite. And, closer to home, on July 11, a US surveillance aircraft crashed off Nantucket, killing sixteen of the nineteen crew aboard.

Developed in 1963, this plane, the EC-121 Warning Star, was charged with monitoring the Eastern Seaboard; a sequence of the aircraft flew continu-

FIGURE 3. Lockheed EC-121 Warning Star. Wikipedia Images.

ous missions over the Atlantic coast twenty-four hours a day for a decade. Producing photographic documents that would be beamed across the United States and interpreted by specialists (in a room very much like Dragon's command control center in *The Eiger Sanction*) at the NORAD Combat Operations Center in Colorado Springs, the Warning Star sought out singularities in its assigned neighborhood, tracing in particular Russian aircraft and naval vessels cruising off the East Coast of the United States.[13] While other jets of this same make provided surveillance for atomic testing in the Pacific and for the war in Vietnam, this squad remained in a kind of permanent holding pattern whose center was less than twenty miles from Eigner at another local airport, Hanscom Field in Bedford, Massachusetts.

"The plane sounds protective," Eigner writes in a May 1960 poem. That October, an Eastern Air Lines flight landing at Logan crashed into the sea, killing sixty-two of the seventy-two passengers aboard. Eigner writes directly of the accident: "planes again hove by / the corridors light   above / sirens, after the crash / this wall off toward the bay" (*EP*, 429). If Eigner's house in Swampscott was nominally protected by the Warning Star, it was also, however, an around-the-clock center for a very different kind of information gathering. Eigner's self-composed biographical statements—which have played a large role in his reception—invariably stress that radio first connected him to his circle of poets. Acting on a desire similar to that articulated by Bertolt

Brecht, who suggests that radio users attempt to "change this apparatus over from distribution to communication," Eigner, after finishing high school at home and completing seven correspondence courses from the University of Chicago, "bumped into Cid Corman reading Yeats, on the radio, in this first program . . . from Boston [in 1949].[14] I disagreed with his non-declamatory way of reciting, and wrote him so. This began a correspondence in which I got introduced to things, and the ice broke considerably."[15] No set of utterances could ever have been less declamatory than the vast collection of Eigner poems that would follow—so this anecdote has served to mark this transformation. More recently, critics have begun to reframe Eigner's statements by exploring his larger relation to radio, whose "aural qualities offer," as Seth Forrest puts it, "a model for the visual and aural parataxis that is Eigner's formal signature." Yet we might ask further just why Eigner would want to sign on to such a project—or rather, just what kind of a broadcast station Eigner developed in his quiet neighborhood on the northern shore of Massachusetts Bay?[16]

As the story goes, Eigner's first contact with a local radio station leads, through Corman, to correspondence with Robert Creeley, then Olson, Levertov, and the rest of the New American poets, as well as their editor, Donald Allen. But if radio is the democratic medium that bounces its waves from the cultural center to the isolated suburban house, allowing this "shut-in" to make virtual contact with a range of like-minded experimental poets and eventually establish a successful career, the boundless address of radio was in fact a source of anxiety for most of these poets, who tended to distrust claims about a generalized public. Creeley makes this point directly in his early correspondence with Eigner. In June or July 1950 Creeley says that he does not "give SHIT for the readers/general. Am looking only for the ONE or TWO men/ cd find sense & stimulus from contents. Useless/ to slant for a 'general' group: their 'taste' is nonexistent."[17] This is a concern that Olson, Creeley's epistolary interlocutor for eight hours a day at this point, will make soon after in his third letter of *The Maximus Poems*: "Polis now / is a few."[18] That December, in a letter that mentions trying to get hold of tapes made of Olson to play along with his own reading and discussion on an upcoming radio show hosted by Corman, Creeley continues: "Since it's very damn likely you'll have heard the program, before this gets to you, rather futile to say much more; only—— IF I stagger, mumble/ only be thinking of the excruciating horror with which I front the whole damn idea, of so becoming 'public'/ the a i r '/ well: so much for that."[19] Always committed to contexts, framing, and intimate dialogue, Creeley seeks out a narrowcast reception framework within the broadcast space of unbounded air.[20] He seeks to close the letters in the word "a i r," to bind its space in a sympathetic listening, hearing. Eigner, too, will spend his entire career contemplating the problems and opportunities of "a i r," a concept to which we will return. For now, though, let us note merely that as crucial as it was that Eigner was able to catch WMEX "on the air," to receive the anonymous Boston radio signal, in fact his daily relations to media were as much about seeking to limit, frame, and contain the external signals that were broadcast into his living environment or at least to relativize their impact by hearing them less as prompts and messages than as part of an ambient surround.

Indeed, radio is also part of a smaller-scale media ecology inside that same Swampscott house, in which the writer with limited mobility, seeking to control his thought regime and cycle of poetic production, is subjected to the less discriminate media consumption of his parents, who, as Eigner puts it, "are receptive to nothing beyond the news, radio tv talk, [Lawrence] Welk etc., and are capable only of flag-waving."[21] Whereas Ginsberg could conceive of his radio listening for *The Fall of America* as a discrete project, and indeed turn off the signal whenever he chose, Eigner had considerably less control over his media environment. And it is seemingly because of this that he writes of "mummies and armchair citizens . . . transported coolly via huntley/brinkley and bob Hope and lawrentian welk etc. nightly to a few of the hot and bright . . . spots around the world."[22] The actual noises of this passive armchair passage frequently blotted out his own attempts at more active passage through reading, as in this example in 1970 with a recent Allen Ginsberg book: "INDIAN JOURNAL i took a look at maybe 14 days ago! 1st page after the dedicatory page. Wow! That d . . .-page. And the page or so after. Words clustering space, hard to get into and stay with, maybe especially here where detective drama and whatnot comes through the walls regularly (the folks' rest, time killer and sleeping-pill)—but it gives promise of adventuring through crowds."[23] Eigner, that is, must journey through the sonic crowds in his living room to focus on Ginsberg's depiction of crowds in India. Published two years before *The Fall of America*, Ginsberg's *Indian Journals* not only depicts an earlier trip—from March 1962 to May 1963 in Calcutta and Bombay—but also a greater faith in the trip itself as a vehicle for self-discovery, and not merely, as the latter trip will become, an inventory of toxic symptoms.[24] Yet even in Eigner's experience of reading this earlier work, the very mediascape toward which Ginsberg will next turn his attention is already making the kind of concentration Eigner would like impossible.

Subject to what he complains of as his parents' "adamantly reasonable routine," Eigner proposes, nonetheless, that accepting their regimen (after long fighting it) affords him "10 or 12 hours daily [on his] own, except for tv etc., through the walls."[25] Such uncontrollable sounds, like the changing contours and textures of his workspaces (periodically rearranged by family members without his say) become the shifting membranes and ambiences of his poems:[26] "suddenly the window seems washed / the newspapers falling in the / opposite bathroom // I'm right in the reflection // permanent / radio ads" (*EP*, 311). This enveloping mediascape is thus an outer shell of contingent sound (and here printed textuality) that periodically registers within the poems, though its doing so is not always at the level of individual references to what is on the radio or in the papers, for instance.[27] More often Eigner reflects on the underlying structure of sound itself: "we're always just missing / the silent life," he writes in a 1959 poem that mentions "the office furniture / all set for acoustics" and suggests that this "silent life" might be always just missed in part because in *actual* acoustic space external sound tends to penetrate the would-be autonomous chambers of contemplation, like his workspace: "It's in fairyland that / things go around themselves / and without a spread   here / there's always some forced in" (*EP*, 308). Perhaps the central agent of this disrupted autonomy is wind, air in movement.[28]

While there are occasional complaints about distraction as in the passage about trying to read Ginsberg, more typically Eigner's approach is like that of a range of post-Cageian musicians who embrace the total spectrum of sound as the scene of a new kind of listening: "Life nowadays is full of blind dates, has been," he writes, "though most have turned out well."[29] These blind dates are, in one sense, the transforming field of his perception (visual as well as aural), the mutating contingencies that generate his open field poetics.

Given all this, it is worth pausing here to draw out a contrast with Ginsberg's media poetics. Their difference inheres not merely in the fact that Eigner was often subject to, whereas Ginsberg could frame and control, his mediascape. The more interesting contrast, which perhaps emerges in part from this condition, is that whereas Ginsberg understands his media intervention as a series of messages designed to compete with the regime of audio broadcasting, Eigner's "intervention" is a more thoroughgoing attempt to undo media's organization of time, its creation of regimes of attention, schedules of daily life, and galvanizing events. Whereas Ginsberg develops a series of countermessages (break your media thralldom to perceive how the radio's bland support for a distant war leads to the dismemberment of actual bodies, then remake your body as a love machine), Eigner goes to work on the temporal structure that makes radio effective in the first place. Perhaps art history can help us in offering a distinction that doesn't quite exist in poetry criticism: between history painting, with its attempts to depict individual events occurring at decisive and discrete moments in time, and genre painting, with its commitment not merely to repetition and ongoingness but, arguably, its critique of the event in favor of attention to the underlying conditions out of which events are constructed.[30] Framed this way, we might speak of Ginsberg as a "history" and Eigner as a "genre" poet. And while traditionally the hierarchy of the genres positioned history at the top, over the course of the nineteenth and early twentieth centuries both genre and the closely related category of landscape (in the work of Courbet, Manet, Cezanne, Hemlock's beloved Pissarro, Picasso, Braque, and others) gradually overtook history painting to the extent that, for the most part, by the early twentieth century the latter appeared self-evidently stilted in relation to the main lines of modernist experimentation.[31] Such a narrative can obviously not be transferred seamlessly to poetry history—especially if it were used to suggest that Ginsberg's work were somehow traditional and limited in relation to Eigner's. Ginsberg was, it bears stressing, trying to invent new modes of historical engagement in the 1960s rather than simply harken back to a series of hallowed conventions; and it was a measure of his success that he had as large a role in the New Left as he did. Yet highlighting Eigner's project as a kind of genre poetry, that is, as a mode that seeks to undo the rhetoric of the event, has the benefit of reframing his practice not as a mode of insular quietism or even a reflexive engagement with the language of representation as much as a profound engagement with his own mediascape—one whose full implications have still not quite been brought into view.[32]

Given Eigner's limited mobility, the shape and texture of his perceptual envelope have a kind of coherence that is atypical among poets and musicians drawn to the everyday contingencies of sound. Also, many of its transformations can even be traced to a common agency: Bessie Eigner, Larry's mother, who cared for Larry at home until the poet moved to Berkeley in 1978.[33] If the open field poetics associated especially with Black Mountain correlates the poet's breath-based being in time with a particularized registration of that temporality on the page, it also has tended to foreground the literal, physical space in which the poet operates. And this is true beyond Black Mountain and into the New American poetry more broadly—from Olson's apartment in Gloucester to O'Hara's familiar walking routes in New York City. It is in this sense that Eigner's space, his open field, is so atypical, depending to a much greater degree on the choices of others, especially those of Bessie Eigner. To grasp how Bessie Eigner's labor was also a framing condition for Larry Eigner's thought, imagine for a second Mary Olson each morning arranging the ship models and laying out the archival documents and maps in Charles's Gloucester apartment, the immediate physical field in which her son will explore his breath-based being in space and time.[34] Imagine Kay O'Hara swooping down from Worcester in the family Oldsmobile to volunteer as a lunchtime crossing guard on Fifth Avenue, before slipping into Larré's restaurant on Fifty-Sixth Street and giving Francis a meaningful look as he contemplates his fourth midday martini; or Genevieve Creeley renting a Bolinas bungalow next door to her son to cook organic dinners, clean bongs, and lay down the ground rules for when her now rather long-haired offspring could sink into acid stupors on Stinson beach. These period fantasies of feminized open fields come first because it was in fact Eigner's mother who both enabled and affected his; yet the dynamic would hardly be less strange were it a pressed-suit-wearing patriarch selecting the jade Buddhas and coarse felt throw rugs for Philip Whalen's meditation hut or the plank dimensions and floor-plan layout of Gary Snyder's house in the Sierra Nevadas. The familial legislation underlying all these not entirely open fields points to the fact that—whether urban or rural, Western or Eastern in their philosophies and aesthetics—New American poets were supposed to *construct* the physical horizons in which their perception would occur and to do so outside vertical kinship relations. Indeed, such fields were understood as "open" precisely to the degree that they resisted such determinations. Eigner's field was in this sense utterly unparalleled:

> Mother again fussing . . . herself—e.g. I woke up this morn to find her mad at the dust in livingroom bookcase she was unexpectedly cleaning and my failure to weed except insignificantly. A general admonition to be more cooperative. Afraid she'd have to send me to a [Nursing] Home if she gets too tired . . . or to St. Louis [one of

Eigner's brothers lives there] where, though, I couldn't, she stated, stay permanently. As passing remarks as ever, as much off the top of her head. Too much thought brings worry. Me and you and the lamppost.[35]

Such threats are a continuous feature of Eigner's immediate surround.[36] Yet the poet could not work were he not able, also, to enlist his disgruntled mother as one of the key scribes and secretaries that makes his production possible—most of the time.[37] "Down cellar are many letters from Creeley and a few from Olson, which I suggested be looked for," Eigner complains as he prepares a Guggenheim grant application, "but ma asserted she wouldn't be able to find em. She does have her hands full, like the rest of us."[38] At work recasting the instrumentalized time of administered media, Eigner cannot help ceding to his often recalcitrant literary secretaries both this kind of archival question and his more basic environmental conditions, including his saturation in their soundscape. And while Eigner will later have a series of poet secretaries, all of this enclosure and sonic penetration may suggest the importance of air for Eigner's poetics.[39]

Connected by radio to the outside world, introduced by radio to the field of poetry, news for Eigner is still not the hum from the other room about rockets and jets launching satellites, dropping bombs, testing nuclear weapons, spewing exfoliates, and crashing into the sea close by. Eigner's poetry, in fact, would seem to be a direct rejection of these kinds of drama, even when its highlights occur within earshot. Rather, Eigner FM tended to register events that could not be noticed, let alone broadcast, by major stations, central among these what he calls "tides of the air" (*EP*, 419) or elsewhere "the inrolled / maps in the sky" (*EP*, 425). Whether his attention is on currents of moving air themselves or clouds moved by air, both involve a kind of durational attention that resists ideas of development, conclusion, and human control more generally. Air offers an undomesticated, fluctuating space that will not permanently retain man's physical or linguistic imprint: "no axiom exists / in the air" (*EP*, 428). Whereas Creeley's concept of a kind of media "a i r" would seem to mark the distressing lack of a context, and thus give itself over to the fiction of a generalized public, Eigner could share a critique of broadcast media without saddling air itself with this fault. In Eigner's poetics, air itself would seem to be a resource for contesting the temporal organization underlying broadcast media—if also at the same time the shifting atmosphere that brings the outside world through the permeable membrane of his research station.

Air is thus at once the noninstrumental force that gives rise to the durational patterning of clouds on which he'll lavish his attention and also the larger medium through which passenger jets, surveillance planes, and even bombers move, threatening to visit another kind of cloud on his neighborhood. In fact, many of Eigner's poems from the late 1950s and 1960s explicitly reflect on the possibility of airborne nuclear destruction. But this engagement is typically understated, superimposed as one among several interpretive registers: "That the neighborhood might be covered / by one roof, occurred / this morning," Eigner writes in a 1959 poem, morphing this image of a dome into a mushroom cloud with the lines, "death when you don't want it   what you like / is a plain object // the long-trunked clouds / a weltered event" (*EP*, 305). Again, most long-trunked clouds and weltered events in Eigner's poetry are less about singular tragic occurrences—like nuclear strikes—than about the ongoing perceptual possibilities of clouds transforming in time. But the fact that there is quiet commerce—or perhaps we should call it air loss—between the durational neighborhood diorama in which Eigner labors and the outer world of nuclear strikes and airline crashes helps us understand the degree to which the former is not so much a repression of the latter as it is a patient and radical remodeling of it with the materials at hand. Or, to put it temporally rather than spatially, the slow process poetics of air always available on Eigner FM was a dramaless, eventless broadcast that achieved its traction dialectically as an aural oozing below the frequency of administered news.

Alan Davies and Richard Dillon capture this aspect of Eigner's project well in a 1974 review of the book *Anything on Its Side*: "May I speculate that he speaks to people who have not thought of listening to, let alone, observing this territory? Isn't he asking Americans to attend to a reality that other voices would not give them time to consider? What sort of person would desire to *do that*?"[40] This was the project of Eigner FM. From FDR's fireside chats of the 1930s and 1940s, to war broadcasting, through to Radio Free Europe and its equivalents in the United States of the 1950s and early 1960s, radio became a central machine of intimate address for the American state.[41] It was, for instance, over the radio and in the cozy setting of a fireside chat that, as radio historian Susan Douglas tells us, most Americans learned of the US entrance into World War II.[42] What was "intimate" about such speeches was not just that, from the late 1930s on, their messages of shared national crises that required timely action from civic-minded subjects were broadcast directly into domestic interiors.[43] Radio seemed also to come from a speaking interior directly to a receiving ear.[44] It was, we might say, media's poetry as opposed to the prose of newspapers and magazines. This ability to penetrate from a distance is what convinced writers like William S. Burroughs to approach recording as a technology of manipulation, of psychic invasion and control.[45] Locating a kind of unconscious metronymic effect, R. Murray Schafer characterizes normative radio as "the pulse of a society organized for maximum production and consumption."[46]

Yet, as Douglas and others have demonstrated, radio did not have an inherent and consistent politics.[47] The explosion of FM radio in the 1960s, for instance, challenged, at least for a time, much of what Schafer and others objected to in radio programming.[48] It's in this sense that one might speak of Eigner's poetics as resembling that of an alternative radio station: his commitment was to a slow, durational present, stripped of drama, conclusions, and temporal projections. "Despite the always hectic, mixedup and unfinished present I've decided," he writes, "that an indefinite future is worse . . . about which you're in the dark, with less and less assurance what's going to come through."[49]

Like Henry Darger's daily meteorological data, or Georges Perec's lavish attention to the micro-occurrences of a single Parisian apartment building, Eigner's extended involvement with his proximate domain should also be understood as an intentional and carefully framed project. As Eigner himself put it, "In order to relax at all I *had* to keep my attention partly away from myself, *had* to seek a home, coziness in the world."[50] Radio was, moreover, crucial in the process. As Eigner writes in a 1971 letter, "One thing that makes bks seem dispensable is radio and tv, which are now more effective here in taking me out of myself."[51] Yet this physiological constraint does not dictate the *kind* of attention Eigner will lavish on the surrounding world. Indeed, rather than see this simply as a symptomatic determination, we might understand it as a generative constraint. As Eigner writes to David Gitin in May 30, 1970, "I figure my exploratory impulse was and maybe you cd say still is sharpened by inability to get around, besides which my need, dire before 1962 cryosurgery tamed wild left limbs, to keep some way outside myself, though not too far either, a fairly precise distance—and it looks intriguing" (EC).[52] This is the reason he objects to a reading like Ginsberg's that sees Eigner's singular open field poetics as a direct mechanical consequence of his cerebral palsy. The type of exterior home Eigner will construct is not a given; nor is his patience, either in Swampscott or in Berkeley. As Eigner writes, provocatively, to his mother's query about the poet's possible loneliness after moving to Berkeley,

"As Rimbaud said, before he quit writing poetry at the age of 18 and became a smuggler of guns and a pirate, 'Je suis un autre' ('I am another')."[53] But if gun smuggling and piracy were not part of Eigner's media sanction, his identification with Rimbaud was not as idle as one might imagine. Eigner continues in the same letter: "I'm for others maybe a little more than myself, relaxing by vacationing from myself if and when I can, especially of course now that I have a feeling of being settled, and trying to see and hear (reach?) what's beyond, out of more . . . indiscriminate and non-selective curiosity so I haven't had much loneliness."[54] We see this kind of allover attention, projected out into his immediate surroundings, in the poem with which I began:

those planes were loud

       asleep
   the degrees   with my head down
    half-way to my lap

   what bird's call
    sounding close
   I haven't
    learned   a flute

     to match silence
and the sea's sound

there's nothing like music
  in the street

     out the opposite window
       along through trees

    a piano hoisted up-
      stairs slung
     level storey

   fire sire
         n   crickets   afterwards
    the hot night
     still to dawn

   the passing earth

    whirls out (*EP*, 671)

Here the external world of planes is a prompt—an alarm clock even—that as

ambient sound often does for poets (think of Wordsworth) begins the focusing process: first, on a rare image of the speaker's body and then on a series of
less dramatic, less loud, sonic occurrences that organize the neighborhood. The
failed identification of a birdcall here is also a rejected identification with birds,
say, famously melodic nightingales, as idealized figures for poetics. Similarly,
the role of the as-yet-unlearned flute would only be "to match silence / and the
sea's sound." Another celebrated melody maker, producer of expressive musical figures, must for Eigner compete against the equally fascinating ground of
silence (more Cagean than absolute) and sea murmur.[55] Here as elsewhere in
Eigner the received hierarchy of event over condition is first challenged and
then exploded—as conditions themselves become micro-events. When Eigner
writes that "there is nothing like music / in the street," he means not that literal music beyond his driveway would be an unmatched experience but that
the actual sounds of the street—on which he's just reflected—would be poorly
described by musical analogies. So flutes and birdsong are poor figures for the
poet's self-assigned role as reflexive transcriber of local audio effects. As he continues, the piano is similarly of interest not for the music that might come out
of it but for the sound its hoisting makes. In the distance fire fathers (or sires)
a siren, and crickets fill the subsequent gap, as the poet briefly tunes out from
the constantly new sounds and visual effects of the "passing earth" that "whirls
out" nearby, drawing his poem to a temporary close, which the next poem of
his street will quickly open again.[56]

As my earlier quotes from Williams and Levertov suggested, Eigner was
not unknown at the time this poem was composed. Yet his most sustained
reception would occur at least a decade later, in the 1970s and 1980s, when he
was taken up by poets associated with Language writing. Barrett Watten published him in early issues of *This*, brought out a book of Eigner's prose in 1978
(the long, elegant sentences of which casually explode Ginsberg's claim), and
then wrote on Eigner in *Total Syntax*.[57] Hejinian, as mentioned earlier, published her Tuumba Press Eigner chapbook in 1980, and Ron Silliman dedicated
his 1986 anthology of Language writing, *In the American Tree*, to Eigner. So
there was both significant interest and significant lag time: the odd temporalities of Swampscott in 1965 getting rereleased, rebroadcast, in the atmosphere
of Berkeley in the 1980s.

But it was not primarily time that caught the attention of the Language
writers. Eigner was recuperated mostly for his rejection of a speech-based

poetics. Following the blast of Robert Grenier's "I HATE SPEECH," the first line of Silliman's introduction to *In the American Tree*, the rest of this essay proposed a rereading of one wing of the New American poetry, now claimed as the radical wing, in which Creeley and Eigner became "two early 'projectivists' whose writing had transcended the problematic constraints of that tendency."[58] But did the negation of speech in fact require 3,070 poems over the course of roughly fifty years? Either it was a very eloquent and protracted renunciation, or speech kept breaking out, like small fires or insect infestations, on Eigner's street, thereby requiring his continual attention, his patient acts of sequential shushing. Understood solely as the sanctioner of speech, then, Eigner's poetics becomes that of the cranky octogenarian neighbor who has always just been woken up. Yet we see, even when he *is* actually woken up, as in the poem we just read, his poetry performs a range of far more specific sonic, temporal, and conceptual operations than can be conveyed by the raised-finger-to-lips commemorative statue fashioned for him by Silliman in his Language writing wax museum of literary history. I've suggested some of these already. But let me now reframe this problem at a larger scale by sketching another way of understanding Eigner historically, one in which his insistence on conditions rather than events might better register as the event it has already become in literary history. Eigner occupies an extreme position within New American poetry not just because he undermined a poetics of speech but also because, unlike Olson, the field of his field poetics was comparatively purged of diachronic references, of collage historicism, and was, instead, identified with an unfolding empirical situation—his Swampscott porch and the street scene beyond it over three decades—that he nonetheless refused to "capture" in pat vignettes. As Martial writes, "Whoever dwells everywhere, Maximus, dwells nowhere at all." It was, indeed, the specificity of Eigner's field that, however much it was occasionally trimmed and reframed by Bessie Eigner, makes his version of projectivism as singular as it is. The project of Eigner's projectivism was at once to insist on and destabilize his literal field by testing relations between its fleeting effects—sonic, visual—and the field of the printed page, where Eigner's lexemes invariably uncouple themselves from any simple, instrumental role and begin to take on reflexive relationships only possible on this second field. But it is the dose of empiricism within this otherwise reflexive textuality, the continued, iterative framing in relation to the porch and its surround, that turns Eigner's writing into such a site-specific, conceptually unified, and singular project: an experimental research station, observation outpost, durational diorama.[59]

What emerged from this diorama was, however, more than a subtly reflexive discourse on the depiction of space. Eigner's attention to minor time, to "another / time / in fragments" (*EP*, 357)—to nonmonumental unfolding, to a micro-temporality diametrically opposed to the would-be major events of Cold War time was in some ways the clearest and most compelling version of a larger temporal project often associated with the idea of daily life and shared by most of the New American poets, including O'Hara, Creeley, Olson, Philip Whalen, Joanne Kyger, Baraka, Jack Spicer, Mayer, and, in fact, Silliman, among others. Silliman would put his and the larger project of Language writing negatively as the critiques of representation and speech rather than as the positive experimentation with the poetics of daily life because he saw the New American version of this latter project as entailing a commitment to representation. But if daily life becomes not merely a spatial picture but a contestatory time, a time below the radar of history with a capital "H," unmanageable by the rhythmic pulses of normative radio, then we can begin to recognize a vast project of the New American poets that put them all, in different ways, in dialogue with official modes of timekeeping, and measuring more generally. Moreover, and this is the rub for Silliman's reading, we see a continuity rather than a break between New American poetry and Language writing. Both seek another time in fragments—a slowing down. If Language writing proposed a higher degree of reflexivity, the implied liberation to be wrested from disjunction was not merely an anatomized space of representation or the suddenly activated coproducer of meaning. No, disjunction was also a temporal project that sought authenticity in a micro-temporality of unfolding linguistic complexity that could be positioned against the rush of administered time.[60]

I

"I do so little / because the drive / of the world / is so much," Eigner writes in 1952 or 1953.

> It meets me, going
>   the other way
> through me
>
> And when there is silence

all naked   I sit here
trying to hold my breath

but sometimes
in the livingroom
the wind
is felt
shaking
the house (*EP*, 59)

A programmatic microcosm of Eigner's poetics, the poem positions a dialectical refusal of heroic action as the necessary antidote to a world bent on the latter. But while the poem at first seems to propose literal silence as this antidote, read in relation to Eigner's massive lifetime production, we might want to imagine this doing of "so little" on another register. Perhaps "trying to hold" one's "breath" is less a matter of the familiar idiom, less the complete cessation of breathing in order to counteract the world's runaway "drive," than it is a matter of physically grasping or controlling the medium of one's linguistic world against the forces or drives that would administer that world as an unconscious, unmasterable pulse from the outside. Such "holding" of one's breath was, after all, a central Black Mountain tenet, a movement away from the standardized measures of iambic and trochaic verse patterns toward the ostensibly more finely calibrated possibilities of individual breath, especially as it was now framed within the wider temporal possibilities of the open field page—as writing, that is. In this sense Eigner carefully and precisely held his breath for about three decades in Swampscott and almost two more in Berkeley.

Yet reading all writers associated with Black Mountain as, essentially, illustrating Olson's "Projective Verse" essay from 1950 has led to a strange reduction of an extremely varied body of poetic production. So let us proceed from a slightly different angle. First, Eigner's breathing is not simply aligned with speech: while Silliman's emphasis on speech as a constitutive negation for Eigner misses the temporal dimension to Eigner's project and conscripts the writing solely as an antimimetic precedent for Language writing, Silliman is right that Eigner's poetics will not resolve itself into a naturalized poetics of speech. Second, inasmuch as one frames Eigner with an Olsonian term like "open field," in which the page becomes a score for the unfolding temporal relations among the poem's elements, then Eigner's field appears, despite his mother's occasional intrusions, far more open than even Olson's. In Eigner's writing,

that is, our attention remains more consistently on the second-to-second relations among the page's micro-temporalities, their shifting modifications of each
other within a single, imaginable duration, whereas in Olson this real time of
the perceiving body in space is far more frequently punctured or displaced by
what we might think of as vertical time vortices that pull one out of a durational
1960s Gloucester and into the town's Puritan seventeenth-century landscape, or
elsewhere. And these vortices are spatial as well as temporal, since others launch
us toward Aztec glyphs, ninth century BCE Greece, Pleistocene Syria, and so
on. Eigner, by contrast, emphasizes an open field of temporal ongoingness not
only by avoiding Olson's collage historicism; he also resists the sudden (if fragmentary) epiphanic conclusions blurted out so frequently by his large, rambling
neighbor. Eigner's project is the most horizontal and present tense of all New
American poets. Finally, it is also the most about developing a countertemporality, a nonmonumental now that would work to contest administered time.

However, as is typical in Eigner, the poet does not present this negation
as a closed, secure economy: there is, again, bleed between this outer world of
enforced activity and the domain of remeasured thinking he cultivates. Even
if the poet's body can be made relatively quiet, still sitting in the living room,
"the wind / is felt / shaking / the house" (*EP*, 59). Given the rest of the poem,
I'm inclined to take this shaking not so much as a matter of climatological
events outside—literal wind or storms—so much as physical registration of
the world's "drive" that initiates the poem. About the same time Eigner wrote
the poem, he composed a short work that, on first glance, seems too slight for
even a pause:

■ ■ ■ ■ ■

What happened?

I've got to blow my nose

Mucous in summer

after so warm
(Aug. 1

Spring so flowery in my holes

the trouble is I have to get clear, you see
as anything might happen and
time   marches   on (*EP,* 74)

These five black squares with which the poem begins are, so far as I have found, singular in Eigner's works. In one sense they are like an extended ellipsis, a short break in time between this poem and the one that might have preceded it—a bit like those in Robert Creeley's *Pieces*. Yet the squares are more mechanical and aggressive than three dots, suggesting as well, perhaps, a filmstrip. Committed to the radical present, Eigner rarely begins a poem with a question about something that happened in the past, even if, as here, it impinges on the present. What seems to have happened, or be happening, is that the perceiving center of Eigner FM has been overcome, briefly and unexpectedly, by snot. Whether it is August or May is unclear; what is more certain is that some temporary bodily disruption—"flowery in my holes"—has made the subject need to "get clear" to be ready for the "anything" that "might happen." I have to blow my nose so that I can be ready to write more Larry Eigner poems; oh wait, that turned out to be one, this poem pretends to realize, before noting that "time marches on." So a minor mucus management problem in Swampscott gets recast as the kind of event that might be the subject of a Time Inc. film short—narrated in Westbrook Van Noorhis's smooth, authoritative, and phlegm-free voice.[61] However ephemeral this small piece of writing may be, it takes on a fascinating function within the larger Eigner corpus by programmatically mismatching the most minor of occurrences (which have, in different ways, been generating poem after poem), with the dramatic phrase that Henry Luce had hammered into Americans. Rather than just poke fun at himself or highlight the discrepancy between these registers, what Eigner is in fact doing is calling to mind "the march of time" as a datum of official time management that his entire project sought to contest. The phrase was the inevitable conclusion of each thirty-minute segment of the Henry Luce film series *March of Time*, which, after eight months of research and development, ran first in theaters on February 1, 1935.[62]

Following twelve years after the founding of the Luce media empire with *Time* magazine, which began in March 1923, *March of Time* marked a shift both in its expanded circulation and in the address the Luce media took: from the more ironic and disengaged mode of *Time* in the 1920s toward a more concerned civic involvement that would soon seek to galvanize support for intervention in World War II. Within a few weeks *March of Time* was in four thousand theaters in 168 cities. By the end of its first year it was, according to Alan Brinkley, in "five thousand American theaters and in more than seven hundred in Great Britain."[63] Seen by an enormous number of people (estimates range from twelve to twenty million), the films were part of a massive, interwoven media platform including radio and print, that, as Robert Herzstein estimates, was "reaching over 40 million people a month, almost a quarter of the American population."[64] Historians and sociologists tend to agree that Luce thus shaped public opinion in the United States.[65] When in his 1951 classic, *White Collar*, for instance, C. Wright Mills mounts an argument for the importance of business interests in the "cultural and marketing life of the intellectual," this is posed in relation to the already *established* influences of "the New Deal, Hollywood and the Luce enterprises."[66] Despite his strong support for US involvement in World War II, Luce was no fan either of the New Deal or of FDR more broadly, and one of Luce's primary methods of undercutting FDR takes us back to Eigner in a strange way.[67]

FDR's fireside chats were, to repeat, a canonical instance of radio as a national tool of opinion building and subject formation—in this case, support for the New Deal. In these implicitly domestic, comfortable chats around the family hearth, Roosevelt put radio's intimate address to use, its ability to establish a familiar, trusted vocal tone that allows it to cozy up next to its listener. But in a public climate intensely unsympathetic to people with disabilities, the president's spell could be broken, as it occasionally was by Luce, by focusing attention on the *body* from which these speeches emerged. "Even before FDR had taken office, *Time* had irritated the White House by referring to the governor's 'shriveled legs.'" While the magazine then came around and praised his recovery from polio, "FDR's relation with Time Inc. quickly soured again, however. *Life*'s publication of a photograph of him in a wheelchair caused a terrible row, for millions of Americans now saw that Roosevelt was a crippled man."[68] Or might have seen, since the photograph was shot at a distance and somewhat ambiguous. In fact, it was not until after his death that close-ups of FDR in a wheelchair were published, like the photograph by Margaret Suckley reproduced here.

It may seem strange to twenty-first-century readers that the American public did not know about FDR's physical state and that it made such a difference in their valuation. But apparently some viewers of the (earlier) *Life* photograph were disturbed by a wheelchair-bound American president both ruling the United States and decisively impacting the world during the war. We capture something of this attitude when we return to Clint Eastwood's depiction of the albino, light-sensitive Dragon undergoing a blood transfusion in

FIGURE 4. President Roosevelt in his wheelchair on the porch at Top Cottage in Hyde Park, New York, with Ruthie Bie and Fala, February 1941. Photo by Margaret "Daisy" Suckley.

his customized lair. As late as 1975, this was the embodiment of a fallen state, a civil servant incapable of the extreme alpine mountain climbing through which the plot will resolve itself and of the most basic acts of self-preservation and physical maintenance. But Eastwood is in fact tapping into an image repertoire of the sedentary tyrant in his overcustomized interior that stretches back through a long string of Cold War Bond villains, to FDR (as seen by his enemies on the right) past countless cruel Enlightenment and early-modern aristocrats—Philip II has often been singled out as the poster-child shut-in Counterreformation sadist—back to a long list of supine classical autocrats lisping death knells from their bejeweled staterooms. While not all these tyrants are strictly immobile, limited or no mobility helps with the idea of a larger world being controlled irrationally and whimsically from a fixed point, its frozen ruler lacking the virility to investigate the situations over which he holds power, to engage in the inquiry or fieldwork that would, implicitly, be necessary to govern more knowledgeably and equitably. Obviously this cruel cliché represses the actual decentralization of most regimes, which makes the kind of firsthand inquiry it romanticizes impossible if not unnecessary. But something of this line of thinking nonetheless underlies the depiction of the immobile center of a vast power structure from Luce's FDR to Eastwood's Dragon.

From the late 1940s until 1978 Eigner was indeed watching and listening to the world from a relatively fixed location and creating in writing a singular cosmos out of these activities. At its edges, this world was crisscrossed with passenger jets, surveillance planes, and the larger threat of nuclear war; inside, at its core, his domestic space was not just saturated with signals of media— the at times distracting sounds of television and radio. These sounds metronomically paced out half-hour sit-com slots and hour-long news programs; they marked morning with one kind of soundscape and the dinner hour with another. They gave shape and structure to the day. Given that this happened in most domestic settings across the country, there was, from one perspective, nothing especially singular in this occurring within a wooden clapboard house at 23 Bates Road in Swampscott, Massachusetts. What was singular, however, was the way that Eigner got to work conceiving of, and practicing, a countertime, a mode of temporal measure that would denaturalize and estrange these available, indeed dominant, frames for the passage of time.

If Murray Schafer is right that "radio is the pulse of a society organized for maximum production and consumption," then the strongest form of this insight is not to understand each micro-unit of radio time simply as an equivalent causal engine; rather, it's to see radio's larger structuring of time as laying the organizational groundwork for these processes of making and buying. In fact, this "pulse" varies importantly both in itself (in the differences, for instance, among hour-long documentaries, broadcasts of experimental music, short news programs, and advertisements) and in relation to the rhythms of its listeners. One of the dominant frames for listeners' rhythm was the opposition between work and leisure, public and private time. Because Eigner did not work outside his house, did not, that is, labor at anything other than his writing, his weekdays were not divided between a workplace and a domestic setting.

This fact might cause us to wonder about the way Eigner concludes an October 17, 1976, letter to his brother Joe: "Taking time, things easy."[69] Such a suggestion—and Eigner's correspondence is full of claims that he is "taking it easy"—most commonly marks a break from externally imposed obligations; it typically functions, that is, within a labor/leisure opposition. While in some circumstances this phrase operates, at least at one level, as an explanation for why Eigner answers a letter later than he might have liked, in the previous example and elsewhere "taking time, things easy" evokes a larger attitude toward time Eigner actively cultivates.[70] It evokes, we might say, the allover attention manifested in his writing, which requires extended and deprogrammed time: "I've gone along giving e v e r y t h i n g the benefits of doubts at that (hence, partly, the indecision), and by this time coming out my ears."[71] In this statement of his broadly attentive poetics, the phrase "by this time" seems to split in half so that we also hear "time coming out my ears." Indeed, Eigner does generate a new kind of extended and noninstrumentalized time with his generous ear. But what I want to stress here about this time is that because Eigner didn't have a numbing office job, or any job that took him out of the house, the temporality he cultivated so carefully in his writing did not operate as a form of compensation or reward in opposition to an externally imposed work schedule, the kind of schedule that might have been hammered home by radio's "pulses," by the temporal parceling that it, together with television, effected inside the Eigner home.

When Eigner ironized the Luce film in the poem quoted earlier, noting that "the trouble is I have to get clear, you see / as anything might happen and / time marches on"—the phrase "anything might happen" points to the allover temporal attention I have been describing: anything might happen here in this corner of the house at 23 Bates Road, or across the street, but within earshot. Anything might happen as words are marshaled to register this happening, as they are spaced, irregularly, at customized positions on the field, via Eigner's typewriter, becoming a second-order happening on the page that in turn generates more happening for the poem. It is in this way that "time marches on"—it marches irregularly out from the left margin of each page and then marches, in his correspondence, in a customized sidebar that at moments operates as commentary on the main text.

To bring the odd time of Eigner's writing into greater relief, let us now turn more directly to the timekeeping undertaken by Henry Luce. Nicknamed

"Father Time," Luce certainly worked to manage and keep official time through his media interests.[72] *Time, Life,* and their filmic offshoots functioned, from the late 1930s through World War II and well into the Cold War, to galvanize the nation around both wars, hot and cold, as *the* contemporary events that required sudden and complete recalibration of daily existence: an instrumentalization of the temporal datum toward results whose productivity would register on a national level. "When *Life,* America's cheerleader, endorsed rearmament, Marshall found that Congress was more receptive to his requests." "When Luce's publications and movies articulated a *single, coherent message,* the polls reflected changes in public attitudes, usually about four to six weeks after they had launched their propaganda blitz."[73]

This dramatic shift in time consciousness and time management depended, not surprisingly, on a series of assumptions about the agents of historical change and the nature of historical time. We might begin with the scale of *Time* magazine: the week. The negative datum against which *Time* launches its project is the "over-detailed" daily newspapers. These it combs and rewrites (there is no investigative reporting until well into the 1930s) in punchy language, offering, as Brinkley puts it, a "comprehensive view of the week's news that could be read in less than an hour" by an educated, affluent audience that lacked the time to edit and correlate their news services.[74] One of the basic principles of organization that allows for this streamlining of historical detail is the familiar proposition that history is largely a function of great men, good or bad. *Time's* covers reflect this theory. On them Stalin appears twelve times; Chiang Kai-shek, ten; Roosevelt, Churchill, Franco, and Mussolini, eight each; and Hitler, seven.[75] "Speaking to a group of advertising salesman, Luce described *Life's* editors as the "real historians of the day."[76] In this world of events stripped largely from underlying conditions, great men, tyrants or heroes, both represented or embodied their historical moments and required timely responses.[77]

The Luce media developed a sense of temporal passage, and contemporary history more broadly, as a vastly sprawling field that required first efficient and reliable summary and, increasingly throughout the 1930s, prompt intervention. This increasing need for timely intervention in the Luce media sense of time peaked perhaps in 1941 with Luce's famous essay (initially published in *Life* and widely reprinted) in which he proposed, as his title suggested, that the twentieth century was to be "The American Century."[78] This plea for intervention in World War II (and, beyond that, for a global role for the United States) centers on the way that Americans' ambivalence about the war causes them to suffer from a crippling nervousness that, implicitly, could be cured by enlisting in the cause. The essay begins by asserting that "Americans are unhappy . . . nervous—or gloomy—or apathetic."[79] Luce then locates "a striking contrast between our state of mind and that of the British people," who have, since the war began on September 3, 1939, been guided by Churchill's assurance that "outside the storms of war may blow and the land may be lashed with the fury of its gales, but in our hearts this Sunday morning there is Peace."

> Since Mr. Churchill spoke those words the German Luftwaffe has made havoc of British cities, driven the population underground, frightened children from their sleep, and imposed upon everyone a nervous strain as great as any that people have ever endured. Readers of LIFE have seen this havoc unfolded week by week.[80]

While Americans suffer vicariously with the help of images from *Life*, the British paradoxically do not suffer at all because they have resolved to instrumentalize themselves against the Nazi war machine. "Yet close observers agree that when Mr. Churchill spoke of peace in the hearts of the British people he was not indulging in idle oratory. The British people are profoundly calm. There seems to be a complete absence of nervousness. It seems as if all the neuroses of modern life had vanished from England."[81] For Luce, the master time organizer, it is as if enlisting entirely in the war effort might, in a sense, turn back the clock to a mythical premodern period of unassailable certainties, banishing "all the neuroses of modern life." This would be achieved by accepting "wholeheartedly our duty and our opportunity as the most powerful and vital nation in the world" and, the clincher, exerting "upon the world the full impact of our influence, for such purposes as we see fit and by such means as we see fit."[82]

Given the title of the article, we may have had an inclination that some such sweeping claim was coming. But in what sense, precisely, can America own a century—own time that is, and not merely space? If the British Empire could control an enormous amount of territory in the nineteenth century, still it was always possible to contest literal space; the shrinking of the empire at the moment of this essay proved this. But how does one resist time, especially an entire century? In one sense, Luce's title is obviously designed to suggest that such resistance is impossible—that if time can be made American, then in no possible space will one have any practical means of casting off this temporal yoke. Such a suggestion, however, begs the question of just how any unit of time, be it a week, a year, or a century, could become American. How, that is, were questions of hegemony transferred from the spatial to the temporal domain, and how did one country step up to control that temporal regime?

Framed this way, we might return to Luce's larger media work as a key instrument in this recoding of control. Indeed, we might understand "The American Century" essay not simply as offering a timely call, in 1941, to abandon neutral nervousness and cast our lots with interventionist calm. The essay does present this as a decisive, momentous event. But to understand it as such—to take it as inaugurating the American century it prophesizes—depends, paradoxically, on acceding to the much longer-term, underlying logic of the Luce media's reconceptualization of time across the twentieth century: its construction, in print, radio, and film, of days, weeks, months, years, and now, centuries. Rather than welcome us into an entirely unknown though heroic present and future of American hegemony, in other words, the essay might be thought instead to reconcile us with the Luce media's time management strategies of the last twenty years—presenting these, in turn, not as the company's instrumentalization of temporal units, its building up of a series of useful forms of attention and modes of summary, but as the country's new temporal, and political, expression of itself. Twenty-five years later, artists would begin to recognize a very similar phenomenon within the temporal structuring of their own genres of discourse. "Art histories may be measured in time," Robert Smithson suggested, "by books (years), by magazines (months), by newspapers (weeks and days), by radio and TV (days and hours). And at the gallery proper—*instants!* Time is brought to a condition that breaks down into 'abstract-objects.'"[83] Laying the groundwork for this regime in journalism, Luce helped naturalize these different temporal measures of discourse, paving the way for their trickle down into art writing. The problem Smithson identifies, in other words, is of course not simply that different media sources appear with different frequencies but that the learned equation of the media source with the frequency—one issue of *Life* magazine with a week, for instance—gradually allows the magazine or book to assume the role of the time it purports to represent, to, in a sense, be the time—the "abstract-object" Smithson proposes. Such a reoccupation and restructuring of time were at the center of Luce's construction of an American century.

So the "American century" might be something a bit different from a simple hundred-year span dominated by an emergent power. Yes, it would be the story of that domination. But in a sense this period, and the control it implies, might only come into being if the story could organize the time in which it all took place: the days, weeks, months, years, and decades whose significant events could be managed by the Luce media. As this process occurs, first the units of media—the publications—are conflated with the time they purport to represent, then those publications' criteria of cultural or political relevance are naturalized—their styles of evaluation, construction of crises, and demands for timely responses. This parceling of time is what made it possible, in 1941, to step boldly into the American century. Time may march on. But the pace of its marching, and the meaning of each of its steps, called for careful orchestration.

II

In 1974 the German S Press, founded in 1970 by Angela Köhler, Michael Köhler, and Nikolaus Einhorn, visited Eigner in Swampscott to record a tape that would be released in a series that included works by John Cage, Henri Chopin, Clark Coolidge, Allen Ginsberg, and Patti Smith.[84] The cassette's liner notes emphasize the poet's exuberant experience of his surroundings and the way that viewing and hearing the immediate environment interpenetrate with media experience: "Larry Eigner has lived almost all his life in Swampscott on Massachusetts Bay's North Shore a few miles from where he got muscle incoordination at birth in 1927—mostly he's been on top of the world and in a wheelchair, while it's a puzzle for one thing, enough is elusive and a lot comes within sight and hearing through glass and radio and TV." The two sessions were recorded on July 1 and July 11 of that year; the tape was released the following year, in 1975.

The very title of the work—*around new / sound daily / means*—could be understood in relation to its media environment: first we might hear the lines as an open-ended statement about the meaning of being around new sound daily, that it means . . . something to be determined anew each time, a value or term to be discovered in time, as it unfolds. In this sense the title would allow the work's meaning to emerge gradually and unexpectedly through daily sounding or sonic exploring. At the same time, however, we can also recognize that it was precisely Eigner's being around new sound daily that provided his "means" of writing. And this second sense of means, typically connected to the word ends, might be understood to recode one of the most instrumental terms in the language toward a noninstrumental end. It's no accident, I think, that Eigner's first media release played on these senses of means and meaning.

The cassette also played on Eigner's literal and figurative position within the map or discourse of New American poetry. Including two poems that reference his neighbor Charles Olson—"For Charles Olson—You Gotta Have Steam" and "At Death Olson's"—the recoding seems to situate Eigner firmly in relation both to the category of Black Mountain poetics and to the geographical location of the North Shore of Massachusetts Bay, be it Swampscott or Gloucester. But these references aren't simply to a preexisting Olsonian authority; rather, they subtly suggest another version of an open field poetics—one less punctured by diachronic references and oracular pronouncements and more open to ongoingness. For reasons that will become clear, I begin with these poems' textual representations before moving into Eigner's tape itself.

"At Death Olson's" was written on January 12, 1970, two days after Olson died in Manhattan. The poem begins,

```
get a            ( at
hand-out         Death,
                 Olson's )
revealed
                 and the
is there         blind
no change        dark


         intricate, bare

  snow  moves

     this morning
       from the cloud

    you can see there's wind (EP, 936)
```

The stanzaic structure makes it difficult to decide on word order, since reading across columns seems, at points, as logical as reading down. However one establishes sequence, it appears that the poem is concerned with the status of energy at death, with, we might say, the field poetics of bodily energy transfer at the moment a body ceases functioning: discerning change in the snow pattern, inferring wind's action, wondering about change—all of these would seem to be bound up with the enigmatic first line, in which a "hand-out" registers, simultaneously, as divine energy transfer after death—the hand of god "revealed"—the last gesture of a dying body, the simple movement of a body, and the larger possibility of something for nothing, of a kind of surplus energy that might, now, be revealed not to exist. The poem's last lines—"implode the gas con- / duction, travel, you / feel this // Kelvin / and" (*EP*, 937)—seem to further these questions, in part by evoking an imploding energy source and in part by linking this to Lord Kelvin (1824–1907), perhaps the most famous measurer both of electrical energy and of heat more generally; it was he who first provided a reliable way to measure absolute zero, a state in which all energy transfer, all movement of molecules, has ceased. All of which is to say that the poem seems to be wondering, quite literally, about the full implications of the shutting down of the Olsonian energy field, which had for some time been pulsing away not twenty miles from Larry's front porch. Yet a key feature of this Olsonian pulsing, which separates it from Eigner's poetics, is the extent to which the Olsonian energy field engages not with the immediate world of sense perception but with a wide range of historical materials. Eigner seems to be thinking this difference in the middle of the poem:

> the past imagined, the back
>   real
>
>   or memory or
>
>   this may be
>   any time at
>   removes
>
>   memory of
>   memory of
>
> when is it you remember (*EP*, 936)

Here the past and memory are simultaneously *of* Olson himself and having to do with Olson, as part of Olson's work. As contingent as Eigner's own writing may be—contingent, that is, on what's happening around him—here the suggestion is, perhaps, that the turn to memory and the past opens an even vaster, more threatening landscape of contingency, set off not just by the double "or" in the line about memory and by the double "memory of" but also by the vertiginous sense that memory opens a relation to a near-infinite and uncontainable set of times. Eigner's diagnostic seems to come in the last line quoted: "when is it you remember," which suggests not just the difficulty of framing or selecting among possible pasts but more fundamentally the problem of the elision of the present tense of the remembrance, inasmuch as this "when" is displaced onto another when in the past. The recording could be said to deal with these problems inasmuch as it includes ambient sounds from Eigner's neighborhood: birds, for instance, are sometimes audible in the background.[85]

The reading I've performed here is, of course, dependent on the printed text of the poem—not merely to parse the visual prosody of the first, potentially interweaving, columnar lines but to capture the importance of the lines' sparseness, of the silence (or perhaps low-level ambient hum) that surrounds their brief articulate sounds. Eigner was the first to note that his own speech, affected by his cerebral palsy, may not have provided the best registration of his extremely subtle textual effects. As is typical with him, however, this did not give rise to laments or self-pity but to a wry, and extremely sharp, engagement with his own and others' recordings of his work.

What he was up against is interesting when framed in the history of poets' recordings: if typically such recordings at once activate poetry sonically and tend to allow future readers to hear the voice as a guiding measure, such an effect may not have been exactly achieved in Eigner's case, where his sensuous caressing of words in the recording did not evoke the complex spatial play on the page.[86] Certainly the traditional idea of the poet's own voice as measure, as guiding metronome for future silent readings, has come under theoretical and practical criticism—from Charles Bernstein and others. What's fascinating about Eigner's case is that he at once partly displaces this function to other poets—David Gitin for a KPFA radio show in 1970 and Allen Ginsberg for the Henny and Boon film—and then offers detailed critiques of these poets' renditions of his work. If, for Bernstein, performance creates singular effects that undermine familiar models of textual authority, here something very close to the inverse happens: text at once resists an array of empirical voices and generates—latently, unrealized in performance—a series of singular effects that complicate the more normative attempts to possess the work in performance.

In a letter that comments on Gitin's broadcast, Eigner begins with an account of recoding his own voice and listening to an audio letter from his brother and sister.[87] After depicting the reel-to-reel as a "driveshaft of my mirror," the poet notes that this "reel" mirror does not quite reflect him: "i was disconcerted at finding i cdnt understand myself," Eigner notes; "i saw the difficulty in that" (EC).[88] This inability to achieve a kind of sonic reflection seems to provide a backdrop for Eigner's account of Gitin's rendering of the poems on the tape: "what an experience, while it lasts!, another one (the machine put in a [chair] next to corner table in the livingroom, low pretty much but the controls, in re listening, a cinch)." Here, the temporal dimension of listening to tape—"what an experience"—emerges through Eigner's attention to duration, "while it lasts!" Subtly, however, what first seemed like a unified experience, an "it" that could "last," turns into an ongoingness that resists such unity, becoming instead "another one." Moving in to the specifics of the reading, Eigner remarks: "Grt realization (appreciation, yeh, what an identity) it brings of the variables of speech." Presumably Eigner is praising Gitin for separating and giving space to the elements of his poem, and thus "realizing" them, in a way the author himself could not vocally. Not surprisingly, Eigner also applauds Gitin's slow pacing: "Wow! Fine that you dont go too fast." But then he moves into an actual critique: "Except in the few lines where you have a caesura and I wdnt—and theres 1 final line in . . . Fragments, of two words ("stirred   on") when I've a lacuna but you haven't."[89] Gitin can, from Eigner's perspective, actualize the poems by giving discrete identity to the variables of speech, stretching them in space. At moments, though, Gitin's construction of the temporal implications of this space are not Eigner's, so the poet feels authorized to remind Gitin of some of the implied notions of scoring.[90] "Memory some one part of re-creation, of varying percentage. There's a line in 'Keep me still . . .' that you do exactly as I wd: 'the peaceful corn salt in the empty night.' Yr end-of-line intoning often rising intonation where i think the opposite."[91] While Eigner is not referring Gitin back to the printed text as an unequivocal record of his intentions, he is pointing, nonetheless, to a series of effects—caesuras, tonal shifts, lacunas, questions of implied pacing—that seem, with the help of Eigner's comments, to find their rationale within the printed text, no vocal performance as yet having brought them out.

Is this merely a familiar idealism of authorial intention and control? For a poet who, himself, could claim to embody the definitive pronunciation and pacing of his work, we might say so; in Eigner's case, the dynamic is stranger. In fact, what seems to be behind Eigner's comments is not so much an idiosyncratic or personal set of preferences for reading but a desire, paradoxically, to realize the *textual* dimensions of his writing when it is spoken out loud, without naturalizing these into implied conversations or normative idioms. Indeed, Gitin's rising intonation at the end of lines makes the work sound closer to speech, to an empirical conversation in which statements suggest the need for response; Eigner proposes the opposite, suggesting that observation occurs without being placed urgently before a second-person interlocutor: the underlying *variables* of speech rather than its representation. Similarly, in his comments on the poem "The Discursive," from *Another Time in Fragments*, Eigner highlights a gap between words that uncouples the line from idiomatic speech and reinscribes it within a network of more complex textual effects; the printed poem reads:

> a pile of screens
> you could leave acquire
> time,   flies
> reverberating
>
> the dark house, and the vast
> sun moving, out,
> slowness, level of it all
>
> approach night
>
> the clouds to the sea
>
> stirred   on (*EP*, 357)

Whereas Gitin does pick up on the pause between "time" and "flies" (at once to evoke time flying but upset it by the idea of acquiring flies), he reads straight through "stirred on"—thus undercutting the sense in which the clouds are simultaneously stirred by the sea and on the sea and making the line more about how the sea is moved.

However significant, these distinctions are far subtler than the ones Eigner notes in response to Ginsberg's reading in the Henny and Boon film *Getting It Together.* Soon after the release, Eigner wrote the Gitins describing a screening that took place on August 25, 1973, at the Salem State Student Union: "Allen at his characteristic speed etc. swallows words and phrases especially on longest piece he does, 'Birthday,' which is missed thus yet a whole ts of the thng is shown on the screen."[92] Ginsberg, in other words, reads Eigner with a familiar beat inflection and pacing, wherein the kind of minutia of perception that occupies Eigner operates, if at all, as a palette cleanser or brief cool-out period between dramatic episodes in an oversaturated world of experiences and interventions.[93] The problem, then, isn't just that Ginsberg "swallows words." To a listener trained on Ginsberg's "characteristic speed," Eigner might seem to offer the scene setters without the events, the passive backdrops without the decisive occurrences that would activate them. Ginsberg seems to undercut the textual specificity of Eigner not merely by rendering his work in a familiar beat pacing and phrasing. The larger problem is that this pacing *itself* comes to suggest to listeners trained on hearing Ginsberg a world of earth-shattering events and scene-making drop-ins that casts writing like Eigner's, with its attention to minute temporal passage, merely as the cool-out time before more heavy "content." So we have the context without the decisive gesture, the ambience without the focal object. Unlike the Gitin reading, Ginsberg's performance cannot be brought closer to the textual implications of Eigner's project by having the author call his attention to a few caesuras or lacunas on the page.

But if the vocal realizations of Eigner's work in the film fall short, the visual dimensions play in fascinating ways with Eigner's larger project—especially with the kind of domestic open field noted earlier in the chapter. After an introductory sequence of a yellow flower opening against a black background to the sound of sitar music, we see—in perhaps the most compelling scene in the film—the outside of 23 Bates Road from across the street, focused on the corner where Eigner writes.[94] Introducing us to Eigner, the opening voice-over makes the mistake that Ginsberg will in the main part of the film: "In recent years, he has mastered one-finger typing—a technique which, unfortunately, cannot keep pace with the speed of his thinking or poetic invention. Larry is getting it together on pure will power." As the camera zooms in, Eigner's head becomes visible in the middle window; as the camera zooms closer, we become aware that Eigner's father is working behind him in another section of the same room. While we see Eigner's head (slumped somewhat, and directly under it his typewriter behind him and several binders of papers), just above this is his father, who either does not think it necessary to leave his comfy chair when Larry is being filmed or worked out this shot beforehand.

A similar effect occurs when Eigner reads to a group at Marblehead bookstore: now it is his mother directly behind him, her face seeming to merge with his at various points as he speaks. The film, in other words, provides a visual instantiation of the fact that Eigner's work environment and soundscape were negotiated in relation to his parents' proximity. Eigner comes into view in the film framed by his parents. While they do not speak for him in the film, his letters make it clear that, through their choices about radio and

FIGURE 5. Film still from *Getting It Together* (1973), Leonard Henny and Jan Boon.

television, they determine the audible effects of language in the house. Is their continuous consumption of radio and television a frame for Eigner's rejection of normative spoken language? With the examples of Gitin and Ginsberg one might grant that Eigner agrees with Grenier and Silliman and demonstrates a strong distrust of any model of poetry that placed a naturalized spoken idiom above the possibilities of words, printed or thought.

But, as I've been arguing, disrupting speech was never an end in itself. To understand the full force of Eigner's project, his cultivation of textuality must be seen not merely as a reaction against the faux naturalism of a speech-based poetics (or, worse, as a brooding jab at his parents' listening habits) but as a larger sanction of the *time* that emerged from that speech, especially as it was managed via radio and television media, as it was cut into half-hour sit-com slots, hour-long radio programs, and regularized days with their coded pulses emerging from media outlets around the house. For Eigner, "taking it easy," cultivating a kind of downtime, involved neither a break from an office job nor the restrictive leisure administered to parents in the next room as they watched Lawrence Welk or listened to the evening news on the radio. Rather, Eigner's daily, self-appointed job of "giving e v e r y t h i n g the benefits of

doubts" involved a highly conscious project of reclaiming duration, of building and testing his own time in horizontal acts of writerly attention. As he
heard, observed, and patiently reacted not just to the views and sounds in and
around his house and neighborhood but also to those of his typed pages under
construction, Eigner produced "another time in fragments" that, in its nonmonumental temporality, might, were it not itself a critique of news flashes,
serve as the suppressed press release of the New American poets as a whole.

Olson's Sonic Walls
Citizenship and Surveillance from the OWI to the Nixon Tapes

Vino la guerra y América toda cambió—las aldeas, las grandes ciudades, el norte y el oeste. El cambio más importante—los jóvenes fueron a pelear.

—Charles Olson, *Spanish Speaking Americans in the War*

Perhaps . . . the growth and development of historical consciousness, which is attended by a concomitant growth and development of narrative capability . . . has something to do with the extent to which the legal system functions as a subject of concern.

—Hayden White, "The Value of Narrativity in the Representation of Reality"

The last two chapters have sought to enlarge the context of poets' involvement with recording and broadcasting practices by situating these in relation to the state's deployment of tape both in private surveillance and in commercial radio. Thus far, in other words, the state has operated mostly as a negative datum. Tracking poets' audio research from the dramatic media critique proclaimed by Allen Ginsberg's *Fall of America* project to the almost diametrically opposed undermining of the media event undertaken by Larry Eigner in Swampscott and Berkeley, I have listened to both poets *against* the state: the EC-121 and the Luce media have brought into relief Eigner's countertemporality, just as the Bureau and Agency listeners have helped frame the recording interventions Ginsberg and Burroughs undertook. But the nation-scaled project of time and consciousness management during and after World War II was not only the work of journalists and politicians. It was, crucially, the work of poets like Charles Olson as well. And it is to this more complicated relation we now turn.

The unsettling political dimensions of Olson's practice, his close relations to American empire, have organized a dissenting current within the poet's reception—from Robert von Hallberg and Andrew Ross to Heriberto Yépez.[1] But even for those critics who dispute the foundational story of how, after a brief political career in Washington, the frustrated Olson renounced the world of politics for poetry, the poet's first book is generally regarded as the 1947 study of Herman Melville, *Call Me Ishmael*, which emerged out of his American studies education at Harvard.[2] In fact, however, Olson's first book was a twenty-four-page pamphlet titled *Spanish Speaking Americans in the War*, produced, with the help of photomontages by Ben Shahn, for the Office of War Information, where, at the time of its publication in 1943, Olson was assistant chief of the Foreign Language Division.[3] Rather than understand the pamphlet either as irrelevant war work or as unformed juvenilia, I want to propose it as the first articulation of a kind of sonic fieldwork that will organize his writing from start to end. Nor does this writing move from the politics of Washington to the poetry of Black Mountain College and Gloucester, Massachusetts. It moves instead from one concept of fieldwork to another— from what I will call the sonic area studies of *Spanish Speaking Americans in the War* to a mode of archival filibustering, where it shares terrain with sound and conceptual art as much as with historiographic poetry epics. While the scale and trajectory of this movement might seem to involve a shift from the nation and its politics to the self and its sounds, the specification of audience and the reduction of scale do not in Olson constitute a turn away from politics. Olson certainly wanted his late cosmological work to be understood politically; that his younger readers within the New American poetry identified strongly with this work at the same time as they sought to exteriorize its personal cosmological dimensions into a series of New Left discourses provides a way to understand his politics that offers more nuance, I think, than readings organized around the question of whether or not Olson supported empire.[4]

But to frame the larger context in which Olson's sonic fieldwork might be best understood, we must also put the cultural cosmos of his war work, and equally his epic, into contact with the state-sponsored programs of language learning and area studies—a project that involves characterizing the related research and methodological writing of a number of CIA and state operatives, especially William Yandell Elliott and Henry Kissinger. It is in this way that *Spanish Speaking Americans in the War* can lead an alternate path through the strange sonic world of Olson's oeuvre. The pamphlet's few commentators have sketched its context as that of building support for the war effort among Chicanos and Latinos, especially in light of the disproportionate number who had died during the Bataan death march (about which the pamphlet served as a public statement of grief). Daniel Belgrad in particular also suggests that it was "meant to counter Axis propaganda encouraging minorities to question their stake in an American victory," to disaffiliate Spanish speakers from the Allied cause—both in the United States and throughout South and Central America.[5] All of this is true. But the pamphlet was also about the sonic, linguistic dimensions of national identity—the possibility that hearing American daily life in 1943 through Spanish might sever subjects from the opinion-forming power of the closely controlled national media. If they could not understand the language of the Luce media, how could they receive the crucial message that they were living not merely in American space but in an American century as well? So Spanish-speaking Americans were addressed in the bilingual pamphlet not merely as one among any number of social groups that might have needed ideological conditioning geared to their specific interests; rather, their interests were seen as inextricably tied to the linguistic medium in which they were articulated.[6] In Olson's prose the US state spoke to Spanish speakers in Spanish, seeking to convince them that, despite some appearances to the contrary, such speakers were in fact already at home and that this home was worth defending: "Vino la guerra y América toda cambió—las aldeas, las grandes ciudades, el norte y el oeste. El cambio más importante—los jóvenes fueron a pelear" (WAR CAME, and all America changed—small town, big city, North and West. One change above all—young men went off to fight).

While we might recognize the telegraphic tone, with its suppressed verbs and clipped clauses, here, unlike in *The Maximus Poems*, history is not a revisionist metanarrative critiquing the mythic Puritan origins of American identity, including the more sophisticated version of that story told by Olson's professor at Harvard, Perry Miller. In *Spanish Speaking Americans* history is inevitability: "WAR CAME," and with that change, "young men went off to fight." We simply cannot ask about which young men, from which countries, speaking which languages within which minority populations, affiliated with which sides. Instead, these lines are translated so that, for Spanish-speaking Americans whose affiliations to the United States might, for good reasons, remain weak, there can be no mistake about the universality of this experience: "Los hijos de todas aquellas razas, de todas aquellas naciones del mundo que vinieron a edificar esta nación en América, salieron a luchar por la libertad en todo el mundo" (The sons of all races and nations of the world, who came

FIGURE 6. Cover of Charles Olson, *Spanish Speaking Americans in the War* (1943). Reproduced from the Charles Olson Archive, the Dodd Special Collections, University of Connecticut, Storrs.

here to make this America, went off to fight for freedom the globe around). Evoking the totality of "this America," these lines mark perhaps the widest social formation an Olsonian reader is ever conscripted to join, the broadest site or context imagined as operative for his address.

Over the course of *The Maximus Poems* the asserted intersocial context, the thematized polis, will consistently shrink: from the residue of New Deal America at war with "pejoracracy" (*MP*, 7) (Truman and Eisenhoweresque civic boosterism and the administered "mu-sick" [ibid.] that greases its constitutive petty business) down, gradually, to "Gloucester" (less the empirical town than a town-sized peerdom of interlocutors), to the late moment when even Gloucester must sail away from the United States, and eventually, the polis or site of the work can be only the single body of Maximus.[7] Whereas we encounter multiple references to "my Portuguese" and "my people" in the early poems, for instance, the implied collectivity and the would-be representative speaker become far less central later in the work. One might map this transformation, however, not only in terms of the empirical size of the thematized audience but also according to the sonic negations necessary to bring this audience into focus. Olson's listeners, in other words, must first be told what *not* to hear before they can hear him correctly. At the beginning of *The Maximus Poems*, it is "mu-sick" that plays this negative role, a kind of sickening sonic ambience generated from signage and, presumably, radio: "O my people, where shall you find it, how, where, where shall you listen / when all is become billboards" (*MP*, 6). The answer, of course, is right here, with the rather large book in one's hands: one should listen carefully to these printed words of Charles Olson's.[8] No longer the kind of unified national story offered in *Spanish Speaking Americans in the War*, *Maximus* begins of course as a counterhistory. However, by its conclusion, what one is invited to hear in *The Maximus Poems* is less an alternative history per se than the sound of a single body at work researching—or so I propose. It is not exactly that the scale or ambition of the work as a whole simply shrinks as it continues. Instead, as the geographical and textual collapse onto the corporeal, so the entire project also seems to mushroom, now as an Imago Mundi, into a global-scale cosmology.

In the 1943 pamphlet, however, the question is not merely the scale of the address but the time as well: rather than say that soldiers *are going* off to fight for freedom (since their choice of whether or not to do so was happening in the present), Olson flashes forward to a near future from which he looks back at the present, rendering it as a scene of inevitability: they *went*. Olson then humanizes and specifies these "Spanish speaking sons" from the "Southwestern states" by focusing on Ricardo Noyola, twenty-six, from "a ranch 'Los Potreras,' in Texas near the Rio Grande," who "like his father . . . could speak no English" because he "had had no schooling, working as a farm hand growing cotton and wheat since he was thirteen. It took war, and the new world America entered, to bring about a change for Noyola and his people, to give him his chance." But what, exactly, is the "chance" offered to Noyola? Education, fluency in English, civil rights, or merely the opportunity to fight for the United States? The pamphlet seems to equivocate, as Olson must tacitly admit that the reason Noyola has not learned English or attended school is that he has been trapped in a pocket of medieval serfdom south of San Antonio. This rather embarrassing fact, however, merely becomes a foil for the army's benevolence: "At Camp Robinson, Arkansas, where Noyola found himself, without English, awkward, confused, unhappy, the U.S. Army stepped in and did an unusual, important thing." What the army did was take Noyola, "and 54 other Spanish speaking boys," and form "a special platoon," led by someone "who could teach them in their own language, share their troubles, advise and encourage," turning them into a battalion that "received high commendation for stamina, enthusiasm, and ingenuity." Training within a native tongue, in other words, lubricates parts of the war machine like Noyola (who is singled out for his daring work of "leading a night reconnaissance patrol") that might otherwise rub, jam, or squeak.

This project of linguistic and sonic tuning was, of course, central to the foreign-language division of the OWI, where Olson worked. Anthropologists, linguists, poets, and musicians were all conscripted to fine-tune the sonic dimensions of war by expanding scales from various linguistic worlds to their attendant cultures and soundscapes. But while much war anthropology, sonic or otherwise, relied on direct fieldwork, it was also possible to contribute to the sonic war effort in other ways, as was the case with Harl McDonald's *Bataan* (1943), which invited listeners to revisit the tragic events of the previous year through an eight-minute tone poem whose middle section seemed to evoke the death march. Here, as the music began to operate as the sound track to an imaginary film of the actual, recent event, listeners were presented a musical scaffolding for an affective relationship to the war in the Pacific. While McDonald's is only one of many commissioned or self-commissioned nationalist musical compositions undertaken during the war, it's of interest here because of the extreme specificity of its reference (a single event rather than, say, a national figure like Lincoln) and because that event was the very one that Olson himself was called in to clean up after through writing a pamphlet.

Language and music, then, were two key wings of wartime anthropology.[9] Though here comparatively rudimentary, and located within the continental United States, such attention to the strategic importance of native languages and music (and the larger cultures in which they are embedded) can be understood as part of a much wider enlistment of anthropological practice toward the war effort. The OWI was at the heart of this weaponization of what had been seemingly benign earlier fieldwork, laying the groundwork for what would become the Cold War discipline of "area studies."[10] Examples of this process are, as one would expect, spread uniformly and neatly across the globe, but a dramatic one is the English anthropologist Tom Harrisson's application of previous studies to the struggle with Japan in Borneo. "While preparing for the mission," David Price tells us, "Harrisson pored over articles from the *Sarawak Museum Journal* describing explorations of Borneo's interior region of the early 1900s and 1930s. With the Japanese occupation of Borneo, these peacetime writings by ethnographers, geographers, and biologists took on a military significance." The eureka moment came when, in reviewing this fieldwork undertaken by the Welsh anthropologist Edward Banks, Harrisson noted "poorly understood . . . independent people [the Kelabits] living right inside Borneo." Thus, "the obscure *Sarawak Museum Journal* articles persuaded the Z Special Unit to parachute to the interior . . . rather than attempt a submarine operation that held high risks of Japanese capture or landing failure." And when these anthropological commandos landed in 1944 with the goal of training the Kelabits into a guerrilla army that could fight the Japanese, the warring scholars were sufficiently versed both in local traditions and in the history of contact that they could motivate earlier encounters to their own ends: "Harrisson and his comrades' airborne arrival produced an awed respect, as the Kelabits making first contact wanted to know if the Z Unit members were humans or supernatural beings." With Harrisson identifying "his commando team to the Kelabits as 'relatives' of the known explorers Edward Banks and R. O. Douglas," the Kelabits were soon won over and "pledged their allegiance to Harrisson and the British Forces."[11]

In this example, in which anthropologists "constructed a secret inland landing strip and undertook training exercises" of the Kelabits,[12] the discipline was fully weaponized with only moderate attention to the sonic domain: knowledge and use of the native language and the staging of what must have been for the Kelabits an unprecedentedly loud arrival by airplane. But the anthropology of sound and music were, elsewhere, even more central to the war effort. Not only were a broad range of musicians (among them Aaron Copland, Virgil Thomson, and Jerome Kern) commissioned to write new works, but more basically, all musicians living in the United States were required—as Annegret Fauser tells us—to fill out questionnaires about their suitability for various modes of war work, including whether or not they could teach the instruments necessary to fill out a marching band.[13] Arnold

Schoenberg's response—a slightly baffled "I guess"—seems to convey the gap he (and one imagines many others) would like to have maintained between the ambitious intellectual world of avant-garde practice and the coarse martial music of the armed services band.[14] Yet the record of war participation by musicians and historians or anthropologists of music suggests the opposite.[15] Beyond the *enormous* number that performed at USO and other military sites, many were employed as well in Olson's OWI, including Copland, Alan Lomax, Elliott Carter, Charles Seeger, Henry Cowell, Samuel Barber, Marc Blitzstein, Roy Harris, Colin McPhee, Kurt Weill, and Harold Spivacke.[16]

Some musicians did certainly pause to consider the odd situation their music (and music more generally) was asked to occupy: the process of weaponizing a sound collection is the subject, for instance, of Henry Cowell's 1946 essay, "Shaping Music for Total War":

> The most exciting feature of my work with OWI was the speed with which material from abroad could be obtained when vitally needed. At the time of the Indo-China problem . . . I remembered the recordings made in Paris during the Colonial Exposition in the early thirties. I sent a cable to our representative in France; within five days a collection had been located at the University of Paris and I had copies in my New York office![17]

At this point gleefully, and at others less so, Cowell sketches the transformation by which the vast international network of the anthropology of music became, within a few days, a world-scale martial soundscape to be pored over by Allied listeners searching for regional advantages.[18] As Cowell continues, he marvels at the rapidity with which benign sonic fieldwork now turns into crucial military intelligence: "A cable to New Delhi produced a list of over two thousand records." This new global soundscape, built at once to frame the world musically and to put American composers on the new map, also becomes a new sonic archive: "The OWI collection thus built up over a period of years contains more folk music of the world's peoples and more symphonic works by serious American composers than any other I know."[19] But if this appears as a one-way process by which academic work was simply appropriated by the state and thus moved out of the university, we are also witnessing the birth of area studies, in which a wide variety of academic disciplines will now work closely with the state over many decades.[20]

In his early Maximus poem "Maximus, to Gloucester, Letter 15," written May 8, 1953, and revised on June 17 of that same year, Olson had proposed that

> The true troubadours
> are CBS. Melopoeia
>
>> is for Cokes by Cokes out of
>> Pause
>
> (O Po-ets, you
> should getta
> job   (*MP*, 75)

The typical way to understand moments like this has been to hear them as part of the poet's self-narrated biography: here, upon Olson's leaving government, the negation of the compromised world of public politics in an attempt to cultivate authentic poetry at a distance from the degraded worlds of propaganda and advertising. Given the sad state of relations between these two worlds— that the most effective troubadours or makers of melopoeia are singing the praises of Coke for network television—poets will need to ratchet up their games or, as Olson puts it, "getta / job." But when we recall that Olson himself worked for CBS news reporter Elmer Davis, director of the OWI, this division becomes a bit more complex.[21] However much we might want to understand Olson's reference to CBS as evoking his inside knowledge of the workings of media and state power, we are left to wonder just how far Olson's work ever actually gets from what he calls "the trick of politics." Perhaps, that is, Olson's own state-sponsored melopoeia, his work convincing Spanish-speaking Americans to participate in World War II, is not unrelated to the institution building and persuasion that underlie both *The Maximus Poems* and Olson's larger construction of a central position within the world of postwar poetics.[22] Perhaps sound and recording can provide a bridge between these two moments. So it is in this heretical context of Olson's war work that I want first to test the encyclopedic, global dimensions of Olson's later epic, especially two famous recordings of it: his 1965 *Reading at Berkeley*, which was transcribed from a tape recording; and his 1975 Folkways LP, *Charles Olson Reads from Maximus Poems IV, V, VI*, which was made in Gloucester in February 1969.

I

Larry Eigner the one day yet, so many years ago I
read in Gloucester—to half a dozen people still—

asked me

why, meaning my poetry doesn't
help anybody.

—Charles Olson, *The Maximus Poems*

Given that most Folkways LPs mobilize sound ethnography to recover marginal cultural practices or repressed folk traditions in tension with modernity, one might reasonably wonder, despite the iconic cover photograph of the
larger-than-life poet taking in Gloucester harbor as he pulls on a cigarette, what
precisely the scholar Charles Olson is doing in this series. In a sense, the liner
notes—written by Barry Miles, who recorded the LP on a Nagra reel-to-reel
in Olson's Gloucester apartment—seem calculated to deal with this possible
objection.

"I had known him when he was staying in Regent's Park, London," Miles
explains, casting Olson as a countercultural figure whose odd working hours
are part of his allure, "so the schedule we used to record came as no surprise
to me: Charles got up at about 8.00 pm, ate breakfast and talked. At Regent's
Park the guests were all gone by two or three and Charles had the still of the
night to work in. At Black Mountain College his classes sometimes started at
midnight. This recording is no exception, it was all recorded well after midnight."[23] But this eccentric schedule seems mild compared to Olson's physical
act of converting his "railroad flat, in an old white-painted clapboard house"
into an extension of his research process. Setting the stage, Miles explains that
"outdoor stairs led into the kitchen where, propped against the huge refrigerator, Charles used to hold forth." It is here, then, that one encounters his
particular research space:

> Everything was in the most almighty muddle, papers, books, dishes, jars and boxes,
> even a storage jar of dried peyote mushrooms, all mixed up together. The window-
> frames had pencil notes of lists of ships and cargoes, forgotten captains and first
> mates and the customs duties they paid, fading in the thin winter sun and a thin film
> of dust. The walls too had notes in Charles' slanted illegible handwriting, details of
> Dogtown and who built which house where. The living room looked like a book-
> shop after an anarchist's bomb!

Within the explosion ring are fragments of still-valuable objects, produced by Olson and others: "bookcases all full to overflowing, bulging with coffee-ringed first-editions, original MSS from Ezra Pound used as bookmarks. Piles of journals and books reaching table-height and used as one. His typewriter balanced amid all this confusion, like a little nest among the papers over by the window." Is this a familiar hippie pad of the late 1960s, or the customized research den of a slightly unhinged nautical scholar who has taken to annotating his walls and window frames? In either case, however, one wonders about the crossover audience between nautical scholars, pop-musicians, and countercultural poets. In fact, the album was first scheduled to come out with Apple—as part of a series of "spoken-word albums" that Beatles' Paul McCartney asked Miles to organize.[24] The series seems to have been imagined by McCartney and Miles as offering democratic access to avant-garde literature through the record player. Their hope, apparently, was that the success of pop music could carry with it, and underwrite financially, a new relation to the poetry from which it often came.[25] That this sort of project reached a broader audience with a poet like Allen Ginsberg than it did with Olson is perhaps not surprising. Telling Olson that he has already been in touch with Ginsberg, Kerouac, Burroughs, Creeley, Pound, Basil Bunting, Samuel Beckett, and others, Miles notes that the records

> would be priced as cheaply as possible to allow as many people as possible to buy them and they would also enjoy not only international record distribution through EMI, Capitol, etc. but also through the book clubs (Evergreen Club for instance), to the book trade in the form of limited signed editions but also on Sale or Return to experimental bookshops throughout the world. Special rates to institutions, the blind and Universities and anti-universities. One record a month like a magazine.[26]

Clearly Olson's record did not fit within this frame, which may have been why Apple ultimately passed on it; yet, to repeat, the LP did not fit snugly within the Folkways context either—unless, perhaps, one rethought the larger epic of which it was a part.

What if, such a line of thinking might go, *The Maximus Poems* were understood less as an individual field recording—the dissident folk poet in New England crooning his alternative histories onto the tape—than as a massive, if somewhat confusingly organized, sound collection not unlike the larger sonic libraries developed by the OWI, but equally by Alan Lomax and Moe Asch, founder of Folkways? As the center of that collection, Olson, head librarian and sound collector, would of course play a special role—a role we might consider not merely editorial but also, in a sense, institutional. If he renounced the instrumental domain of politics when he left Washington in 1945, Olson nonetheless built and maintained a position at the institutional center of postwar poetry: he opens Donald Allen's epochal 1960 *The New American Poetry* anthology and gets the most pages; he uses his voluminous correspondence and teaching not merely to work out poetics, develop contacts, and traverse multiple fields but also to enlist young recruits who will be his bibliographers and annotation writers, a small army of postwar North American and English Eckermanns who will create the domain of Olsoniana.[27] Such a reading, in other words, would not depend merely on the morphological parallels between a Folkways or an OWI sound library and Olson's; it would also depend on the power a collection of documents generated by far-flung fieldwork around the world could come to have when, as we saw in the case of Henry Cowell's work for the OWI, one regime of use shifted over to another.

We see something like such a transformation in Olson's reading at the Berkeley Poetry Conference on July 23, 1965, when encyclopedic Maximus, a perhaps virtual figure of historiographic thought, asserts himself as the literal embodiment of contemporary poetics.[28] In this three-hour rambling talk/reading, Olson, in a proto-performance-art dynamic, seems in a way to have taken the audience hostage, calling out to his many poet peers in the room (Allen Ginsberg, Lew Welch, Robert Creeley, Robert Duncan, and Ed Sanders, among others) to affirm his right to stage his seemingly endless free associations as the would-be focalizing event itself. At one point, for instance, Olson interrupts his own discourse to free-associate about whether a particular reference of his is to Pindar or Anacreon; then, weaving in comments about Ed Sanders, Robert Blaser, and Robert Duncan, Olson pauses, enlisting Duncan's support in what seems to begin as auto-critique but spirals out into its opposite: "I'm confusing two poets, ain't I? . . . Am I Robert? Tell me. Show the people how unknowledgeable I am. How ignorant. Please do. . . . Because . . . I sound so goddamn intellectual and so knowing and so literate." When Olson cannot (or pretends not to) hear Duncan's response, it must be repeated *three* times to the crowd: "You're the boss poet here, daddy!"[29] This repetitive affirmation literalizes what Olson's performance has been designed to enact: less his abstract significance and authority than his real-time position at the physical, literal center of contemporary poetry, with its assembled representatives

FIGURE 7. Charles Olson, cover of *Reading at Berkeley* (1966).

attentively participating in an abject endurance ritual that dramatizes how that position emerges from his large, powerful body, as much as from his voice or intellect.

At other moments within the performance, Olson's tactics for maintaining control might be taken to evoke his war work in Washington—both for the OWI and for the Democratic National Convention of 1944. When, for instance, nearly an hour into the performance, the first dissatisfied listener finally gets out of his seat and heads for the Wheeler auditorium exit, Olson stops and addresses him directly: "If you don't know, brother, that politics— poetics is politics, poets are political leaders today, and the only ones, you shouldn't have come, and I'm happy you left. If there's a world to be left, it's

FIGURE 8. Vito Acconci, *Claim*, 1971. Vito Acconci / Artists Rights Society (ARS), New York.

simply society."[30] Though the man's decision to leave could have been based on any number of other factors (boredom, annoyance, Olson's incoherence, and so on), Olson effectively recodes the simple fact of walking out as an exemplary misunderstanding of Olson's political project, of Maximus's special mission on earth.[31]

Calling the poets to attention, putting them in their places, extracting further authorizations to continue, and framing this all within an elevated rehearsal of his special calling that makes any objection or qualification impossible—these are dynamics that performance artists like Paul McCarthy and Mike Kelley would have well understood. Viewers of McCarthy and Kelley's collaborative films, like those of Vito Acconci's early performances, have taken the pathological dimensions of these works as intentional devices designed to amplify social dynamics to the point where they became perceptible: in *Family Tyranny* (1987) McCarthy, as father, humiliates his "son" Kelley in a cheap Hollywood set, while droning on about how "you can do this to your son"; in Acconci's *Claim* (1971) the artist sits blindfolded at the bottom of a basement stair holding a crowbar and taunting audience members upstairs, via a video monitor, not to come down into the basement because he'll attack them.

Safely contained within the genre of "performance art," these activities have always been seen as distant from the plain old bad behavior Olson displayed at Berkeley. While Olson at Berkeley may not be in control of the models of (poetic) kinship, social relations, or audience domination he evokes, his performance staged all of these dynamics with diagrammatic clarity. And it is this that allows me to wonder whether his might be understood as a special kind of symptomatic performance art. In fact, one hears an echo of this performance context when Barrett Watten describes Olson as an unyielding "wall of sound."[32] But if in events like his reading at Berkeley this effect of the embodied wall of sound emerged from dynamics of confrontation, abjection, and ritually recited hierarchy, the social dynamics that subtended Olson's Folkways LP might be thought to occupy the opposite pole of his practice. They take us back, instead, to the quiet sea scholarship Barry Miles noted as the organizing logic of Olson's customized Gloucester apartment. A brief turn to one other contemporary sound art piece will help draw this out.

II

On January 9, 1961, the artist Robert Morris strolled into a downtown Manhattan hardware store, bought a 4 × 8-foot sheet of walnut, and lugged it back to his loft on Bond Street, where he lived with dancers Simone Forti and Yvonne Rainer. There, in his seven-foot-ceiling room off to the side of the main loft, he spent three and a half hours cutting, drilling, connecting pegs and sanding the hardwood into a cube just under ten inches in each direction. For the duration of his home carpentry project, Morris turned on a reel-to-reel tape recorder and captured the sounds of his sawing, hammering, and planing. Morris's last move was to include the sound track itself. While this first emanated out of a base on which his box sat, more recently the reel-to-reel has been digitized, the base has gone away, and the sound now emerges from a speaker inside the original box.[33] *Box with the Sound of Its Own Making* has been hailed as a key early conceptualist artwork; from its legendary first listener (John Cage, who is supposed to have silenced Morris's own speech *about* the artwork and instead listened intently for the duration of the more than three-hour recording), the work has been taken to undermine the myth of the autonomous inspired artist by detailing sonically (with excruciating completeness) the work's coming into being, its process. While the walnut box's audio record of its construction history has also constituted *Box with the Sound of Its Own Making* as a key event

FIGURE 9. Robert Morris, *Box with the Sound of Its Own Making* (1961). Seattle Art Museum. © 2017 Robert Morris / Artists Rights Society (ARS), New York.

in the history of sound art, what has been less remarked is the work's close relation to the history of home and portable electronics.

Given the dimensions of the tasteful walnut console and that it does emit sound, viewers might be excused for missing at first that all of its sides are solid and that what they hear is, contrary to the advice of good audio engineers, coming from a speaker submerged inside solid wood, without sections cut away to release the sound. Indeed, at the moment that *High Fidelity* magazine was popularizing an emergent audio culture that promised to bring listeners closer and closer to the sonic events about which they were most curious, *Box with the Sound of Its Own Making* was, in effect, a high-fidelity artwork—an artwork with a newly intimate relation to the soundscape of its creation.[34] As Susan Douglas suggests, high-fidelity enthusiasts linked their care for precise, referential sound to an ethic of "technical tinkering" in which the ideal audio subject was also the builder of his own, customized system. This tended to mean, in a kind of proto-minimalist aesthetic, that one did not cover such industrial products in "finished cabinets that matched existing furniture designs such as French provincial or colonial" as was the case with commercially available stereos from Magnavox and RCA.[35] In this sense, too, Morris was participating in hi-fi culture, since high-fidelity enthusiasts wanted viewers to be aware that they had made, and not simply purchased, their components: their minimalist, industrial aesthetic foregrounded this process. Morris, then, seems to have found a slightly different way to elevate this powerfully mundane process to the status of attention-focalizing occurrence—to allow viewers to see and hear the relation between the box and the home carpentry that fashioned it. Morris's artwork perhaps counts, if we enlarge its context somewhat, as a new mode of audio research.

Let us return to the sense in which Olson's Folkways record might constitute a mode of audio research. If Olson was concerned to project and amplify his status at the center of the institutions of postwar poetry, what role did a recording like *Charles Olson Reads from Maximus* play in this campaign? In what sense might the encyclopedism of *The Maximus Poems*, for instance, have cycled back on (rather than simply split off from) the modes of instrumentalizing knowledge Olson learned during the war? One way—as I have suggested—is to understand Olson's sound collecting in *Maximus*, despite his undeniable interest in alternate histories and contestations of familiar humanism, as a form of sonic area studies that builds off his work for the OWI. In such a reading *Maximus* would operate as a kind of Folkways world ethnography condensation, with Gloucester fisherman talk and their quaint nor'easter idiolects operating as the first regional frame, beyond which is a global soundscape that extends not merely across Europe, Scandinavia, the Middle East, and Asia but to the Caribbean and Central and South America as well.[36]

There are, however, several limitations with such a reading: first, most obviously, Olson's citations are often arcane and historical rather than topical and synchronic; the global "knowledge" produced by his epic would not, it hardly needs saying, find CIA celebrants eager to act on it. But the problem is also sonic: while *Maximus* does *mention* and at points discuss a very long list of countries, this is quite different from the geographically organized sound samples offered by so many Folkways records. *Maximus*'s references may be global and encyclopedic, but they do not tend to coalesce into a representative world soundscape, historical or otherwise. In fact, one might say that the dominant soundscape of *The Maximus Poems* is, despite its citational sweep, ultimately that of the apartment rooms in Gloucester where Olson composes it, as he shuffles papers, coughs, and creaks the table while reaching impetuously for books or pointing at maps. These deictic sounds, indeed, become a kind of theme music, a bildungsroman of progress through the home archive encoded in grunts and squeaks, that at times seems to drown out *Maximus*'s ostensible reference field.

For all media theorists' talk of recordings separating speaking bodies from auditory effects, recorded poetry had always carried within it a site-specific dimension. What one heard, for instance, in the early, extremely popular Caedmon recordings of Dylan Thomas was not just the sonorous, high-toned, intensely rhythmic character of Thomas's delivery—its Poetry with a capital "P."[37] One also seemed to be hearing Thomas's Wales, its whole linguistic life world.[38] If this is true and generalizable, as I think it is, then recorded "voice" operates as a spatial and geographical marker. However haughty or demotic, oracular or tentative, recorded poetry seems to betray the sonic traces of place, to point, as if indexically, to location in a way that is more difficult for printed lexemes.[39] One site-specific effect of listening to *Charles Olson Reads from Maximus Poems IV, V, VI* is that the cosmological, encyclopedic poet of *The Maximus Poems* announces himself, sonically, as a New Englander, one who speaks of Glaauster Haaber, and how its wata connects to the local riva. Olson talks of the daakness, the aair, and of his shoulda.

But Olson's recording is site-specific not merely in that it registers the poet's own regional accent; rather, his, like all recordings, encodes the literal scene of recording as well: the room, where papers shuffle, chairs and tables creak, and his failing body struggles to produce organized and articulate sound. We hear the famous poet of breath as measure unable completely to control his decaying, emphysema-suffering lungs.[40] This, however, is not merely a tragedy particular to Olson's late life but also a reminder that voice recordings always document nonarticulate corporeal sound: we heard it with the somatic sounds logged in Ginsberg's van, in Eigner's German tape and in his movie, and now in Olson's Folkways record. Each of these recordings is site-specific both in registering the immediate environment of the recording (the envelope of the van, the room, the studio) and also in pointing us toward the body at work articulating sounds and producing effects that do not quite allow alphabetic registration. Attention to this dimension of recording has been a rich concern both for sound art and for the at times overlapping project of ethnopoetics, which is worth mentioning here inasmuch as it is a movement that Olson's own anthropological poetics, in fact, helped launch.[41] As Dennis Tedlock puts it, in the context of an essay about recording spoken myths,

> The information on the tape is not limited to what that voice sounded like at the moment it left the lips. Even the performer's bodily movements are in evidence,

affecting the sound of the voice as the head moves with respect to a microphone that was not tied around the neck. Also on the tape is evidence of the remarks or movements of an audience (including the mythographer), along with evidence as to whether the performance took place indoors or out, whether seasonal birds or insects were singing, and whether there was a violent wind or a thunderclap.[42]

Tape recordings inevitably trace bodies, their movements, and the spatial envelopes or sites in which all this occurs. But if Olson's LP can be compared to Dylan Thomas's in that the former, too, evokes a site and not merely a voice, first it does so much more literally—moving as it does from region and culture to the body and its immediate sonic environment. In other ways, however, *Charles Olson Reads from Maximus Poems IV, V, VI* radically departs from Thomas's 1952 recording. As much as he might have liked to, Olson was not popularizing poetry. His reading style is not a demonstration of the romantic, dramatic powers of poetry recitation. Nor does Olson's work traffic in a mood of nostalgic wonder. Inasmuch as there is a pathos of distance, it seems to have to do, instead, with a string of minor, unrecoverable historical events that exist only in fragmentary records. To recite the existing documentary record of these, as Olson does for instance in a poem titled "Further completion of Plat," is to produce an auditory event that fails to perform many of the most basic functions associated with recorded poetry. Here, as in Berkeley, Olson grabs the mike, gathers our attention, and perversely refuses to give us the payoff we expect.[43] While the violence of that former event is explicit and social, here it is implicit and conceptual. Instead of the high-toned, rhythmic recitation of a discourse audibly identifiable as poetry, what we get is a mumbled set of eighteenth-century dates (1717, 1725, 1719, 1713, 1727), names (Joseph Ingersoll, Bryant, Samuel Davis, William Hilton, Jabez Hunter, Elwell), and places, both proper names (Lower Road, Kinnicum, Smallmans, Upper Road) and common nouns (a reservoir, a swamp, and wood lots).[44] In this and the next poem, "Above the head of John Day's pasture land"(which is dated July 24, 1968, and appears as *Maximus*, 590), we are occasionally offered a point that relates thematically to the founding of the city; however, the overall effect is a meandering and at times out-of-sequence string of colonial dates partially framed by open parenthetical questions.

In *The Maximus Poems* Olson twice proposes "to build out of sound the walls of the city" (*MP*, 600). There is plenty of reason to take this city as the ideal Olsonian community, the polis, and the sound as the discussion or dialogue that would be constitutive of a polis's actual democracy, not the false, administered discourse of what Olson calls a "pejoracracy," where the absence of real democratic decision making is smoothed over by piped-in "mu-sick." But perhaps Olson was also building "out of sound the walls of the city" in *Spanish Speaking Americans in the War*, cozying up to the linguistic world of Chicanos in the Southwest to urge them that despite speaking Spanish, coming from Mexico, and not receiving education, economic opportunity, or the full rights of citizenship in the United States, it was nevertheless these national walls that they would now need to defend against the Axis menace.

When we encounter what might pose as the parallel instance of such an address in *The Maximus Poems*, however, the national frame simply drops away: after sympathizing with his close friend LeRoi Jones's turn toward Black Nationalism, Olson proposes that Gloucester too "sail away / from this / Rising Shore" (*MP*, 499) of the United States. "Gloucester" now becomes a project, a social formation, not merely an empirical location. So we might take the "sound" needed to build its walls as the epistolary, discursive network that keeps Olson closely connected, not just early on to Creeley, Corman, Frances Boldereff, and Edward Dahlberg but later as well to the transatlantic audience he develops with Dorn and Prynne and others.

But if such sounds built the social and institutional walls in which Olson operated, where does that leave us with the literal sound of Olson's LP? Despite being dressed up in the hipster veneer of its liner notes (odd working hours and speech habits, legendary countercultural status among poets, graphomania, bibliophilia, and custom construction of his apartment into a time-traveling research vessel), the LP systematically refuses to provide the expected folk counterhistory and indeed to sound much like anything listeners would recognize as poetry. In perversely negating these potential roles of recording, Olson instead turned to a model of proto-conceptual process that, in insisting on the actual time spent in research and the ongoing mood of uncertainty that attended and structured that time, seems "to build out of sound the walls of" an ambiguous archive.[45] Looping back to Robert Morris's walnut box with which we began, perhaps *The Maximus Poems* might be thought of similarly as, say, *Colonial New England Diorama with the Sound of Its Own Making*—ever pictureless as a totality, ever incomplete, even as it sought to stretch cosmologically across the globe.

III

Olson's late work, including his Folkways record, insists on a deictic dimension that links it to conceptual and performance art and uncouples it both from the dominant conventions of poet LPs and even from most versions of sonic research undertaken by poets. But the seemingly narrowing trajectory of his address, which in a sense moves from nation to polis to epistolary network and even to the body, is not the full story of Olson's sonic politics and linguistic fieldwork. Indeed, these shifts of scale are best understood not simply as antisocial turnings away from an accessible public toward less ambitious and empirically smaller reception networks but rather as carefully constructed rejections of available models of publicity toward various coterie countermodels of situated address and reception. And, as strange as it may sound, Olson's thinking on such matters was formed in part by his work on the foreign-language press (both in the United States and across the world), for the Foreign Language Division (FLD) of the OWI.

Olson's OWI archive includes material on Italian newspapers; Czech publications; and Portuguese, Spanish, Polish, Hungarian, and many other national presses (OC). But if the Foreign Language Division's concerns extended across the globe, its immediate concern was foreign-language publications within the United States—German, Italian, and to a lesser degree Japanese.[46] Though newspapers associated with Axis powers receive the most attention, in fact the FLD read *all* foreign-language publications in the United States. An analytical spreadsheet in Olson's archive breaks newspapers down into the categories of title, location, circulation, daily or weekly, and politics, noting, for instance, that Detroit's *Abendpost*, with a circulation of twenty-eight thousand, is "50/50 Hitler" while the Chicago paper of the same name (circulation twenty-one thousand) is listed as "80% pro-Hitler" (OC). Beyond the German and Italian papers, the spreadsheets also include exhaustive information on foreign-language newspapers in Yiddish, Polish, Spanish, and sixteen other languages.[47] Much of the actual analysis that generated these spreadsheets does seem to have preceded Olson's work at the FLD. That they remain in his file, however, suggests that these were the kinds of documents he was poring over. All of this information seems to have gone into the Foreign Language Division's March/April 1942 "Report of Press Survey of 21 Languages," a document that widens the context of Olson's pamphlet, *Spanish Speaking Americans in the War*. What this report suggests is that while Olson may have been asked to *intervene* in the US management of language politics and war morale with this one group of foreign-language speakers, he did so from within an institution that was closely studying the daily press production (and from it projecting shifting levels of support for the war effort) of all major foreign-language groups in the United States. Olson was studying what the war sounded like to Americans hearing about it in other languages. He was also studying how publications composed within the United States but not in the dominant language of English could complicate affiliations with parts of the state's agenda. Could experimental poetry, too, be conceived as a minor language in relation to the articulation, in standard English, of would-be national concerns via dominant radio, television, and print?

Perhaps the most permanent result of Olson's work in this context was the February 1945 confidential publication *Foreign Nationality Groups in the United States: A Handbook.*[48] The signed and numbered copy of this document in Olson's archive notes that it was "prepared in the Foreign Nationalities Branch for use in the Office of Strategic Services." Olson, that is, helped work on a survey of foreign-language publications designed for the CIA's predecessor, the OSS.[49] Yet it would be inaccurate to suggest that this exercise was a dress rehearsal for his later labors—that, over the course of his career, he identified with the centralizing, nationalist (indeed anti–civil rights) perspective from which this analysis was conducted. We know that Olson resigned from the OWI when he saw it veering away from its more intellectual, left-leaning Rooseveltian orientation, toward its later pro-business, proto–Cold war, "mu-sick" stance, from, as Michael Denning puts it, "the Popular Front vision of the anti-fascist war" to the "corporate vision of an American century in the OWI."[50] But, again, the suggestion that this negative experience simply turns Olson *away* from politics is inaccurate. What this densely textured foreign-language research suggests for Olson's later writing is perhaps something a bit different. When we now look over its table of contents and consider the micro-linguistic communities in the United States on which it comments, with various levels of concern about their politics and about how such groups' interests might be mobilized against the United States, we see a dynamic that, oddly enough, maps itself onto Olson's later work in cultivating a poetry community.[51] Like the Albanian, Swedish, Portuguese, and Romanian publications researched by the OWI, Olson's later work involves the possibility of an alternative polis that might reject the allures of ready-made American citizenship. It was this he cultivated by teaching at

Black Mountain, by lectures, magazines, and thousands upon thousands of letters. Olson, in other words, seems to have moved across his career roughly from the left-center, synthesis-seeking nationalism of the early OWI to a position at least structurally closer to the foreign-language publications he monitored (in his case more extremely left, while for many of the papers, roughly equivalently far to the right)—that rejected national unity and cultivated instead a discursive community out of other points of identification. Was this war work the causal source of Olson's later social thought? Probably not, or at least not only. Olson's thinking seems to have been affected both by the larger heating up of politics throughout the 1960s and by the specific New Left role in this process. Olson was sympathetic to Black Nationalism and, as we have seen, made explicit parallels (via his close friendship with Amiri Baraka) between the Black Nationalist movement and the shift in his own project away from the larger context of national politics. Yet the turn away from the category of the nation that will become pronounced in his later work will also be, in a sense, a doubling back on this early apprenticeship in how minor languages could—when focalized around active and well-distributed print or radio sources—produce alternative sonic/social formations that might resist integration at national scales. It seems to have occurred to Olson that avant-garde poetry might operate in a similar way: a counternation of nothing but poetry.

IV

When Olson turned away from the American Civilization Department at Harvard in 1939, one of his main concerns had been to expand Harvard's narrow, Protestant-centric canon of what might count as a usable American past. Key members of the Harvard American Civilization program—especially Perry Miller (1905–63) and Kenneth B. Murdock (1895–1975)—had in fact been engaged in a thorough reframing of the American Puritans as ambitious, informed intellectuals. But even these rebranded Puritans were offensive to Olson.[52] In composing *Spanish Speaking Americans in the War*, Olson was not just performing a patriotic duty; he was also picking up on William Carlos Williams's interest in including a wider canon of Spanish and French speakers as part of the country's past and, implicitly, present—a historiographic project Olson would continue in *The Maximus Poems*.[53] But if addressing these recruits in their native language was understood by many Americans as a remarkable act of state benevolence, then the problems underlying this shift in attitude toward the political stakes of language acquisition (in other words, a move, roughly, from early-century isolationism to Cold War diplomacy) would not disappear once the army had Spanish-speaking units. For the United States after World War II, the pluralization of linguistic communities domestically paralleled the rise of foreign-language instruction within the emerging discipline of area studies.

Olson's job for the OWI was at once to acknowledge and contain this pluralization by helping Spanish speakers feel themselves to be American. However, by the beginning of the next decade, Olson was coming to think about his linguistic labors in a different light. By 1951, Olson had struck up, developed, and burned through a close relationship with his prime modernist mentor, Ezra Pound, then confined to St. Elizabeths Hospital in Washington, D.C., because of his pro-Mussolini World War II radio broadcasts. Olson had published his book on Melville, *Call Me Ishmael* (1947), his first book of poetry, *Y & X* (1948); begun work on the counterhistoriographic epic *The Maximus Poems*; started teaching at Black Mountain College; and in February 1951 headed south to Yucatán to investigate the kind of larger genealogy of North American civilization that might include Mayan culture. If Olson's trajectory from American studies at Harvard through the OWI and into experimental poetry was not one *away* from politics, it was nonetheless a trajectory that, despite its global sweep, did not map easily onto the postwar US consolidation of power through area studies.

That fall of 1951, back in the Cambridge from which Olson had fled in 1939, a thirty-one-year-old immigrant from Belgium, displaced by the war, was offering a language lesson in French to a middling student named Henry, a native German speaker with an awkward accent. Paul de Man wouldn't be admitted to the PhD program in comparative literature at Harvard for another year, so he was making ends meet by lessons like these and others at Berlitz and by translations. Because Henry was a graduate student at Harvard at the time, such private lessons would have been complemented by work at the university's language laboratory. There, using a plastic disc player, Henry could practice basic phrases in a soundproof room—hearing them first in French, then trying to repeat them. Such language-learning centers, or phonetics laboratories, as they were first called, were in the years just after World War II becoming a crucial part of many universities, a component dictated from on high and administered widely as the United States rethought its role in global politics and thus the importance of language study as an aid in that role.[54] It was, in fact, as a secondary use of such technology, and an after-hours affair, that many recordings of poetry during the 1960s were made.[55] A state-sponsored demand for university-level language learning, in other words, provided the technological infrastructure not just for the recording devices that this student would have used at Harvard but equally for the same reel-to-reel tape recorders on which many university poetry reading series would have been recorded.[56]

Harvard had such a center by 1940, which moved to its own building— Cannon House—by 1946. The center had "two sound scribers and three record players," along with "700-odd records kept in the Center's recording-studio," as part of what were referred to as its "linguaphone facilities."[57] According to a 1949 article in the *Harvard Crimson*, the center was designed to give students "the opportunity to continue beyond the limits of the classroom their efforts to understand and appreciate foreign cultures" in part by learning languages. "Some students report as regularly as five times a week to use the linguaphone facilities," the article continues, quoting the wife of the center's director, a Mrs. Leggewie: "American ears are just not tuned to foreign languages, . . . and so hearing these records seems to help them tremendously." While his ears weren't American, and were in fact tuned to foreign languages, Henry's too seemed to need prac-tice, and tuning. So it's very likely that he, too, would have made regular use of the linguaphone facilities at Cannon House in between his sessions with de Man.[58] In their one-on-one sessions, Paul de Man was teaching Henry Kissinger the French the latter would use to negotiate with Charles de Gaulle about Vietnam in Paris in 1968.[59] What were the exemplary sen-tences de Man selected to instantiate the French language? Perhaps he relied on one of his favorite lines from Stéphane Mallarmé's "Tombeau de Verlaine": "Le noir roc courroucé que la bise le roule" (The dark rock angry that the high wind rolls)—savoring the strangeness of the word combinations by slowing down his pace. Or he might have chosen lines from later in the poem: "Cet immatériel deuil opprime de maints / Nubiles plis l'astre mûri des lendemains" (This insubstantial grief burdens with scores / Of nubile folds the future's ripened star).[60]

Perhaps, faced with these odd lines, Henry again stumbled. Kissinger was, after all, born in Bavaria and had not moved into the English-speaking world until anticipatory rumblings of World War II had displaced him, in 1938, first to London and soon after to the United States. He remained self-conscious about his Frankish accent. Nonetheless, it's unlikely that, sensing Kissinger's anxiety about his accent, Paul de Man would use a word like *détente* (relaxation). There was, one imagines, no *détente* in de Man's language instruction. Indeed, should Kissinger have mentioned his slight alienation from these second and third languages, English and especially French—his lack of coziness in these borrowed tongues—de Man might have offered an amused half smile instead of a quick reassurance, since de Man simply did not believe in the possibility of coziness in *any* language, including one's own.[61] Despite (or was it because of?) speaking French, Flemish, German, Italian, Spanish, and English, de Man did not subscribe to the idea that there could be a snug and reassuring fit between an empirical human being and his ostensible mother tongue. Indeed, de Man is supposed to have *forgotten* his own Flemish mother tongue after living in the United States for a decade or so. Late in his life, in a talk on Walter Benjamin's essay "The Task of the Translator," de Man would show not merely that Benjamin's English and French translators had made basic mistakes in their translation of this famous essay on translation but that this had been bound up with a systematic blindness about what Benjamin was in fact saying, which was, according to de Man,

> We think we are at ease in our own language, we feel a coziness, a familiarity, a shelter in the language we call our own, in which we think that we are not alienated. What the translation reveals is that this alienation is at its strongest in our relation to our own original language, that the original language within which we are engaged is disarticulated in a way which imposes upon us a particular alienation, a particular suffering.[62]

It seems safe to imagine that these sentiments would not have emerged quite so directly in 1951, in, say, de Man's job interview at Berlitz or his early conversations with Kissinger about becoming the latter's French tutor.[63] Whatever de Man said to the young Kissinger, something about his French teacher impressed the diplomat-to-be enough to ask de Man to become one of the main translators (and summarizers) for his new magazine, *Confluence*, which quite neatly embodied the Cold War model of area studies. De Man's first assignment (for issue no. 4 in 1952) was to provide summaries in French of articles in the journal. Other writers provided summaries in German and Italian. This suggests that, from the start, Kissinger was, like Olson working for the OWI, pitching *Confluence* within the linguistic world of readers who did not know English.[64] If, as it appears, these translations for the young Kissinger were somewhat more than grunt work, perhaps de Man did engage to an extent with the larger discussion generated by *Confluence*. The magazine was, after all, directed very much to Europeans seeking new cultural and especially political bearings after the war.[65] From our current vantage, and perhaps equally from that of the later poststructuralist de Man, many of the articles appear as bald attempts to produce Cold War consensus. The de Man of 1952 was perhaps closer to the anticommunist atmosphere that had permeated occupied Belgium than he was to the more nuanced reading practices of his philosophical future.[66] But however one understands de Man's degree of identification with *Confluence* in the early 1950s, its instantiation of a model of area studies helps us flesh out the negative datum against which I have been reading Charles Olson. Moreover, problems surrounding the media infrastructure underlying this model contribute directly to our narrative.

Consider Rudolf Vogel's essay "Press and Radio in Germany," which de Man may have summarized in French.[67] The essay begins with the claim, which Kissinger's work implicitly supported, that "all the problems of the Western World seem to be concentrated in particularly acute form in Germany."[68] Though Vogel does not remark on Germany's pioneering use of audiotape during World War II (to ensure the simultaneity of broadcasting and increase state power), his essay does address German wartime radio's terrifying power.[69] Initially "reduced to the status of 'His Master's Voice'" with Hitler's broadcasts, radio became later in the war a practical means of survival "when the air raid warnings broadcast night after night meant the difference between life and death for its listeners." But if radio was a means of social control that then, as the Germans began to lose the war, became a nominal means of survival, one of the oddnesses of Vogel's account is the way that, after the war, radio seems to appear again as an agent of social control—Vogel calls radio "the most powerful factor in public opinion"—without any attempt to differentiate this new state from the "His Master's Voice" period.[70] Rather, with its citizens subject to the competition not merely among the American, English, and French models, but the Soviets as well, postwar German radio would appear to be a pluralization of masters' voices, one per occupying power, in which, as Vogel notes, "each pursued its own policy with regard to radio." The Russians, for example, "as experienced totalitarians, continued and perfected Dr. Goebbels' policy of nationalization." Meanwhile, the British and the French, both "accustomed to centralization," set up single broadcasting corporations to cover their whole zones; it is only the Americans' commitment to federalism that allows them to establish several, regional stations within their zones.[71] For Vogel, national political cultures map directly onto the media spaces they control.[72]

This competition between German and Soviet airspace was a direct concern for the editors at *Confluence*, since the magazine's masthead director, William Yandell Elliott (1893–1979), was involved "with the launch of Radio Liberty (originally Radio Liberation), a U.S. broadcaster targeting the Soviet Union" (*K*, 263).[73] A historian, literary critic, and political adviser to six US presidents, Elliott was also the director of Adams House at Harvard, where Kissinger lived as an undergraduate.[74] Elliott was the reason that New Critics both published in and were on the board of *Confluence*; he had been an undergraduate at Vanderbilt, where he was part of a group of poet-scholars known as the Fugitives, including John Crowe Ransom, Allen Tate, and Robert Penn Warren. The circle was one of the earliest manifestations of what would become New Criticism.[75] An anglophile who supported British colonialism even as the enterprise collapsed (his contact with England had come during an MA at Oxford), Elliott had been warmly embraced first by the Democratic and later by the Republican Party.[76] He was a member of the Roosevelt Brain Trust, accompanied Roosevelt to Yalta, and was on the National Security Council (NSC) after the war.[77] By 1960 he was a scriptwriter for Nixon; despite this, Elliott was retained by John F. Kennedy as a special presidential consultant after the latter won the election that year (*K*, 493).

Yale is historically the American university tied most closely to the cultural Cold War generally and to the CIA specifically. But Harvard also had its share of both Cold Warriors and direct Agency operatives.[78] Elliott was both. Or rather, Elliott *had been* associated with the Agency in the late 1940s as an "occasional consultant" (*K*, 260) to Frank Wisner, the CIA's deputy director for plans. But by 1953 Elliott was forced, despite his best efforts, to accept inactive status and to work for the CIA from then on in a pro bono capacity. He also tried to bring Kissinger in, writing in 1951 to his old contact Wisner, asking that Kissinger be granted "an inactive consultant status similar to my own, but one that could be changed at need" (*K*, 278). As Niall Ferguson explains, other members of the Harvard faculty remained more active within the Agency and within the larger Cold War cultural imperatives: A professor of history, William L. Langer was "director of Research and Analysis at OSS" and later of the "CIA's Office of National Estimates" (*K*, 258). Another professor of history and dean of the Faculty of Arts and Sciences, McGeorge Bundy, became national security adviser for both Kennedy and Johnson. Harvard's version of area studies grew directly out of its faculty's proximity to the OSS and later the CIA.

> Bundy was proud of the fact that the postwar area studies programs at Harvard were "manned, directed, or stimulated by graduates of the OSS—a remarkable institution, half cops and robbers, half faculty meeting." It was desirable, he told an audience at Johns Hopkins, that there should be "a big measure of interpenetration between universities with area programs and the information-gathering agencies of the United States." (*K*, 258)

Elliott, for instance, maintained this link by thinking of his educational programs as extensions of what the OSS had called, rather bluntly, "psychological warfare." This term may jar slightly in an educational context. It was, though, in common use in the OSS and the OWI, especially among Ivy League–trained intellectuals. Indeed, about the time Olson was thinking of leaving the OWI, he received a promotion offer with the new job title of "psychological warfare executive."[79] It is no accident, then, that Elliott was supportive of both the Harvard Summer School (of which he was the dean) and *Confluence* or that Kissinger ran their daily operations: both the summer school and the magazine were not only conceived within the matrix of psychological warfare but also funded by organizations that directed their largesse toward such explicitly Cold War–oriented projects.[80] As Elliott wrote to the Ford Foundation, asking for financial help for the magazine, "It seems to me the best possible propaganda is not to propagandize. . . . Therefore we are purposely inviting characteristic statements by people who do not share our own views . . . painfully and even slowly, in spite of every wish for speed, [to] build up the moral consensus without which common policies are really impossible" (*K*, 280).[81] The summer school would work, as Kissinger explains it, "to swing the spiritual balance in favor of the U.S." (*K*, 275).[82]

To effect this swing, Kissinger needed not only a journal and a summer school but also a Belgian language instructor and a recording infrastructure to improve his language skills: indeed, after several issues, Kissinger himself is listed as one of the translators from French. With Paul de Man launching exemplary French sentences to Kissinger in the latter's apartment in the fall of 1951, we have, in a way, a prefiguration of the two Yale schools, of CIA surveillance, and American poststructuralism, together in one room—almost twenty years before de Man will actually move to Yale.[83] Despite not being a Yale-trained Agency-based theorist of espionage like Angleton or Pearson, Kissinger is nonetheless a central figure in the surveillance culture of the 1960s and early 1970s—already a high-level consultant to President Johnson and then Nixon's national security adviser and secretary of state, and thus privy to the president's audiotape fiasco.[84]

It is to this latter context we now turn in an attempt to draw out the perhaps counterintuitive theories of research that underlay both Kissinger's and Nixon's projects of audiotape surveillance. When US presidents and secretaries of state taped their conversations, they were performing what might seem like a very different kind of audio research from that of the poets: the state listening (mostly) to the state, the government in effect undertaking surveillance of itself, one branch or fiefdom against another. One function of such recordings was merely mnemonic. Executives as busy as the president could not be relied on to remember, verbatim, a conversation that occurred several months or years ago. Yet verbatim memory was often necessary. So tape was, in its most mundane capacity, a device for aiding in the conversion (with the help of trusted transcribers) of live conversation into printed text.[85] But obviously this use was not the function for which White House tapes became infamous. Audio surveillance—whether initiated by Kissinger, Nixon, the Bureau, or the Agency—could always be justified either through practical exigencies like those mentioned previously or through the model of hypothesis and potential substantiation, suspicion and possible verification. The claim that documentary research on a potentially guilty party was necessary justified most surveillance, including that of the Bureau on MLK. That the Bureau neither always believed its own claims nor used its findings to substantiate them has been well documented. What is of interest here, however, is less the obvious ethical breach than the status of research in this more cynical mode—whether conducted by Hoover or Kissinger.[86]

Such tapes were potential evidence awaiting their occasion. Rather than try to determine in advance who might offer useful audio proof of what,

Kissinger (like Hoover and others) seems to have proceeded from the more politically pragmatic stance that any current ally might soon become an enemy; thus, all discourse could be sifted after the fact for a wide variety of useful documentary elements.[87] His recordings, in other words, logged less the pursuit of a preexisting research hypothesis than a branching set of hypothetical scenarios or narrative sequences that need not be theorized or articulated in advance. Once manifested, however, a potentially useful scenario—a flipped position, a stabbed back, a broken promise, or even just a compromising phrase—was immediately documented and logged for future enlistment.

Given this theory of evidence, it's not surprising that Kissinger was extremely concerned about being recorded by others. In 1968, for instance, when he was about to come on board with Nixon, Kissinger insisted on speaking to Richard Allen by payphone and using German.[88] Three years after he had joined the administration, the secretary's telephones were still, Seymour Hersh tells us, "repeatedly swept for signs of wiretapping, but Kissinger insisted that such surveillance not be placed on a routine basis with any single agency. Special Secret Service, CIA, FBI, or National Security Agency teams would be summoned at random and on short notice to inspect the telephones" (*H*, 314). Distrustful of the process by which each of these agencies researched, retained, and deployed secrets via tape, Kissinger played them all against each other to retain a level of autonomy. His strategy was informed especially by the close relationship he had developed with the Bureau, from whom he regularly received wiretap reports, including many "on foreign embassies in Washington—as well as politically sensitive FBI information on an 'Eyes Only' basis" (*H*, 208). These Bureau dossiers involved both "salacious information on such black antiwar leaders as Martin Luther King Jr." and Hoover's "'raw FBI files'—always replete with malicious gossip and unproven allegations—on people the NSC was considering for staff vacancies or as consultants" (ibid.).[89] Certainly Kissinger would also have had access to the Bureau's COINTELPRO files on the New Left and the counterculture, the files that, perhaps more than any others, turned popular opinion against the Bureau when they were discovered in 1971 and published in 1972.[90] This revelation, together with Watergate (the break-in happened in 1972 and was revealed the following year) and a 1973 book by Victor Marchetti on the CIA, brought surveillance-aided state research to the center of public debate.[91]

But while the Bureau, the Agency, and the Nixon presidency were all forced in some capacity to deal with the public revelation that their "research" was both brought to bear beyond its claimed hypotheses and, in most cases, was more fundamentally illegal, Kissinger, who had been a key agent in the expansion of audio surveillance, managed to sidestep this kind of inquiry.[92] In fact, when Nixon decided to install the infamous taping system in the White House in 1971, he did so largely because of Kissinger. "Nixon realized rather early in their relationship that he badly needed a complete account of all that they discussed. . . . He knew that Henry was keeping a log of those talks, a luxury in which the President didn't have time to indulge. And he knew that Henry's view on a particular subject was sometimes subject to change without notice" (*H*, 316).[93] Similarly, the plumbing campaign taken up against White House leaks was also closely aligned with Kissinger, though administered through the Bureau's William Sullivan (*H*, 319). Strange as it may seem, the Bureau was actually reluctant to perform audio surveillance in the early 1970s because its "crime-fighting image was at an all-time low."[94] Concerned about this and about being forced to "defend the FBI against charges of violating the constitutional rights of United States citizens," Hoover had in fact recently "called a halt to illegal wiretaps." According to Sullivan, Hoover was persuaded to change his position and begin electronic surveillance once again "when President Nixon and his security advisor Henry Kissinger asked Hoover to tap the phones of a number of government employees who were suspected of leaking highly classified information to the press."[95]

It was this attempt to plug leaks by testing the various potential "pipes" via surveillance (seventeen people were singled out for this taping) that in turn became a key part of the White House's own tape morass. Audio evidence about both this project and the related one of breaking into the Watergate apartments was captured on tape, and Nixon was eventually impeached. Hunter S. Thompson refers to "those reels of harmless looking celluloid that had suddenly turned into time bombs."[96] The explosion to come involved a reversal of the power relations that typically underlay state audio research. The state, which had used its cutting-edge audio equipment and Ivy League–trained literary critics to research New Left poets, had now turned this kind of special audio attention on itself, one fiefdom against another. While Olson had been successful at the milder form of state-sponsored sonic tuning undertaken during the war, now the state could no longer agree on a program, a method, or even an object of attention; thus, its own (now illegal) behind-the-scenes operations became public. That the results were divisive and that illegal state surveillance now moved to the center of public discussion have long been known. But that this state surveillance culture is closely bound up with language learning, area studies, and literary education at Harvard, and that in Kissinger's hands at least, surveillance approached an avant-garde structure in which the more traditional model of hypothesis and verification was abandoned in a manner comparable to historiography after the linguistic turn, has been what I have tried to demonstrate here.

V

In May 1972 (Hoover died that month and the Plumbers were arrested in June) the historian Hayden White, then teaching at UCLA, began to notice a surprising number of clean-cut faces in his lecture course on the history of historiography from Herodotus to the present.[97] These budding historians seemed especially curious. Were they captivated, perhaps, by the bold (and for many historians unthinkable) critique of narrative that was emerging in White's thought; drawn to his engagement with figures often marginalized within history departments, like Nietzsche and Hegel and Michelet; or perhaps taken by White's program of rendering historical inquiry itself historical, of putting it into contact with the latest developments in art and philosophy? Indeed, even before the publication of *Metahistory* in 1973—which would remain White's most famous work—the historian had, in a 1966 article titled "The Burden of History," articulated an experimental and disciplinarily unstable path for historians:[98]

> It may well be that the most difficult task which the current generation of historians will be called upon to perform is to expose the historically conditioned character of the historical discipline, to preside over the dissolution of history's claim to autonomy among the disciplines, and to aid in the assimilation of history to a higher kind of intellectual inquiry which, because it is founded on an awareness of the *similarities* between art and science, rather than their differences, can be properly designated as neither.[99]

However much such a passage may be legible as an early moment in the American version of the linguistic turn, here this reflexive trajectory went perhaps a step further than the claim that history shared crucial features with literature and could not be regarded merely as a window onto the past. White seemed to be inviting young scholars into the field of history precisely so that they could take down its institutional walls and "preside over the dissolution of history's claim to autonomy among the disciplines." Whether they were fully conscious of it or not, many people, including many of White's students, relied on these walls in their everyday activities. History's claim to autonomy, in other words, was operative not only among academic disciplines but also within all manner of practical operations in the social and legal world outside academia.

Given that White had articulated this radical position as early as 1966 and that its key features would only be amplified over the 1970s and 1980s, it seems safe to assume that something of this orientation would have organized his view of historiography during his lecture course at UCLA in 1972. Still, the full implications of his position may have taken some time to sink in among his students. When White was proposing, for instance, that history draw more fully on the resources of modern art and philosophy, he was suggesting not merely that it come up to date. Rather, in doing so, history might also cease to be recognizable to many of its current practitioners—it might even, for instance, abandon narrative.[100] Were there, perhaps, some blank stares from the audience at this point? Were the seemingly progressive California youths more attached to traditional history than White had first imagined? White began to have doubts about one of these new students in particular and to suspect that, from one point of view, he was not even a student at all but in fact an undercover police agent from the LAPD sent to monitor his and other classes and to build dossiers on faculty and students. These doubts, however, were not based on hostile questions or poor class performance but on the fact that a person quoted in the *LA Times* offering testimony on a surveillance case for the LAPD shared this student's name.[101]

White's hypothesis seemed to be verified by three subsequent observations, the first two of the student, the third of the LAPD as a whole: First White witnessed the student getting into a car on campus with someone who looked to White like a plainclothes officer. Second, and more important, the historian (and many others) witnessed the student both explode in a heated exchange with White (upon being confronted about his identity) and attempt to flee the scene, even driving his car into another professor in an attempt to make a quick exit. As White explains about the encounter and its aftermath, "This attracted a crowd which surrounded the car and the officers panicked, tried to flee the scene and in their haste knocked down a faculty member."

The third, and seemingly clinching, observation: later that night LAPD Chief Edward M. Davis went on the George Redding television show and presented White as "the most dangerous radical on the West Coast" (much to the chagrin of Fredric Jameson, one imagines). To substantiate these claims, the "police officers' jacket, torn and mutilated, was shown as evidence." The suggestion was that White had "torn the jacket from the officer's back and that he had to flee for his life."[102] Whereas one might have had some slight doubt that perhaps the student shared a name with a police officer or even that the public charge (in 1972!) of being an undercover cop posing as a student might cause an innocent student to lose his composure and make a rash driving decision in an attempt to flee, neither of these scenarios would have resulted in the LAPD chief appearing on television to denounce White as a coat-tearing radical, and so White's hypothesis seemed to be confirmed.

Nonetheless, White was confronted with several problems. There was, to begin with, the basic factual account, the narrative, of what actually occurred on the UCLA campus. "Needless to say, I had not laid a hand on" the officer, White writes; "he was not in uniform, [i.e., the torn police jacket prop bore no relation to the man's actual outfit that day] and the whole thing was the typical police defense (really heavy handed) against my daring to confront them."[103] If it was possible to establish a more reliable narrative of the events, then it might also be possible to contest LAPD's right to perform surveillance on campus more generally. But finding a way for his narrative to prevail would involve contesting the authority of the police department and its access to media, a problem that takes us back to White's claim that "narrative in general, from the folktale to the novel, from the annals to the fully realized 'history,' has to do with the topics of law, legality, legitimacy, or, more generally, authority."[104]

As it turns out, White *was* able (with the help of the American Civil Liberties Union [ACLU]) to secure his own narrative. He sued the LAPD's Chief Davis and, as sole plaintiff, won his case in the California Supreme Court in 1975, establishing a still-extant precedent (*White v. Davis*) governing the limits of state surveillance on university campuses. The state must demonstrate "reasonable suspicion of a crime" before it can send fake students into campus lecture halls. White himself, however, is skeptical about the extent to which the case represents a victory, citing the fact that the LAPD and the FBI "continued to do this kind of work."[105] My interest, though, is less in whether the case was a success or a failure than in its relation to

White's own work on historiography and the larger questions of hypothesis and verification.

Indeed, the arguments by which the case was won bear a fascinating (and as-yet-unexplored) relationship both to White's writing and to the differing modes of state research under consideration in this chapter. White's case rested on the commonsensical claim that, in the absence of "reasonable suspicion of a crime," police cannot engage in such surveillance on college campuses; intellectual life on campus, that is, was not understood as immune from all surveillance—just from what was deemed unreasonable surveillance. Such a concession might have been insisted on, from the state's point of view, as a mechanism for dealing with another kind of fake student—the KGB plant designed to foment student activism. Certainly the state also could have justified surveillance on homegrown activists engaged in crimes. But the possibility that these latter activists were (1) (knowingly or not) following Soviet orders or (2) working with actual Soviet plants on college campuses reminds us of the narrative frame, or interpretive theory, discussed in Chapter 1. In our current context, it seems to silence any effective objection that campuses should be considered entirely immune from modes of surveillance that involve officers impersonating students—a tactic that was central to the COINTELPRO's incursions into and disruption of the New Left.

Despite the obvious and well-documented ethical breaches involved in such covert actions, the hypothetical narrative scenario of a Soviet plant on a university campus, of more mediated Soviet influence among students, and even of certain brands of native radicalism, would appear to set a limit or horizon condition whereby university faculty and students in fact had no right to expect full freedom from city or government agents posing as students. These hypothetical narrative scenarios had too much power for them to be dismissed either as totally implausible or as nominally plausible but unworthy of the ethical compromises involved in combating them with the technique of police officers posing as students.

So White and the ACLU mounted their case on slightly different grounds. They did this, again, by pointing out that state surveillance within democracies is supposed to be predicated on just cause, or on what a more traditional historian like Sherman Kent might call a workable hypothesis, a narrative of criminality that was at once based on a verifiable piece of evidence and a reasonable expectation of expanding that evidentiary basis through the collection of more materials by undercover agents on campus. What faculty and students could expect, then, was not that lecture courses on historiography would remain free of police officers posing as budding historians but that such plants would not attend "without reasonable suspicion of a crime." After *White v. Davis*, police officers posing as students need approved surveillance theses.

Putting matters this way allows us perhaps to double back on how this model of state research relates to White's own pathbreaking work in historiography. In his essay "Interpretation in History" (published in *New Literary History* in 1973 and thus presumably in progress at the time he filed his suit), White argues that the historian "does not bring with him a notion of the 'story' that lies embedded within the 'facts' given by the record. For in fact there are an infinite number of such stories contained therein, all different in their details, each unlike every other."[106] In one sense, this distinction should be legible as that between classic research and the more narratologically complex mode undertaken by experimental historians like White and others, but also by Hoover, Kissinger, and those state researchers whose data collection transcended any organizing, focalizing thesis, any "reasonable suspicion of a crime." This structural similarity should not be taken as proof of any ethical problem inherent in White's model; rather, it points to the complexity involved in *any* research, including state research.

To take White's proposition seriously for the LAPD researchers, for instance, would be to recognize that an original hypothesis (backed by just cause or not) could give rise to an infinity of potential narratives and that these potential narratological branches would continue to increase during the process of research, as documents were uncovered, or in this case, produced by the police scholars in their note-taking sessions. Thus, the final reports would not be a matter of "finding the story which lies buried within or behind the events" but of framing the multivalent events into one of many stories whose limiting condition is really only that of plot.[107] But even the backstop of plot structure does not, in itself, clear up the contingency native to narrative. Indeed, White proposes in his classic essay "The Value of Narrativity in the Representation of Reality" that "unless at least two versions of the same set of events can be imagined, there is no reason for the historian to take upon himself the authority of giving the true account of what really happened."[108] While for Chief Davis this second version of the events does seem to have been "imagined" quite literally, more typically this imagination has to do not with the matter of inventing evidence for an invented crime as much as with the subtler question of choosing the kind of story for which one would select and conscript various and multivalent events. White's own research into the history of narrative suggests an inherent link between the multivalence of events and the legal and political need for one version to win out over another. In fact, White's "suspicion that narrative in general . . . has to do with the topics of law, legality, legitimacy, or, more generally, authority" is prefaced by the suggestion that "we cannot but be struck by the frequency with which narrativity, whether of the fictional or the factual sort, presupposes the existence of a legal system against which or on behalf of which the typical agents of a narrative account militate."[109]

Let me be clear that my aim here is not the more familiar one of seeking to demonstrate the "unworkable" or "irresponsible" dimensions of White's historiography; I think he's absolutely right, not to mention heroic, for confronting the undercover officer and bringing suit against the LAPD. The question becomes why the sophistication he makes possible within historiographic discourse cannot be extended to the state. The simplest answer is that Hayden White did not represent himself in court, and the ACLU lawyers who took up his case were neither particularly interested in its relation to White's own writings on historiography nor convinced that these would help them win the case. Had White been involved in preparing his case, he might have assumed that the state could not hear his own historiographic discourse as anything but an evasion of the models of causality that were necessary for it to understand an argument as convincing, and thus that it was a practical necessity to argue simply that an old-fashioned notion of hypothesis and verification was the groundwork on which acceptable surveillance should proceed. Such a stance, which we might think of as a "strategic traditionalism," might be compared to the array of "strategic essentialisms" that became necessary to perform certain modes of political representation and work at the same time as essentialism was itself a heated topic of critique.

A perhaps slightly more compelling answer is that, for all this discussion of hypotheses and verification, note taking and student gatherings, White couldn't quite recognize this police officer as a researcher or, more to the point, historian: despite teaching him Herodotus, White did not want to grant this officer the active model of historical fieldwork Charles Olson would draw from the Greek historian, taking the "'istorin" as a verb meaning "to find out for yourself" (*MP*, 249). White could not see, or did not want to see, the interpretive activities of this undercover pseudo-student as sharing certain unavoidable structural dimensions with his own. So, quite understandably, he wielded a narrower, less sophisticated version of his own discipline in order to shut down the more narratologically complex, open-ended enterprise this scholar had taken up at UCLA, researching all topics related to the New Left, building several narratives as he encountered new evidence, and constantly expanding his field of inquiry. White proposed a more classic educational itinerary that, he hoped, would find no takers because it would find no basis in the evidentiary world recognized by the law.[110]

VI

On April 23, 1971, Henry Kissinger taped a phone call from Allen Ginsberg, who had hoped to arrange a meeting between key members of the antiwar movement and the most powerful players in US foreign policy. Ginsberg appears to have been given Kissinger's contact information by Senator Eugene McCarthy (1916–2005), who had run for president in 1968 on an anti–Vietnam War platform and who remained on the Senate Foreign Relations Committee: "I am calling at the request partly of Senator McCarthy," Ginsberg offers.[111] "Senator McCarthy told me to call you. My idea is to arrange a conversation between yourself, [CIA Director Richard] Helms, McCarthy and maybe even Nixon with Rennie Davis, Dillinger and Abernathy.[112] It can be done at any time. They were willing to show their peaceableness and perhaps you don't know how to get out of the war—" The suggestion that Kissinger simply *doesn't know* how to get out of the war and needs peace activists to show him may be what causes him to interrupt. Yet the first words out of his mouth are not about this offered antiwar pedagogy but about the problem of private speech being made public, being leaked (a problem that's especially ironic given that Kissinger is himself taping the conversation): "I have been meeting with many members representing peace groups but what I find is that they have always then rushed right out and given the contents of the meeting to the press. But I like to do this, not just for the enlightenment of the people I talk to but to at least give me a feel of what concerned people think. I would be prepared to meet in principle on a private basis." By the end we notice that Kissinger has reversed Ginsberg's suggestion: The secretary of state enlightens people he talks to and also finds out what the "concerned" among them think. He does not, that is, learn from them. Bracketing Kissinger's aggressive claims about who does the learning when he meets with peace groups, Ginsberg circles back on the first problem of the press leak, which he sees as "a question of personal delicacy. In dealing with human consciences, it is difficult to set limits." Kissinger then tries to introduce a distinction, presumably about leaking information—"You can't set limits to human consciences but—" whereupon Ginsberg interrupts, seeming to grasp the secretary of state's concerns and pacify them: "We can try to come to some kind of understanding." But when Kissinger then tries to build on their implicit previous understanding, offering the second part of his sentence—"You can set limits to what you say publicly"—Ginsberg doubles back:

Ginsberg:	It would be even more funny to do it on television.
Kissinger:	What?
Ginsberg:	It would be even more useful if we could do it naked on television.
Kissinger:	(Laughter)
Ginsberg:	It might be too [word inaudible] but under some kind of circumstances. What shall I tell them that would be encouraging?
Kissinger:	That I would think about it very seriously.
Ginsberg:	Good deal.

While at first this exchange might sound merely like an instance of Ginsberg trying to provoke the straight politician, in fact it includes two key components, indeed a representative microcosm, of his poetics: first the flesh (the body or "meat") that is in Ginsberg both ground zero for a noncombative affective relationship and the locus of violence that media representations of wars must inevitably repress. Staging flesh has, for Ginsberg, an ethical imperative for this reason. Second is television as the larger media apparatus that performs this repression, now "corrected" by broadcasting Ginsberg and the US secretary of state discussing Vietnam in the nude. The proposed image is thus a media oxymoron—foregrounding both a type of dialogue that television makes impossible and the typically repressed site of prone, vulnerable human flesh. In a way, this is exactly the kind of fantasy scenario—a televised naked conversation with Kissinger—that could have, but didn't, conclude *The Fall of America*, the bringing together of its two components of media critique and bodily contact or expression. It was, in a sense, an attempt to document the repression and violence underlying dominant media in the United States that led Ginsberg out on the road in the first place, led him into his own version of media ethnography or sonic fieldwork.

The insistence that history involve first-person fieldwork has been central to Olson's career and reception. Less known, however, is the fact that this formulation of the historical activity rubs shoulders with a negative account of the documentary capacities of tape recording and television. This comes in Olson's January 15, 1962, "A Later Note on Letter #15" (the poem with which we began, with its characterization of CBS as the "true troubadours" and "Poets" needing to "getta / job"):

In English the poetics became meubles—furniture—
thereafter (after 1630

& Descartes was the value

until Whitehead, who cleared out the gunk
by getting the universe in (as against man alone

& *that* concept of history (not Herodotus's,
which was a verb, to find out for yourself:
'istorin, which makes any one's acts a finding out for him or her
self, in other words restores the traum: that we act somewhere

at least by seizure, that the objective (example Thucidides, or
the latest finest tape-recorder, or any form of record on the spot

—live television or what—is a lie

as against what we know went on, the dream: the dream being
self-action with Whitehead's important corollary: that no event

is not penetrated, in intersection or collision with, an eternal
event

        The poetics of such a situation
are yet to be found out   (*MP*, 249)

The posthuman poetics toward which Olson strives must transcend "man alone" and instead include "the universe" as well. One might have supposed that tape would help with this project. Certainly in Ginsberg's van and in Olson's kitchen tape transcends man alone and brings in his immediate environment—be it road sounds in Ginsberg or, precisely, the creaking meubles in Olson's Gloucester apartment. Indeed, as Barry Miles mentioned in his liner notes to the Folkways LP, it was the problem capturing Charles's voice alone that led to Miles's setting up his equipment in Olson's "bedroom where the fridge couldn't get itself on the tape." That sonic problem solved, Olson added another, sitting "in an upright chair which creaked alarmingly but was the only possible one for him to use so he said." Beyond this loud ambient antique, the poet and his audio engineer are, though it is the middle of the night, "sometimes disturbed by the muffled roar and crunch of snow as a truck slowly passed by." Finally, there is Olson's sonic relation to his books, his table, and his performing body:

> The room contained a trestle table stacked two deep in maritime books, spine out. Hundreds of books, making the table sag, and to which I added a directional microphone. I arranged it as close as I dared, avoiding Charles' gesticulations as he read and the fading as he looked away or down at the page. I sat on the floor by the door with my headphones.

Despite Olson's copious production of ambient, nonlexical effects here, the poet nonetheless equates recording (in the poem just cited) with mystified claims about complete and adequate representation—the "seizure" of "the objective." This negative media essentialism might find as its example the tape that sits at the center of government vaults on IBM reels, perhaps deep in the Cheyenne Mountain Complex. Tape, understood this way, cannot be repurposed by Allen Ginsberg in his van or even by Barry Miles in Olson's bedroom, capturing the poet's contingent squeaks, bangs, and huffs while Olson instantiates the research process of his counternational epic. Instead, Olson presents tape as an ideology of complete reality capture that lacks key elements of representation. Yet, as we can now hear, some of what Olson was after, some of the external "universe" situated close by, "around the bend / of the nest" (*MP*, 5), was in fact in play in the comparatively indiscriminate registrations of Miles's tape recorder. Like Ginsberg, Olson couldn't quite hear it or understand its potential importance for his poetics.

But there is another way we can hear Olson's claim about tape as a partial representation right on the Folkways record where such a claim should, in fact, make its main difference. I mentioned earlier that, despite the record's trappings of a countercultural cult figure who might tell alternate histories of the United States, the poem seems to call attention instead to its own present-tense building or construction, the ongoing researching of which it is an instance: Colonial Ship Model, or New England Diorama, with the Sound of Its Own Making. The record does contain, it is true, a few quasi-narrative poems woven in. We might nonetheless gather something of the sense in which Barry Miles's tape recorder is "a lie" when we hear, for instance, Olson's "3rd letter on Georges, unwritten." This is a poem that might be taken to stage, explicitly, the kind of inadequacy or incompleteness to which Olson refers in his remarks about tape recorders. First, the text tells us that this letter is as yet "unwritten" (though we can learn of this only by reading the text that stands in its place). In what sense do we take this gesture, since the poem *does* in fact narrate a story of one of Olson's beloved ship captains performing a dangerous act of taking his vessel across the shallows at the eastern edge of Georges Bank (a raised and therefore treacherous area of the seafloor between Cape Cod and Nova Scotia) in order to get his fish immediately to market? The suggestion, apparently, is that these are notes toward some later, fuller composition, so are a placeholder in *The Maximus Poems*. They are a placeholder in part, we learn from the poem, because Olson's nautical research remains somewhat incomplete: he can't determine whether the captain is Bohlin, or Sylvanus Smith, or Marty Callaghan—and this matters. So we are left, again, suspended inside Olson's ongoing research. But in this case that suspension is slightly different. What he can convey of this ship captaining instance, without providing the identity of the captain, is the sense of navigational precision, confidence, and risk: "and I want that sense / here, of this fellow going home" (*MP*, 277). Olson wants to register this energy—"here."

But where, exactly, is this *here*? Or rather, which here do we take this deictic pointer to evoke? At one level it seems to be the "unwritten" poem that stands in for the poem in a later, more finalized version within a completed *Maximus Poems*. Here is, in this sense, a temporary set of notes pointing to the fuller elaboration that will never occur. At another level, however, here is less one version of the poem as it awaits completion than the larger *institutional* space of *The Maximus Poems* as a whole. Pointing to the capacious here of his would-be canonical epic, this second here ensures cultural transmission across time even if the research is not final. Yet this evocation of *The Maximus Poems* as a canonical work still under construction emphasizes the ongoing research necessary for this construction to complete itself: actually writing the "3rd letter on Georges" is not merely a matter of composition but of time-consuming archival inquiry. So we are left with a third here: neither the provisional poem nor the institutional space but the ongoing *activity* of Olson researching, the thematized process that stretches Maximus's role beyond that of the composer of discrete poems and into a quasi-performative process of real-time archive spelunking. As we have seen in the case of the Folkways LP, Olson could be quite literal minded about representing the time involved in his research. This dynamic is captured well by Henry Kissinger's French tutor: "The writer's language is to some degree the product of his own action; he is both the historian and the agent of his own language."[113] A durational theme song of atonal creaks and coughs, this third here might be understood as Olson's historiographic version of Robert Morris's *Box with the Sound of Its Own Making.*

But on the Folkways LP there is a fourth sense of here as well: the audio event of the record, the singularity of the voice on tape and then vinyl. This medial here points not merely to the provisional poem, the institutional space of the epic, or the activity of generating that epic in archives; rather, in a manner impossible for printed text, it points to a specific room in which a specific person uttered a specific set of words. In another poem recorded on the LP, "Now Called Gravel Hill" (*MP*, 330), Olson explains: "it isn't so decisive / how one thing does end / and another begin to be very obviously dull about it / I should like to take the time to be dull" (*MP*, 331). For Olson, when he distances himself from tape, the eternal must remain a mythic process rather than the nonhuman world of his apartment, the sonic elements of the recording that resist his control and intention: from his own decaying body to his refrigerator's hum, his squeaking chairs, and his bodily gesticulations. Tape exists instead as a fictive "objectivity" that Olson must contest in his path from sonic area studies to archival filibustering.

As different as their philosophies of research, audio aesthetics, and basic political orientations might otherwise have been, Olson perhaps surprisingly shares with Kissinger a sense of the official and normative power of an audio archive—though turns against it for precisely the reason Kissinger embraces it: despite its radical partiality, tape can become the juridical basis for institutionally recognized claims about what occurred at some particular spot at a discrete historical moment. That this process can escape what must have appeared the tightly controlled power dynamics by which government surveillance is conducted must have been something of a surprise to Kissinger and his colleagues in the early 1970s, as the celluloid time bombs Hunter Thompson had remarked on suddenly exploded and the Nixon administration came crashing down. Had Olson lived a few more years, he'd have relished this result while remaining perhaps slightly skeptical about the final documentary powers of tape.

One did not need Olson's particular distrust of tape, however, to recognize that after the early 1970s a certain phase in American audio culture was over. The case studies I've here educed in part to track the emergence and dissolution of this midcentury audio optimism have stretched from the sonic tuning of Olson's war work with the nation's Spanish speakers and its foreign-language publications through the at-times-aggressive sonic conceptualism and process orientation of his mid- to late 1960s performances and LPs that worked not "to build out of sound the walls" of the country but to enact and articulate counternationalist coterie social formations. To give this episode in literary history a plausible outside, a larger social and political field, I've sought to link it, at key junctures, not merely with the wider postwar project of area studies as it was practiced in Olson's home institution of Harvard and elsewhere but also with the emergent infrastructure of foreign-language learning that was necessary to export and implement the American century. This infrastructure is of interest both because it places Paul de Man as Henry Kissinger's French tutor and translator and because, after Kissinger had spent the afternoon practicing his French with recordings at the linguaphone facilities, the center's recording devices (like those at research centers across North America) could be wheeled over to the auditorium to document the reading by Allen Ginsberg, Jackson Mac Low, or Charles Olson, providing much of our documentation of 1960s poetry performance. In addition to concretizing the institutional basis of postwar area studies, Kissinger's somewhat extended cameo I hope focalizes both the early optimism of an audiotape culture (which in his hands can also simply be called surveillance culture) and its later Cold War implosion. Moreover, Kissinger's model of audio research (like Hoover's) demonstrates the more complex strategy of allover surveillance in the service of ever-emergent (unknowable in advance) needs for documentation—a model that would gradually overtake the more classical paradigm of hypothesis and verification proposed by Sherman Kent and other CIA theorists. As practical as this new model was, it also, of course, had more wiggle room for explosion.

If presidents after the early 1970s, learning from this awkward history of White House audio surveillance, manage increasingly to mute sound recordings of their culpability, this is obviously not because of a decline in state surveillance. Instead, as it shifts from analog to digital in the 1980s and 1990s, the state's access to information about the daily lives of its citizens becomes more generalized, seamless, and total, as Hayden White feared when he suggested that, despite a nominal victory against the LAPD in his own battle, citizens ultimately lost that war. What is increasingly interesting about this early form of surveillance culture is not only its grainy, partial quality—its sound of coming from a remote technological regime of patchy incompleteness that seems to offer pregnant gaps and hiding places. This may simply be how analog now sounds: reel-to-reels as the audio training wheels of our current digital regime of total sound recall and control. What is perhaps more curiously alien about this period is the confidence and even enthusiasm that attends this sonic older regime, a faith in the power of, and above all the control over, audio documentation: negatively, in Olson's case, as a fictive objectivity; and positively, in Nixon's or Hoover's or Kissinger's cases as a reliable record that might always be mobilized against one's enemies. Was this the last flourishing of a midcentury audio modernism, an ambitious culture of sonic research—theorized by a wide range of Harvard- and Yale-trained Agency operatives—and pursued by the state and poets alike?

Ginsberg's embrace of his Uher might incline us to agree. Yet what we see finally in his and in Olson's examples is that the poets do not fully take advantage of those ambient, nonhuman dimensions of tape that situate it in specific, information-laden space, and thus endlessly irritate Agency audio theorists like William Johnson, who love above all clean audio registrations of self-compromising speech—the Agency's theory of the lyric. But if consciously 1960s poets tended to use tape merely as a voice registration machine, the very imperfection of this machine might be understood now, paradoxically, to aid their larger projects of situating subjectivity or human agency within a larger field—be that a field of energy or media or simply social relations. In the Folkways LP and in *The Maximus Poems* Olson cultivates such an effect tentatively—an effect we might identify, despite the mountains of contrary testimony, as one of genre, not history.

To claim that Olson, like Eigner, is a genre poet is not, of course, to discount the former's profound interest in, and involvement with, history; it is rather to locate Olson's insistence on the real time of research not as a personal quirk, a filibustering designed only to waste time, but as a project that sees as its negative datum the monumental, causal events of normative history. But if the Olson that insists on the real and reel time of his Gloucester apartment researches, more than on any ostensible reference they make, is a genre poet, then his genre of genre poetry is a bit different from Larry Eigner's. The Sage of Swampscott gave his attention to an ongoingness under the texture of normative history, engaging with the conditions that underlie discrete events. All of this was based on a kind of empirical attention to sight and sound that becomes increasingly self-reflexive as it discovers and then responds to the language in which it is already occurring. Such scenes of reflexive empiricism do at moments occur in Olson. But it would be more accurate to describe his basic temporal continuum, his involvement with ongoingness, as a time of research—a time of finding out and assembling. While this time is, indeed, punctured periodically by sudden rushes of sensations that appear to be epiphanies, these also follow less the logic of historical events than of mental events within the process of history making, of research. Thus, we can say finally that Olson's archival filibustering is not so much, or not only, a perverse withholding of reference and narrative but an insistence on an ongoing time of research that is the final ground for their production and deployment. It is this ongoingness that Olson's New England history-making-in-progress dioramas attend to in high fidelity.

The Strategic Idea of North
Glenn Gould, Sergeant Jones, and White Alice

> Imperialism is the word used to refer to the extension of an empire or
> ideology to parts of the world remote from the source. It is Europe and
> North America which have, in recent centuries, masterminded various
> schemes designed to dominate other peoples and value systems, and
> subjugation by Noise has played no small part in these schemes. Expansion
> took place first on land and sea (train, tank, battleship) and then in the air
> (planes, rocketry, radio).
>
> —R. Murray Schafer, *The Soundscape*

Frederick George Scott's poem "Quebec" begins: "Like some grey warder who, with mien sedate." Little known today, Scott (1861–1944) was, during his life-time and shortly after, noted for his Christian, patriotic poetry; for his support of British imperialism (he enlisted to fight in World War I at more than fifty years old); and for his attachment to the Laurentian Mountains in southern Quebec.[1] Taking exception to the "grey warder" line (which he does not deign to credit to a proper name or associate with a poem title), Robert Creeley goes on what we might hear today as something of an excessive rant against Canadian poetry as a whole:

> Canadian poetry might always be this attempt, not so much to fit, say, into an envi-
> ronment but to act in the given place. If there is no "major" poet in Canada, if there
> never was one, etc., I think it is a part of this same problem. A theoretic embarrass-
> ment of "culture," all the tenuosities of trying to be local and international at the
> same time, etc., take an energy otherwise of use in the making of an idiom peculiar
> to the given circumstances. In this way Canadian poetry, in its earlier forms, has
> much in common with the American poetry of Lowell, Longfellow, et al. The model
> is English, and it is precisely the English which is of no use whatsoever.[2]

One wonders how much Canadian poetry Creeley had actually read in 1953 when he made this comment and thus what gave him the sense that Scott might stand in for the nation's output as a whole. It helps somewhat to know that this blurt was printed before the emergence of many of the better-known Canadian experimental poets of the 1960s and early 1970s. Fred Wah was fifteen years old; George Bowering, eighteen; Daphne Marlatt, eleven; bpNichol, nine; and Steve McCaffery, six. These are all poets that Creeley will later know and respect. A decade later, in 1963, Creeley will be at the Vancouver Poetry Conference, and from about that time on his work, like that of Olson, will be part of an international poetic dialogue with these Canadian poets.

This is perhaps somewhat surprising given the gauntlet Creeley laid down in his initial rant: "The impact of the place is dulled," he continues, "in the overlay of the English rhythms, and the politeness which couldn't have been actual." Affectedly polite English rhythms mute poetry's possible relation both to spatial and idiomatic dimensions of location and to the social antagonisms latent within any location, Creeley says, antagonistically from across the border. Against this, Creeley nominates "the Frenchman who came over with Champlain" as "the first Canadian poet"—this in part because he has written ("before leaving, and almost on the dock") his "Farewell to France," and it is this renunciation that, to Creeley's way of thinking, opens up the new world for him. Echoing William Carlos Williams's attempt to recuperate French missionaries like Père Rasles (who to Williams both made "contact" with Native Americans and displayed curiosity more generally about their actual location in the New World) over and above Colonial English Puritans (who for him did neither), Creeley claims that "the Frenchman with Champlain was, finally, a poet in a much, much deeper sense, and it was he who catalogued a good many of the plants around their camp, and also made a garden which kept them all in vegetables." The *real* Canadian poet forsakes what has counted as "poetry" for a more intimate relation to the sounds that surround him, to idioms in space, the involvement with which then becomes actual—if nongeneralizable—poetry: "I don't see any other way to do it. The problems of form and content, and all the other contentions of poets, are utterly intimate with each man writing, and where he is writing, and what he tries with what's around him. Canadian poetry becomes, in each instance, which man or woman it is, and what their work can effect."[3]

From one perspective this is Black Mountain 101: renounce received metrics and cultivate the particularity of your own breath, your own occasion and space, and the idiomatic world in which you *actually* live; score and register all this in an open field poetics. Shifting the perspective just slightly, we might say that this is advice on actually listening, on not being distracted by one's presuppositions about poetry, offered as something of a presupposition and without listening much to the culture where it's destined. However shrink-wrapped for export this Black Mountain™ product was, the Canadians seemed to have listened patiently, not so much to Creeley's specific rant, perhaps, as to the specificity of Canada's sonic environment—to the extent that, in the works of Glenn Gould, R. Murray Schafer, and others, Canada now seems inextricably bound to the birth of sound studies. That Canadians have, in turn, taught generations of listeners across the globe to hear the singular characters of their sonic environments, or what Schafer calls soundscapes, renders Creeley's blurt all the more ironic. This inductive attention to the actual character of one's sonic surroundings is, arguably, the goal of sound studies. If the soundscape has emerged as a transportable concept that expands beyond Creeley's Black Mountain frame, then it is worth pausing on the Canadian origins of this attention to one's sonic neighborhood.[4]

Schafer's *Soundscapes of Canada* project is a pioneering, early instance of sound studies' attention to the immediate sonic environment. The fieldwork for the project was undertaken in 1973, with the help of Howard Broomfield, Bruce Davis, Peter Huse, Barry Truax, and Adam Woog. *Soundscapes of Canada* was aired as ten hour-long radio programs from October 21 to November 1, 1974, on the CBC. It was part of Schafer's larger "World Soundscape Project" undertaken at Simon Fraser University.[5] This larger project was then the basis for perhaps the foundational text in sound studies, *The Soundscape: Our Sonic Environment and the Tuning of the World* (1977). Yet *Soundscapes of Canada* was aired before sound studies as a discipline or a global soundscape popularized through Schafer's writings had gained much institutional traction. Canadian sounds, therefore, seem to have played a special role in training sound theorists' ears.[6]

For Schafer, this training involved both dangers and opportunities: the Canadian sound subject needed to be alerted, on the one hand, to the fact that oppressive industrial noises were not inevitable and uncontrollable and, on the other, to the opportunities involved in listening more closely to a wide swath of human and nonhuman sounds, especially those that were threatened with extinction and therefore needed care and preservation. Once conceived this way, the totality of these sounds could then be designated a "soundscape" and even engineered. In the program, after introducing us to the idea of the soundscape via a set of themes (rhythm and tempo, ambience and acoustic space, language, gestures and texture, the changing soundscape, and silence), Schafer walks us through listening exercises devoted to what he calls "ear cleaning," which operates as a prerequisite for the successful hearing and reengineering that is Schafer's ultimate goal. If man's acoustic envelope is now, suddenly, a matter of design, this design should not involve only intentional sounds that reflect his humanity. Rather, much of the ideal soundscape—and certainly much of the time of the radio program—is devoted to sonic textures produced by the Canadian landscape, with its rushing or splashing water, its wind, its animals, it physical materials stretching, cracking, or buckling.

Whereas the downsizing of human presence within a sonic landscape presented problems for many poets working with tape in the 1960s, for Schafer, his colleagues, and his students, such nonhuman sounds could and should play a crucial role within the new sonic landscape. Here, the overriding concern was not human expression but a sonic shielding from what were defined as oppressive sounds. These, as it turns out, were primarily the sounds of industry, construction, and transportation infrastructure. While it would be possible to argue that, to a large degree, these were *working-class sounds*, from which the middle-class sonic citizen (in effect created by texts like *The Soundscape*) now demanded insulation, whatever problems there were with the negative articulation of noise and sonic oppression in Schafer, his work did initiate new modes of site-specific, and not entirely anthropocentric, listening. Like a landscape, a soundscape too can be related to the subjective ears that bring it into being. But the soundscape is something other than a simple projection of that organizing subject out into sonic space. Rather, the subject of the Schaferian soundscape encounters—at least in his Canadian radio broadcasts—a heterogeneous collection of aural events that, though taken to signify "Canada," often do so without situating the human at the center of national space.

Even the most human aspect of the soundscape—speech—is cast as a set of irreconcilable differences. In program six, "Directions," Peter Huse for instance traces "a cross-Canada polyphonic composition of dialects and accents." As Schafer puts it, "What the listener heard were directions on how to get from one village or town to the next, clean across the country, given in all the dialects and languages and with all the idiosyncratic speaking styles of informants from every region between east and west."[7] As Canadian subjects tell listeners how to navigate the physical space of the nation, their telling becomes a linguistic map of the same nation. Schafer seems to include this vast branching sonic network in part because listeners tend to be more familiar differentiating minor variations in accent than they are in hearing the differences among nonhuman landscapes. Thus, surprise and fascination that so much linguistic variation obtains within Canadian space would seem to be only part of the project; the other is a kind of training, or ear cleaning, that helps one hear comparable differences in the world outside human speech.

Throughout, Schafer pays attention not merely to the character of sounds but also to their spatial implications. Suggesting that the population of Plato's ideal republic is generated by the size at which a community can be addressed by a single speaker, Schafer goes on to point out that the community-making functions historically effected by church bells and minarets were now, in most Canadian towns, taken over by air and train horns, whistles, cannons, fog horns, and a wide array of "noon signals," such as one in Vancouver that Schafer and his crew analyze from a variety of distances.[8] This one may be louder and more industrial than those in the rural enclaves in the middle of the country. But the Vancouver air horn, too, is treated as a community-forming audio event worthy of Schafer's sonic pedagogy. Throughout *Soundscapes of Canada* the underlying assumption is that to register the particular character of each of these horns, whistles, cannons, and so on is to hear the singularity of each community; so while we may be able to describe sonic networks via speech, any extensive sound, in Schafer, is also in some sense insular. Defining a "soundmark" as "a community signal that has been present in a community for some time" and is "usually regarded with special affection," Schafer then suggests that each soundmark "gives the community its unique acoustic character."[9] For Schafer, the singular sonic character of each community is to be preserved and, in a sense, amplified by the pedagogical exercises he develops: his brand of close listening was intended to produce subjects who, increasingly attached to the specific texture of their sonic environment and concerned to preserve it against generic noise, would engineer that soundscape—an act at once aesthetic and political. The nature of this sonic engineering was the final frame for Schafer's new Canadian sound subjects: listening to the threatened soundmarks allows for recognition of the loss of specific sounds, preservation, and, in a sense, insulation against unwanted, unintended sounds. At some level, then, Canadians would be those citizens whose hearing would bring them together, whose imagined community would be derived in large part from a sonic preservation campaign that would spur the largest sonic engineering program ever undertaken by humans. Yet, when those same Canadians heard an air siren in Vancouver, it was also quite possible that its origin was not local or even national but international and that it was part of a massive defense infrastructure whose operations undermine the claims about the *individual* character of community soundmarks fundamental to Schafer's fieldwork-based audio programs.

I

A key precedent for Schafer's research into Canadian sonic space is the experimental sound documentaries of Glenn Gould. Despite the undeniably generative status of these works (and of Gould's writing more broadly), a dominant note in their reception, especially among critics interested in the avant-garde, has been an invidious comparison with the works of John Cage. Gould's essay "The Prospects of Recording" (published in *High Fidelity* magazine in April 1966) has been taken as a negative landmark in sound studies. The Italian philosopher Paulo Virno, for instance, positions Gould's investment in multiple takes in an idealized space as the "reversed image" or symptomatic opposite of John Cage's investment in one take, or rather one unrecorded performance, in a literal space.[10] In his book *Records Ruin the Landscape*, which also celebrates Cage's pro-live-performance/anti-recording stance, David Grubbs argues further that despite Gould's avowed interest in counterpoint, his famous 1967 radio documentary *The Idea of North* "thematizes the solitude of the individual, mass-mediated listener—the radio listener, the record enthusiast—by finding a subject echo in the solitude of the five geographically remote individuals who make up the cast of this radio documentary."[11] But if Gould's celebration of the studio and his cultivation of the isolated listener would seem to turn him toward the nonsite of a postproduction utopia, his work from the 1960s was, nonetheless, integrally bound up with both the formation of sound studies and a site-specific story of struggles over airspace and military infrastructure that has not as yet been part of his reception history. This story, moreover, links the nationalist moment of the 1967 centennial of Canada's founding (whose echoes ripple through Schafer's *Soundscapes of Canada* project as well) with questions of the country's spatial and political autonomy amplified during the Cold War in relations with its southern neighbor.

The project of discovering and articulating Canadian space is already under way, for instance, in Gould's 1967 radio program (and later essay) "The Search for Petula Clark," which begins and ends in the Canadian landscape: "Across the province of Ontario, which I call home, Queen's Highway No. 17 plies for some 1,100 miles through the pre-Cambrian rock of the Canadian Shield."[12] Like Schafer's *Soundscapes of Canada* program, Gould's was broadcast in the CBC's *Ideas* series.[13] As is typical of Gould's baroque, almost Smithsonesque prose, discourses intertwine contrapuntally, and often ironically, in a single paragraph; here, the second sentence moves us from geology to Hollywood movies, space travel, and eventually bomber design:

> With its east-west course deflected, where it climbs the northeast shore of Lake Superior, it appears in cartographic profile like one of those prehistoric airborne monsters which Hollywood promoted to star status in such late-late-show spine tinglers of the 1950s as *Blood Beast from Outer Space* or *Beak from the Beyond*, and to which the fuselage design of the XB15 paid the tribute of science borrowing from art. (*GG*, 300)[14]

The highway, that is, seems to move in big spaceship- or bomber-fuselage-like curves as it skirts bays, coves, and rocky necks on its way through a desolate logging country whose towns at intervals of roughly fifty miles become the object of Gould's quasi-anthropological attention. Each of these displays "two indispensable features of any thriving timber town—its log-shoot breaking bush back through that trackless terrain and an antenna for the low-power relay system of the Canadian Broadcasting Corporation" (*GG*, 301). But since "these relay outlets, with their radius of three or four miles, serve only the immediate area of each community" (*GG*, 302), it is only for this very small fraction of the travel time that media from the outside enter his experience. Because the most popular music at the time, in this case pop singer Petula Clark's "Who Am I?," gets played on the radio at the top of the hour in each of these evenly spaced towns along Route 17, Gould can time his trip accordingly: "I contrived to match my driving speed to the distance between relay outlets, [and thus] came to hear [the song] most hours" (*GG*, 302). With this timing mechanism established, Gould's car radio becomes a tool for registering the odd discrepancy between the narrowcast of the individual radio stations (weak signal, not niche marketing) and the uniformity of their broadcast "content." His brilliant analysis of this latter, of Clark's "discrete gyrations," her fierce loyalty to the song's "one great octave" (*GG*, 303), as well as the song's more general "short-term need to rebel and long-range readiness to conform" (*GG*, 304), seems to parallel Gould's car trip's spatial structure of seeming difference, exploration, and release undergirded by rigorous, even mechanical, uniformity: the town planning is "1984 Prefab"; its social ambience, best characterized by the "fantasy prose of the late Karel Capek," inventor of the term robot (*GG*, 301). Just twenty-nine years earlier, Alan Lomax had combed the southern edges of this same lake searching out indigenous folk songs, stopping at towns including Baraga, Marenisco, Ontonagon, and Munising in Michigan's Upper Peninsula to record 249 discs' worth of music in his car-based recording studio.[15] Against this backdrop, Gould's trip would seem to document radical soundscape pollution and diminution, a tour of the sonic monuments of the blighted Great Lakes, a path through an audio terrain previously characterized by invention and variety that now, like the once species-rich lakes these towns abut, merely echoes an imposed language of commerce, be it floating barges or using pop songs to sell what these barges carry.

But the clarity of his project seems to dawn on Gould only once he has been subjected to the same Petula Clark song over the airways in each new logging town; the essay's suggestion, in other words, is that the accidental car radio background music on his trip across Queen's Highway 17, broadcast in each small-station radio bubble, eventually becomes his explicit object of inquiry: "After several hundred miles of this exposure, I checked into the hotel at Marathon and made plans to contemplate Petula" (*GG*, 302). At an immediate level, the result of this contemplation is of course the essay; at a larger, more abstract level, sound studies as articulated by Gould and Schafer also provides a narrowcasted answer to Petula Clark's question, "Who Am I?" While Gould's response is considerably less earnest than Schafer's, both agree in a sense that the widely various sounds latent in Canadian space provide one way to uncouple oneself from the mass-mediated, placeless subjectivity that Clark's song broadcasts over each subsequent radio station, as if keeping the slate blank to be filled again and again by ongoing programming.

As much as Gould was sidetracked by his encounter with Clark's song, we know from one of his biographies that, on the same trip, he also stopped in Wawa to work on his better-known and larger project, the sound documentary *The Idea of North*, which can be compared to "The Search for Petula Clark" both in its exploration of Canadian national space (the program was commissioned for the centennial) and in a basic geometric way. Rather than traverse

Canada east to west by car along Route 17, Gould now moves from the south, Winnipeg, a thousand miles north by rail to Churchill on the Muskeg Express. Contingent sound again organizes his trip through Canadian space. Here debate about the status and function of the north within Canada gets enacted formally by the comingling of five different speakers—Bob Phillips, a civil servant who had worked in the Department of Northern Affairs; Marianne Schroeder, a nurse; Frank Vallee, a professor of sociology in Ottawa; James Lotz, a British anthropologist; and W. V. (Wally) Maclean, an aged surveyor whom Gould met on the Muskeg.[16] These speakers, who do not ever meet each other, are conscripted to play the roles, respectively, of a government budget watcher, an enthusiast, a cynic, someone "who could represent that limitless expectation and limitless capacity for disillusionment which inevitably affects the questing spirit of those who go north seeking their future," and a figure that might synthesize all these positions (*GG*, 392–93). The piece begins with about three minutes of their overlapping voices after which Gould introduces the project briefly (the only time we hear his voice), explaining his distant fascination with "the north of our country" before passing on authority to his subjects, especially Maclean, who, after train sounds alert us to the beginning of our aural journey, becomes in effect the narrator. In general, the speakers focus, as Grubbs points out, on the granular scale of individual experience: the role of solitude, the clichés and realities associated with isolation, the forms of small-scale sociality, with occasional references to social difference and race—the status of the Inuit people in particular. All of this is framed by a set of questions about what drives Canadian citizens north. To this end Maclean, in his first monologue, positions a hypothetical stranger beginning the two-night and one-day trip to the north:

> Before long he's going to have to, perhaps, say hello, you know, pass the odd word with his fellow man. And, indeed, it isn't long before we've heard what he has to say: why, for the first time, he's going north. With what? Well, with the army, with the navy, with the air force? With these initials that he always throws at you: DPW? What's that? Oh Department of Public Works. With DRNL. What's that? Defense? Research? Northern Laboratories? Well, you're studying the Northern Lights then? Well, well. Now you can listen for a while, because what do any of us know about the Northern Lights?[17]

Work for the military is apparently the most common engine of travel to

Churchill. Nowhere else in the documentary, however, does the nature of this work within the overall social life of the north come up for discussion. In fact, when toward the end of the piece another of the speakers, seeking to dispel the myth of the untouched, innocent north, lists the technological feats that have already occurred there, his examples are limited to private construction and oil drilling. As Maclean puts it (apparently for Gould as well, since this is a key part of the piece's extended introduction), only once one has moved *beyond* discussion of the military can one begin to listen, which is, of course, the great opportunity offered by this experimental sound documentary: "Now you can listen for a while, because what do any of us know about the Northern Lights?" But what did any of these people, Gould included, know (or pretend to forget) about the military uses of the north? Why, indeed, were so many people associated with the military heading to Canada's arctic region at this time?

One reason this might have been hard to hear as part of a sound documentary on "the north of our country" is that these uses did not originate or end in Canada. About a decade earlier, the remote northern edges of the Canadian landmass had been, under agreement with the United States, claimed by a string of radar stations stretching from Alaska to Greenland. Once these Canada-traversing missile- and aircraft-monitoring sites became operational on April 1, 1957, they constituted the US Distant Early Warning Line (the DEW Line), beaming information to the same command control US Air Force station in Colorado Springs (NORAD) encountered in Chapter 2. In Colorado, this information was synthesized into a real-time map of North America's strategic boundaries that registered airlines (or missiles) as they entered this space. But it was the northern, Canadian arctic edge of these boundaries that was of particular interest to the United States, since it was most likely across this frontier that Soviet missiles would be launched in an attack on American cities, this being the shortest distance between the Soviet Union and the United States.

Recall Gould's references both to Hollywood and to the American X-15 bomber in his essay on Petula Clark. While these might first appear mere as campy scene setters, in fact Gould's trajectory through radio space in this essay, as in *The Idea of North*, also maps a strategic radar frontier constructed and monitored by Canada's southern neighbor. Searching for Petula Clark, Gould lingers on the town names along his path: "Names such as Michipicoten and Batchawana advertise the continuing segregation of the Canadian Indian;

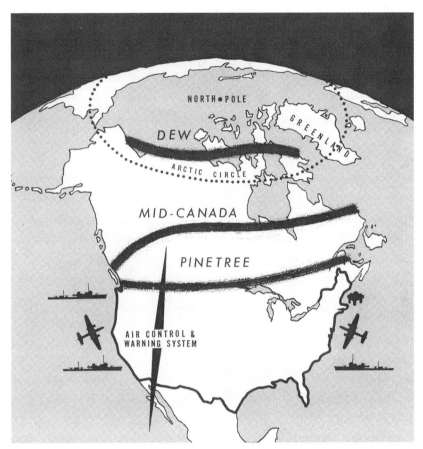

FIGURE 10. Diagram of the Pine Tree, Mid-Canada. and Dew Line Radar Defense
Systems. Wikipedia Images.

Rossport and Jackfish proclaim the no-nonsense mapmaking of the early
white settlers; and Marathon and Terrace Bay . . . betray the postwar flux of
American capital" (*GG*, 301). But it was not just American capital that was
infiltrating Canadian space; indeed, as Gould moved northwest along the
edges of Lakes Huron and Superior, he was already tracing a string of weak
radio transmitters as well as a parallel line, about a hundred miles north,
of much more powerful radar stations known collectively as the Pine Tree
Line, its sites including Pagwa, Lowther, Edgar, Falconbridge, Ramore, and
Foymount. This radar defense system, initiated in 1946, had become obsolete
by the late 1950s: the moment at which it could inform the US military about
a strike was now too late either to get planes off the ground or retaliate with

missiles. Even a second line of defense, the Mid-Canada Line, begun in 1956 at the 55th parallel north (about the position of Churchill, the northernmost point of Gould's journey), no longer provided enough advance warning. The DEW Line, with its string of American-built radar stations that runs from Alaska across the Canadian Arctic, thus came into being because of the inadequacy of two *previous* lines of Canada-spanning radar defense systems.

If Gould's two episodes of sonic fieldwork—his Clark exploration and his journey to Churchill—may have sounded at the time like pioneering attempts to explore a new Canadian soundscape, both were also tours, at a very basic and diagrammatic level, of the reticulated network of Cold War radar defense systems set up by the United States. We may now be in a better position to answer one of the central questions posed in *The Idea of North* about what one encounters at the very northern edge of Canada, at its most typically Canadian, wild, and uninhabitable spot: one meets there a permanent American radar defense system hard at work beaming a continuous string of real-time images of this exotic terrain to a belowground fortress command-control vault in Colorado Springs.

This strategic rush to the northernmost points of the Canadian Arctic, twice as far as Gould ventured, was caused in part by the development of intercontinental ballistic missiles (ICBMs). Early Soviet rocket development had focused on Western European targets. But in 1953 Sergei Korolyoy was bankrolled to develop ICBMs. After initial failures, on August 21, 1957, a Soviet R-7 ICBM was successfully flown more than thirty-seven hundred miles— within range of American cities, that is, if directed over the top of the globe and across Canada. Two years later, on February 9, 1959, the Cosmodrome at Plesetsk in the northwest of Russia (in a position, that is, to make use of the proximity to Canada) became operational. The West knew about the larger, earlier Baikonur Cosmodrome in what is now Kazakhstan because it was the launch site of the first artificial earth satellite, *Sputnik* (October 4, 1957); the first manned spacecraft in human history, *Vostok* 1 (April 12, 1961); as well as the first extravehicular activity (March 18, 1965), in which Alexey Leonov exited *Voskhod* 2 for a twelve-minute spacewalk. That *Sputnik* had an effect not merely on Americans more generally but specifically on the counterculture is borne out by Amiri Baraka's first wife, Hettie Jones, who remarks that, during the fall of 1957, "after the Russian sent up *Sputnik*, the world's first spacecraft, the suffix 'nik' was added to beat, putting us square in the enemy

FIGURE 11. White Alice Communications System, Boswell Bay, Alaska. Wikipedia Images.

camp."[18] As technology averse as the Beats might have been, their resistance to American Cold War politics seems to have linked them, in someone's mind, to new senses both of "far out" and of subversion linked to the emergence of Soviet satellite technology. But if the Baikonur Cosmodrome's launches were helping give new names to a burgeoning group of disaffected youths associated with Kerouac, Ginsberg, Corso, Burroughs, and Baraka, the launch site's secret partner, the Plesetsk Cosmodrome (though located by the West in 1969 and suspected earlier) remained off all official records until as late as 1983. Still, it was because of the inevitability of the Soviets developing a northern site like it from which to launch ICBMs that the northern tip of Canada was converted into a string of functional radar stations.

While Gould was, as late as 1967, subject to the three- to four-mile radius of Canadian radio broadcasting, sites at the DEW Line were, already a decade earlier via the eerily named White Alice Communications System, in regular communication with the rest of the world—or at least Colorado Springs. When Gould was crossing Canada by car and listening for the range of various radio stations, he was not only using the media's projection of the Petula Clark song to time his movements; he was also tracing the first, and now obsolete, line of radar defense against Soviet air strikes, the Pine Tree Line on its path from the St. Lawrence Seaway to Vancouver Island, from Quebec through Ontario, Manitoba, Saskatchewan, and Alberta to British Columbia. Similarly, when Gould went north to Churchill, he was not only marking the edge of train accessibility but the second line of air defense, the Mid-Canada Line. It was from here that, a decade before he began his project, thousands of American-paid Canadians had made their way another one thousand miles to the Arctic Circle to install the DEW Line. Operational from 1957, the DEW Line put a highly detailed real-time image of the extreme north of Canada constantly in front of American military personal. With its eighty radio stations using tropospheric scatter to beam information from huge parabolic antennas to secure technicians buried, after 1966, in the underground Cheyenne Mountain Complex in Colorado, White Alice gave American intelligence a continuous picture of Canada more reliable than the short bursts of Petula Clark Gould was offered in the immediate vicinities of logging towns on his quaint trip along the eastern edges of the Great Lakes.[19]

Cheyenne Mountain is a five-acre site excavated a mile horizontally into a mountain, with another two thousand feet of solid granite above it. Separated from the surface by these two masses of granite (spanned by a tunnel) and by two twenty-three-ton doors, the center of the complex consists of fifteen buildings that sit, far under the mountain, on independent spring systems allowing them, in the event of a nuclear explosion, to bounce independently without touching their protective shell of granite eighteen inches away. This means that operations at the site can continue, uninterrupted, even after a direct hit by the largest Soviet nuclear bomb. What happens within these buildings is that the streaming pictures of Canadian airspace, and its possible penetration by Soviet jets or missiles, is beamed down by White Alice and converted into a unified, real-time picture of the entirety of North America. The extreme architecture and engineering of this Cold War–moderne silo for martial screen monitoring seems just as implausible as connecting and unifying Canada's remote surveillance sites into a single, reliable picture.

This is the space of *Doctor Strangelove* and of the crisis scenes of innumerable later Hollywood movies; it is the kind of setting in which the cruelest of William S. Burroughs's characters would seem to be at home. Is it more implausible, then, to note that it was in fact William's family's business, the Burroughs Corporation, that managed the feat of connecting and uni-

FIGURE 12. Film still of the War Room, *Dr. Strangelove or: How I Learned to Stop Worrying and Love the Bomb* (1964). Directed by Stanley Kubrick. Courtesy Sony Pictures.

fying these data streams within this heavily guarded pit in the mountains of Colorado? Indeed, the Burroughs Corporation was solely responsible for the design of what was known, fittingly, as the command and control system, which both centralized and automated data from the far-flung surveillance sites at the extreme points in Canada's landmass. All of this should also give us something of a new vantage on Gould's sound documentary. During the Cold War, the Canadian "Idea of North" was also an international, strategic idea.[20]

II

By May 1960, when Larry Eigner from his Swampscott home wrote a poem beginning with the line "The plane sounds protective," he was in correspondence with former air force sergeant LeRoi Jones, who solicited work for issues 5, 6, and 7 of Jones's magazine *Yugen*. In addition to poems, Jones wanted a letter of Eigner's, which he hoped would help articulate "a first change": the move from the typical collections of a magazine, which, "after a bit, become odious ... into a stance or something."[21] The changes and stances we're acquainted with in Jones's career are those that, beginning after his July and August 1960 trip to Cuba, push him first farther to the left and then (at least spatially) away from his poet friends downtown.[22] It is fascinatingly contrary to received literary history to pause on the image of Baraka-to-be, just a few months before his transformative journey to Cuba, soliciting Swampscott's Larry Eigner for help articulating a first change and a stance.[23]

Even after the most important site visit of Jones's career, it took some time for him to work out how this would affect his sense of literary and political territory.[24] He would write to Olson, a couple of days after returning, that Cuba was "marvelous . . . everything there. What those people do . . . are doing. Despite all bullshit of rotting colossus del norte," noting also the fact that the United States "bugged all the Cuban planes."[25] Then two months later, after his famous "Cuba Libre" essay was published, Jones would suggest that the political transformation he experienced *should* produce new distance and disaffiliation—both from friends like Olson and from his old self: "Also glad you 'liked' the libre piece. (Tho I spose there's *got* to be some 'objections.' Some objectivity, &c. for anybody I bring all that back to. Nobody can throw over their lives, &c. Me neither, finally." This letter is worth quoting, however, not only because it initiates the terms of this disaffiliation to come but also because it explicitly stops short of severing ties from the concept of the nation. After bemoaning feeling "brutalized" in the United States, Jones writes: "But the thing is, I guess, I don't know now if I cd be 'alone.' I mean, without a country! It is a frightening proposition. And maybe I won't just now be up to it."[26] For the time being, the social/aesthetic formations emerging out of poetry would provide that space. It was in this larger context, then, that Jones wrote to Eigner of a need to "get into thicker material," to "focus" and establish "EDITORIAL delineations" so as to make Eigner "& those people generally aligned w/myself (from whatever useful angle) CLEAR, finally. To make a clearing & stand in that boy all day & all night."[27]

Just what did this clearing look like for Jones in 1960? As poetry, perhaps, it looked quite a bit like the countercultural poetic territory claimed and focused by *The New American Poetry*, edited by Donald M. Allen, in which later that year Jones, Eigner, and Olson would appear. Close-up, in empirical not literary space, it might have taken on some of the rocky features of Eigner's Massachusetts Bay region, from Swampscott to Gloucester.[28] Jones, in other words, was part not just of the social/literary formation that Olson called "Gloucester"; in taking field trips to visit Eigner as part of a literary-space-articulating campaign, Roi was also a participant in the durational, fragmentary temporality of Swampscott. Perhaps counterintuitively stressing Eigner's role in the athletic act of around-the-clock endurance ("To make a clearing & stand in that boy all day & all night"), Jones's phrase takes us back both generally to an armed avant-garde of territorial conflict and specifically to the former sergeant's earlier trip to the Caribbean: his guard duty at the Strategic Air Command Air Force Base in Puerto Rico. Jones had joined the air force in 1954, and after basic training in South Carolina and weather school in the winter and spring of 1955 in Rantoul, Illinois (learning to operate a rawinsonde, a weather balloon that transmits atmospheric information by radio), he had selected to go to Ramey Air Force Base in Puerto Rico.[29] Jones, in other words, was part of the defense infrastructure that awaited that fateful message from White Alice about Soviet planes or missiles crossing one of the Canadian radar lines. As we saw, this message would have been generated at the Dew Line, where the breach would have occurred, and then sent by White Alice to the Cheyenne Mountain Complex, where a SAC general would have confirmed the intrusion and sent a new message to one of several SAC bases, including Jones's in Puerto Rico, where bombers would have been scrambled and a counterattack begun.[30]

In preparation for this scenario, one of Jones's main jobs—in the B-36 bomber, the Peacemaker—was to practice how all this would work, going on "mock bombing raids that SAC stages pretending to bomb large cities in the U.S. and other places" (AB, 152). Baraka describes this period of his life (the chapter of his autobiography is titled "Error Farce") as a mistake that allowed him, however, to deepen his education primarily because, through a librarian near the base, he was able to form a group that allowed for a kind of "collective resistance" through its "salon elitism" (AB, 167). His emphasis falls on the uninformed view of American literature and culture that operated as an "alternative" to the terrifying reality of "day-to-day air force life." Annoyed by his "daily grind of guard duty," Baraka is less enamored by military "sound marks" than his Canadian colleagues. His "fortnight 'alerts,'" he complains,

> announced by the screaming of hellish sirens which sent us scrambling down to the flight line and up into the very wild black yonder, were driving me up the wall, or at least to drink. Yet the reality from which I wanted to escape was replaced by my reading, which often was the most backward forces in American literature, teaching me the world upside down and backwards. (AB, 167)

As in many accounts of military service by postwar writers, here it operates

FIGURE 13. B-36 Peacemaker. Wikipedia Images.

as an irrelevant preliminary to writing: a real terror that gives rise at first to a fake alternative, which it will be the burden of the rest of the career, with its bildungsroman-like structure, to render authentic. But in just what sense was Baraka's experience in the air force the negative datum against which he would gauge his alternatives? Did, perhaps, the dreaded message from White Alice echo beyond these mock bombing raids?

> At least once a month we'd have an "alert." The sirens would rage and we'd all have to get up in the middle of the night and dress and fly off to "bomb" some city, usually American, and then return. It was a recurring nightmare to me. The siren, after midnight, was like hell's actual voice. You'd throw on your flight suit, the grey slick coveralls, check out a parachute, get your weapon, load your cannon, wait for orders, and take off. (*AB*, 171)[31]

Awakened by the system of Uncle Sam's hell, Baraka, in other words, would routinely fly from the Caribbean across the Gulf of Mexico or the Atlantic to practice leveling various American cities: San Francisco could play the role of Leningrad; New York might star temporarily as Moscow; and Philadelphia could make a cameo as Vladivostok.[32] The agents of these imaginary firestorms were not merely conventional bombs (the B-36 could carry ten times the payload of World War II bombers) but thermonuclear weapons that were about 450 times as powerful as those dropped on Nagasaki. What made the plane particularly effective in delivering such apocalypses, fictive or real, was not just that it could stay aloft for forty hours without refueling but also that it could fly at the unheard-of altitude of almost fifty thousand feet, making it nearly impossible to intercept. Despite this, the most powerful hydrogen bombs used during the time Baraka was in the air force (Mark 17s) were deployed without parachutes to ensure explosion. This meant that even at fifty thousand feet, the B-36 that dropped them would be incinerated as well. While there was considerable period debate about the extent to which a nuclear war with the Soviet Union might be limited and/or survivable, Baraka's structural position within the US war machine thus assured his death in any strike scenario.[33] So what was hellish about the air-raid siren was not merely that it interrupted Baraka's sleep or sent him on long, cold errands of imaginary destruction in the sky but that this practice incineration might at any point during the mid-1950s Cold War have become real; and if it had, it would have signaled his own (and many others') inevitable destruction.

"The plane sounds protective." As the crow or the B-36 flies, Boston (or Swampscott) is about eighteen hundred miles from Puerto Rico, making it within a similar striking distance as New York, Philadelphia, Washington, and New Orleans. But with a range of ten thousand miles, the Peacemaker didn't have to look for conveniently located cities. It could select any it wanted, orbiting them at inaccessible heights before delivering its payload. Thus, while the EC-121 Warning Star was circling around Eigner's neighborhood and region looking for signs of Soviet submarines off the Atlantic coast, the Peacemakers in which a frozen huddled Baraka was practicing this odd atomic target study were swooping up from Puerto Rico, pretending that cities like Boston *were* Soviet and simulating the flattening of them with Mark 17 thermonuclear bombs.

In a 1959 poem, Eigner paused to relate his own act of hearing in his neighborhood—his hearing of planes overhead in fact—to the kind of mechanical listening apparatus that was in operation in the EC-121 and the larger warning system of which it was a part.

> everything that happens

> by mechanical means, actually
> (but not mechanical)
> we can now hear
> out there, the speed
> of 2 syllables

the second, so
bound up   it is spinning
the heavy globe

       this

our ears,   energy
of paint

            a plane interferes
from overhead

what was there to learn
but to die
however we come to it

    the big plane
    or is it the common weather
    lumbering over
    no longer the cut ceiling

              the out of range (*EP*, 297)

One among many poems during this period that situated the scale of Eigner's perception in relation to a larger Cold War context, this one blurs the distinction between event and context by posing the plane both as an interference (a disruption of listening) and as the kind of event for which mechanical listening would be established—because its range would determine whether the plane, as it lumbers over, could teach those on the ground to die by cutting the ceiling with its bombs. But what is of interest in this poem is not just a familiar Cold War concern with the possibility of nuclear destruction or even conventional warfare. It is, instead, the relation between these two forms of listening: Eigner's and the larger mechanical listening he identifies. If it is true, as the poet somewhat optimistically proposes, that "everything that happens / by mechanical means, actually . . . we can now hear," then we might wonder just what might recommend an individual scale and style of hearing in a mechanized, precise, far more extensive context of sound registration.[34] In the immediate context of the poem, the experience of music seems to play this role: Handel, Mozart, and Rameau are all mentioned and all at the opposite end of the spectrum of the mechanical listening of radar. But even in the articulation of this easy answer, Eigner points to the more compelling one that his large project floats: "a falling off // or Handel, some mistake /

for the years // until the water / music // the years are lost, you may come / sufficiently / back on that sound." The replaying of music seems to allow a specific form of looping back on previous times; thus, a poetry of duration like Eigner's, attuned as it is to ambient neighborhood sound, might usefully stage, and even in a sense compensate for, the larger experience of temporal succession, of years lost. Poems like this allow one to "come / sufficiently / back on that sound," perhaps to reestablish a "Handel" on sounds as they emerge and disperse, on the water music he hears on Bates Road from the nearby surf. Still, the context in which this occurs is not just a general existential or temporal consciousness: it is, rather, an instrumentalized world in which one is forced to listen for planes and in which, the same year, Eigner writes, "We let you know / in case of attack, so / keep tuned in / every day (all day" (*EP*, 292).

For Eigner, being tuned in all day, remaining attentive to sound, resulted in the opposite kind of sonic ambience: a dedramatized landscape that contested radio's eventful urgency. This might seem neatly opposed to Jones/Baraka's later action- and event-oriented writing. But in fact Eigner's deprogramming of radio was a stance that resonated clearly with Baraka's later engagement with sound.

III

On March 4, 1965, Baraka gave a reading at the San Francisco State University poetry center.[35] His last poem that day was "The People Burning," which would appear in his 1969 book *Black Magic: Sabotage, Target Study, Black Art.* As was done for most readings in the series, a magnetic reel-to-reel was used to record it. On the recording, Baraka offers a brief contextualization: "This was, ah, written around the time, ah, Kennedy got killed. It's called 'The People Burning' and there's a little epigram [*sic*] 'May-Day! May-Day,' which is pilot talk."[36] The poem as a whole can be read as a lament about an imagined return to conservative order that would drive former radicals out to the suburbs under "some thin veneer of reasonable / gain."[37] But while these last are familiar concerns in Baraka, the title, the crashing plane, and pilot talk are, I want to propose, not merely general references to violence. Rather, they help us reframe Baraka's description of the sonic dimension of his nightmarish, midnight bombing runs.

Baraka was, throughout his career, drawn to thinking of sound not merely as symbolism or reference but as actual territory. In "Black Art" he writes of "Airplane poems, rrrrrrrrrrrrr / rrrrrrrrrrrrrrr . . . tuhtuhtuhtuhtuhtuh / rrrrrrrr . . . Setting fires and death to / whities ass."[38] Also published in the same collection, "Black Art" was recorded in 1965 and released in 1967 as part of Sonny Murray's *Sonny's Time Now*, which was brought out by Baraka's Jihad Records.[39] This was the first in a series of records that would include *A Black Mass* (1968) with Sun Ra and *It's Nation Time* (1972).[40] On the 1967 LP the "rrrr" is read like a siren; it is not, that is, the sound of the airplane slicing through space, beginning to fire, but the warning sound, the siren, heard by those on the ground while the planes are still at a distance, or heard by those waking up at 2:00 a.m. to begin (mock?) bombing raids. When Baraka writes of a SAC siren as "hell's actual voice" and then features a siren as the positive culmination of one of his most famous poems, perhaps we can think of this transformation of a toxic sound as structurally related to his recoding of hate speech and symptomatic language more broadly. However we think of it, the literal soundscape and larger destructive imagination to which he was subjected by the American state in the air force hardly disappear from Baraka's mature work.

Consider Baraka's 1972 LP *It's Nation Time*.[41] Setting itself against intensely symptomatic sound like the air-raid siren in its manifestation as oppressor, "hell's actual voice," this record proposes itself, in contrast, as the *actual sound* of a black nation—a twelve-inch vinyl insta-country that could fill various-sized spaces with its nation effects, depending on amplification possibilities—a bit like the clearing he had proposed establishing with Eigner, only concretized in literal space and organized along racial lines. If radio listeners in the 1930s were brought into the fold of the nation sonically by FDR's fireside chats, during which he explained the New Deal, by the late 1960s and early1970s African American listeners could be welcomed into a counternation while listening to an LP like this, where Baraka's lyrics would intermingle with chants, emerging from or dissolving back into free jazz and funk environments. "The direct expression of a place . . . jazz," Baraka proposes elsewhere, "seeks another place"; however, "as it weakens," this other desired location becomes "a middle-class place" (*BM*, 180). Powerful jazz for Baraka, that is, pulls apart normative middle-class space. Yet this does not occur simply (as we might expect) because it never overlaps with or temporarily shares its terms.

Baraka is careful to construct this counternational sonic space not simply as a refuge or solace but instead as a prompt, an enticement, a tenuous possibility that might vanish. Sonically, for instance, the other place that the opening track "It's Nation Time" (4:13) expresses is a transitional one in which African Americans are emerging from disparate locations and merging into the black nation: "come out niggers come out / come out niggers come out." While this may not be the SAC siren, it comes off on the record as the kind of imperative public announcement that would be broadcast over a loudspeaker. Apparently it came off powerfully live as well, at least according to the FBI agent who smuggled a recording device into the Shrine of the Black Madonna on May 18, 1969, in Detroit, where Baraka was performing. Responding to the same lines—"Come out Niggers, Boom Boom Boom"—the audio surveillance fieldworker comments for Baraka's FBI file: "In interpreting the poem the 'Nigger' is one who refuses to work in behalf of the revolution, an 'Uncle Tom' is one who does business with the establishment, and the 'Boom, Boom, Boom' represents the guns firing during revolution in the United States cities as riots or revolution occurs."[42] While debate might remain about whether the term "Nigger" here is meant solely as an insult and not also as an instance of former hate speech recuperated to mark African Americans' actual marginality, most subsequent interpreters have agreed with the anonymous FBI scholar, who understands the "boom, boom, boom" of the live performance as part of, rather than a preliminary to, the revolution. However, on the record this is, in fact, ambiguous.

After an initial drum roll, a bass riff underlines and organizes this activity, as Baraka plays with the sped-up voice of a radio announcer fitting more product information into a tight temporal slot than it seems to want to hold.[43] As in "Black Art," in the "realization" of this poem's promise—after "niggers come out," "brothers take over the school," "change up," and "come together"—the song breaks down into an onomatopoetic evocation of revolution as explosion:

Boom
Booom
BOOOM
Boom

Dadadadadadadadadadadadada

Boom

Boom

Boom

Boom

Dadadadadad adadadadad

Again we are situated sonically in a world in which something like the hell-embodying air-raid siren that had conscripted Sergeant Jones for SAC's Strangeloveian "target practice" has been converted into the liberatory detonations of a Black Nationalist coup. My point is not that the two are interchangeable or that the former is the simple and singular condition of possibility for the latter; it's that Baraka's later work suggests a doubling back not merely on the military force of the state but also on its *sonic regime* so that a record like *It's Nation Time* might be understood as a sonic alternative to both SAC sirens and fireside chats.

Nation time, however, is not entirely a rich, accessible duration that coincides with that of the LP. Even in the immersive midst of the record, one is projected temporally into a range of pasts and especially futures—both to the moment of impending nation formation and to a halcyon future from which Black National subjects look back and encourage those in the present. The track "Answers," for instance, which includes text printed in *In Our Terribleness* (1970), proposes that Black National subjects from the future "would appear right here to /say these things but do not want to / frighten you / instead they speak thru / me."[44] What's of interest here is not merely the mediation proposed by Baraka, his claim to channel (or at times prophesize) a future to which others do not have access; it is that this access is also a *displacement* from the rich duration of the Black Nationalist present. In projecting an Afrocentric future, Baraka at once leaves the LP's now and, in doing so, claims to establish a mode of contact with futurity that might, at any moment, break off, as in this passage when this nation of the future speaks, briefly, to the prenational present:

Do not despair gentle ancient

Groovy ancestors.

We have conquered

and we await the rich legacy

of hard won blackness

which you create to leave

us

here in the black fast future

here among the spiritual creations

of natural man

Do not despair ancient fathers and

Mothers there in old America

We are here

awaiting your gorgeous

Legacy . . .

//

Here the contact is broken. . . .

Since this is the end of the song, this break in contact might first appear as the edge to the record's project of bodying forth a sonic nation: we hear the contact with nation as occurring *inside* the LP itself, not as the entirety of its sonic terrain. And since "Answers" is the second of seven songs on side one, the end of transhistorical contact with nation is not the end of the LP, or even of side one. Instead, coming into and falling out of contact with various pasts and futures constructs "nation time" less as an affirmative present that greets African American listeners who slip into it merely by sliding a needle into the vinyl grooves than as an elusive temporality that, evoked by the LP's suggestive fragments, nonetheless remains to be built.[45] So Baraka in 1972 is not at all done with making "a clearing & stand[ing] in that boy all day & all night." What he appears to be done with, instead, is a political and sonic regime that would have him waiting all night for a call from White Alice who, using parabolic antennas to beam news of Soviet penetration of the Canadian DEW Line from there to Colorado to Puerto Rico, would use "hell's actual voice" to wake the sergeant for a world- and self-incinerating errand in the air.[46]

IV

In *In Our Terribleness* Baraka writes: "John Coltrane must rule us. That sensibility." This line appears both in the text of the book and in the *It's Nation Time* recording. "The energy," Baraka continues, "must be harnessed, so that *our forms* will be given power." What and where are these "forms"? "The spirit of the stiff leg or the screaming horn will be in the institutions we build." In *Fieldworks* I've provided an account of the logic of institution building in Baraka's work, especially in Newark, which takes as its object of inquiry first revolutionary speech acts; then urban bodily bearings among economically and socially marginalized African Americans; then the architecture that would enclose those bodies; before turning (as Baraka leaves Black Nationalism and associates his work with third world Marxism) finally to the economy that enclosed architecture. At each phase in his practice Baraka recoded hate speech, turning to it as a tool for focalizing—and thus rendering vivid and palpable—the actual marginality experienced by African Americans, before at least partially detoxifying it in an act of appropriation. The account of Baraka's involvement with recording offered in *Narrowcast* builds on this argument; I hope to situate Baraka's sonic nationalism as a parallel enterprise to his inquiry into how one might institutionalize change at the scale of the speech act, the body, the building, or the economy. While the (from one angle) immaterial nature of sound suggests that it cannot quite be situated among the upper levels of this ascending order of concretization and enclosure, and thus that it would share territory exclusively with the first phase of Baraka's nationalist practice, his work with the speech act, Baraka's audio recordings, are in fact intimately involved both with modes of bodily bearing and with propositions about the ways that sound might recode physical territory. The last part of this chapter characterizes the particular kind of recoding Baraka seems to have undertaken both in his frequent returns to the sound of SAC sirens and in his enlistment of John Coltrane as the sonic core of Black Nationalism to suggest a series of counterintuitive links between Baraka's sonic nationalism and the national dimensions of sound studies as the discipline emerges in Canada.

Like many later critics, the LP Baraka sees as announcing Coltrane's full arrival is *My Favorite Things* (1961).[47] This view gets articulated in Baraka's 1963 article "A Jazz Great: John Coltrane." Here Coltrane's transformation "from being just another 'hip' tenor saxophonist to the position of chief innovator on that instrument" could usefully be charted "from the beginning of his recorded efforts." Still, the trilogy, "starting with the first Atlantic album, *Giant Steps* and proceeding through the next one, *Coltrane Jazz*, and coming finally to the last one, *My Favorite Things* shows Trane's entire development, from sideman to innovator, in microcosm" (*BM*, 58). After a quite technical description of this emergence—seemingly designed to rebuff know-nothing dismissals of Coltrane as "non-musical"—Baraka begins to account for Coltrane's more recent movement into "fresher areas of expression on his instrument" (ibid.), citing Ira Gitler's description of the saxophonist's "sheets of sound" (*BM*, 59). Here, to emphasize the analytical and experimental nature of Coltrane's project, Baraka describes one concert he saw live, just after Coltrane had left Monk, in which the former approached the song "Confirmation" from every conceivable angle: "It was as if he wanted to take that melody apart and play out each of its chords as a separate improvisational challenge. And while it was a marvelous thing to hear and see, it was also more than a little frightening; like watching a grown man learning to speak . . . and I think that's just what was happening" (ibid.). This logic of pulling out each element of a pregiven song as an occasion for improvisation, and conceptualizing this as a matter of relearning speech, seems central to the title track on *My Favorite Things*.

That same year Baraka had talked to a Howard University philosophy professor who, apparently, had told him: "It's fantastic how much bad taste the blues contain!" Baraka then uses this as a prompt to sort bad taste into several varieties, some of them useful: "To a great extent such 'bad taste' was kept extant in the music, blues or jazz because the Negroes who were responsible for the best of the music, were always aware of their identities as black Americans and really did not, themselves, desire to become vague, featureless, Americans as is usually the case with the Negro middle class" (*BM*, 11–12). Useful or productive "bad taste" in Baraka's reformulation would seem to involve not an aesthetic failure but a resistance to assimilation. In this instance bad taste appears as a buffer against received bourgeois values; yet these values seem to percolate through the song Coltrane chooses to recode. That is, contrary to the anti-assimilation model just sketched, bad taste in Coltrane does not involve a domain of culture deemed low or bad because it is not recognized by official white culture. Instead, in selecting a Broadway jingle, Coltrane plunges right into the heart of mainstream white culture, what we might call broadcast culture. Baraka points to this complication gradually in his reading, first designating the song a "*tour de force*" and "a beginning," both in Coltrane's use of the soprano saxophone and in his turn to melody, wherein "the repeated scale of 'My Favorite Things' is so simple and final that the only means of getting out of it is to elaborate on that tender little melody" (*BM*, 61).

Turning then to the piano in the song, Baraka begins to draw out the sense in which this "tender little melody" might constitute a "beginning": "Listen to McCoy Tyner's fantastically beautiful embroideries on that scale and melody, sometimes breaking down into almost maudlin piano exercises, sometimes hurdling two centuries to sound like rococo cocktail music, but containing as much invention and subtlety as any piano solo I've heard in the last few years" (*BM*, 61–62). Understood as an anachronic emergence of "rococo cocktail music" hurdling from the eighteenth century into the lounges of early 1960s New York, Tyner's solo perhaps surprisingly falls into the category I have been calling genre, rather than history; it evokes ongoingness rather than a discrete cut in time—a distinction also borne out by Baraka's suggestion that Coltrane's work can go on indefinitely and need not stop.

But before pursuing this problem of genre and its relation to duration, let us directly note the source of Coltrane's "tender little melody" and Tyner's "almost maudlin piano exercises." "My Favorite Things" was perhaps the most famous song in the 1959 Rodgers and Hammerstein musical *The Sound of Music*. For those in my generation the timing may be somewhat confusing, since we knew this almost entirely through the 1965 movie starring Julie Andrews and Christopher Plummer. But the 1959 musical, which starred Mary Martin, was also released as an album. At one level, it's arguable that Coltrane was simply using the popularity of this tender little melody as a scaffolding for his own improvisation; he was ensuring a degree of familiarity, even security, that might ease listeners at first, making it more likely that they would then remain focused during his innovative deformation of the melody.

Yet "My Favorite Things" was also an instance of a less combative bad taste—a mode that had *already* been assimilated by the middle class. To make this claim, however, is to move metonymically from the tender little melody to the lyrics it frames. This is not much of a jump; indeed, it is almost impossible to hear this song merely as a melody and not also as lyrics. And these lyrics are, in fact, rather remarkable—for their banality: "Raindrops on roses / And whiskers on kittens / Bright copper kettles / And warm woolen mittens / Brown paper packages tied up with strings / These are a few of my favorite things." With the possible exception of the brown paper packages (which might, of course, contain cool books), the first verse seems to offer an inventory of poetic clichés: precisely the kind of middle-class taste against which Baraka will align his writing. This is a world of comfort, leisure, material ease, and homogeneity. It is also a world answering to the most received ideas of beauty, most administered notions of value, of the "poetic" image: the precious, greeting-card-ready snapshot of cuteness, comfort, or reassuring homey familiarity. In the second verse, these clichés coalesce increasingly into a European setting, perhaps the winter Austrian world of the von Trapp family: "Cream colored ponies / And crisp apple strudels / Door bells and sleigh bells / And schnitzel with noodles / Wild geese that fly with the moon on their wings / These are a few of my favorite things."

One way to gauge these as objects of desire—as an inventory of "favorite things"—is to consider what it is they work to counteract, which is outlined eventually in the chorus: "When the dog bites / When the bee stings / When I'm feeling sad / I simply remember my favorite things / And then I don't feel so bad." Dog bites, bee stings, pouts, or fights that produce sadness. This does, for instance, seem a bit different from what might cause John Coltrane or many of his African American listeners to feel sad in the early 1960s. For them, when the anti–civil rights dog bites, when the redneck police baton stings, sleigh bells and apple strudels were not always at hand to ease the pain. Woolen mittens and cat whiskers were of limited effectiveness in bringing down the Jim Crow regime.

Despite the fact that the Rodgers and Hammerstein lyrics are evacuated from the Coltrane version of the song, the listener must, I think, retain some rough memory of the world they evoke in order to get the thrust of the new version—to grasp just how different John Coltrane's favorite things are. One hears the title track, in Coltrane's hands, inflected with contestation, difference, and recoding, saying in effect, No, *my* favorite things, and moving, as Baraka seems to hear it, from the broadcast sensibility of the Broadway song to the narrowcast framing of a sonic Black Nationalism. "The direct expression of a place," Baraka wrote, to repeat, "jazz . . . seeks another place . . . as it weakens." A Black Nationalist sonic space is, in this sense, not a discrete, removed domain but the space right in front of one, recoded. It is as if Coltrane has sought out this image reservoir of banal though manicured material comfort and leisure specifically for the challenge it poses in recoding it, in turning *even something this trite* into a new musical landscape of actually viable favorite things. So if Coltrane can make even *this* song harbor and extend his values, we will perhaps understand the disruptive power of his musical project in a new way—just in what sense it is a beginning, to take us back to Baraka's read-

ing. What's fascinating about setting up *My Favorite Things* as the announcement not merely of Coltrane's arrival but of a new audio Black Nationalism
is that Baraka does not claim, as his sonic exemplar, a piece of music that
begins by announcing its marginality, a piece that seems pure, untainted,
utterly unrelated to white middle-class culture. Rather, he selects an example
that actively implodes received white musical taste from within, a musical
example that reoccupies a hostile, alien host in order to reveal, latent within
it, an entirely different landscape of values or favorite things.

> Girls in white dresses with blue satin sashes
> Snowflakes that stay on my nose and eyelashes
> Silver white winters that melt into springs
> These are a few of my favorite things

We hear the distant echo of this insipid poetry in Coltrane's deformation, made
now to march, or rather dance, against its original kitsch orientation. Like the
return to the air force siren, this appeal to Coltrane's *My Favorite Things* is
structurally in line with Baraka's larger project of recoding hate speech and its
subject positions. We might say that Baraka was drawn to *diagnostic* cultural
forms, ones in which troubling power relations percolate up to the surface,
where Baraka seeks to foreground them and, at least in his own writing, re-
motivate their implications. Thus, the echo of Rodgers and Hammerstein lyrics in Coltrane situates the musician's intervention in a way that the residue
of hate speech does, obviously more confrontationally and violently, within
Baraka's writing of the 1960s and early 1970s. This points to a perhaps surprising conclusion: at key moments in Baraka's thinking a truly marginal position
tends to emerge not from engineering it at a distance but from reoccupying
and then deforming a hegemonic one.[48] This is not simply a matter of inversion but of establishing a recognizable frame of reference—here we can use the
term "broadcast" to indicate its wide exportability—to reassemble the cultural
object or practice with key differences: negations, complications, extensions
that constitute the new sonic work, in Baraka's estimation, as the model of a
narrowcast social formation.[49]

But while Baraka's writing on Coltrane in 1963 is still within the genre
of criticism, by the late 1960s his understanding of the musician has shifted
fundamentally to a matter of institution building within Black Nationalism.
"John Coltrane must rule us. That sensibility . . . the spirit of the stiff leg or

the screaming horn will be in the institutions we build." Yet there are indi-
cations even within Baraka's writing from the early 1960s that he is drawn
to Coltrane not merely as a singular occurrence but as a life condition—not
merely, that is, as an individual, revolutionary event but as an ongoing, underlying condition that, in the matrix I've sketched so far, would be aligned with
genre, not with history: "You feel when this is finished, amidst the crashing
cymbals, bombarded tom-toms, and above it all Coltrane's soprano singing
like any song you can remember, that it really did not have to end at all, that
this music could have gone on and on like the wild pulse of all living" (*BM*,
66). The challenge, then, on *It's Nation Time*—an album released five years
after Coltrane's death—is at once suggesting this new, rich, and, as Baraka
sees it, Afrocentric duration as a palpable potentiality while at the same time
motivating listeners not merely to passively appreciate it on a recording but to
build it actively—which means inventing and securing institutional change.
As much as we associate Baraka with individual, power-relation-changing
revolutionary acts—"Up against the wall motherfucker, this is a stick up"—
the change underlying his central example of sonic Black Nationalism is an
immanent recoding of a Broadway musical associated with rococo cocktail
music, a recoding that draws as much on the ongoingness associated with
genre as it does on the discrete cuts of historical action.[50]

V

"Brown paper packages tied up with string." On October 18, 1961, a Wednesday,
LeRoi Jones was awakened roughly by three irritated government employees.
As Hettie Jones describes it, these "charming creatures, an FBI man and two
postal inspectors, came to the door, quarter to eleven in the morning." Jones,
apparently, was still asleep:

> He's under arrest, they say. For what says I all atremble, hair standing on end. Wake
> up, *Leee*-roy, says the FBI, shaking him (he was fast asleep) and me all the time yell-
> ing what for, I have a right to know what he's being arrested for, until the mother-
> fucker tells me "shut up or I'll arrest you too." Roi sat up in bed pretty calmly there
> in his underwear and said what am I being arrested for and the guy finally spit out
> the obscenity charge.[51]

The postal clerks, it seems, had untied one of Jones's packages bound for a
reader in a penal institution, pulled open the paper wrapping, read the printed

sections in his magazine *The Floating Bear* from William S. Burroughs's "Roosevelt after Inauguration" and from Jones's own *The System of Dante's Hell*, and declared them, positively, not among the US government's favorite things. The passage from Jones's book was "The Eighth Ditch," which involves a homosexual encounter between men who may be military officers or are perhaps Boy Scouts. More extreme, Burroughs's vignette is a baroque fantasy of graft and corruption that follows Roosevelt into office: "In short, men who had gone gray and toothless in the faithful service of their country were summarily dismissed in the grossest terms—like 'You're fired you old fuck. Get your piles outa here.'—and in many cases thrown bodily out of their offices." In their place, "hoodlums and riffraff of the vilest caliber filled the highest offices of the land," while a purple-assed baboon rapes and maims those governmental officials not lucky enough to have yet been thrown out the doors with their paper piles.[52] Among the replacements are, for head of the FBI, "A Turkish Bath attendant and specialist in unethical massage"; for postmaster general, "'The Yen Pox Kid,' an old-time junky and con man on the skids" who plants fake cataracts. Not surprisingly, the postal authorities did not see the humor in this, so, when they enacted their enormous power as literary critics, Jones found himself in court, with the threat of jail time. Frank O'Hara was one of those who immediately came to Jones's defense. His remarks about the postal authorities' policing of so-called obscenity—framing it within the genre of "pornography"—underline the state's odd status as interpreter (and here evaluator) of literature: "Personally, I wish the postal authorities would ban the detective novel, the autobiographical novel and the *roman à clef*, which, like the sonnet, are simple forms requiring only application, and let pornography run rampant."[53]

Having developed a set of what might seem loose threads across the space of this chapter, let me now tie them back into something resembling a coherent package. We have moved from the Canadian origins of sound studies, seen spatially in Schafer and Gould's field trips across the country and toward the north, to the American technological infrastructure that preceded and controlled that move, and sent images of the northern border to an underground moderne war bunker in Colorado Springs via the White Alice Communications System. From there we have followed a case study of an individual soldier—Sergeant LeRoi Jones—who was on the other end of this messaging system, part of the mechanized air-power response to a potential Soviet breach of North American airspace. The chapter frames his early work as a responder to air-raid warning sirens in relation to his later work as a fashioner of prototypical sounds of Black Nationalism, especially those of John Coltrane in his recoding of the banal poetry of Rodgers and Hammerstein, where we discover a surprising interest in rococo cocktail music as well as revolutionary explosions, genre as well as history. Part of my argument—in demonstrating the infrastructural presence of American war technology at the edges of Canadian national space—suggests that Canadian claims toward autonomous nationalism via the approach of local sounds and weak radio signals represented a will not to hear or see the rather enormous signs of Canada's southern neighbor reticulated across its landscape. Not thinking about the extent to which the perimeter of the northern landscape had been turned into a series of strategic checkpoints for the United States did allow Gould and Schafer to recast their northern landscape as an autonomous soundscape organized around community-serving soundmarks and to articulate a national project of finally hearing the Canadian land's sonic singularity. In this context, Creeley's 1953 injunction against the Canadian ear becomes laughable. But the nationalist repressions and international triumphs of Canadian sound studies are not this chapter's full story.

We know that nationalism is not so much a present experience of collective identification as an imaginary one and that this imagination often requires displacement across time.[54] In this chapter, by using the radar system underlying the American B-36 to join the unlikely case studies of Canadian sonic nationalism and American Black Nationalism, we see how such temporal displacements fundamental to nationalism are managed by claims about a new education in sound. For the pioneers of sound studies, the new Canadian sonic subject that will be encouraged to emerge via these sonic field trips across this seemingly uncharted northern landscape is one that will come to know itself and from there operate within the collective space of the nation, not merely by thinking or seeing but by hearing, or rather hearing anew. He or she will, when these sonic training exercises have at last worked their office, finally *hear* both the immediate domain of daily existence (electricity hum, step patterns, elevator rumble, noon air-raid sirens) and the country's vast untapped sonic reservoirs. These last might, indeed, improve the quality of that daily sonic regime, especially when mixed in or amplified to counteract the effect of degraded or oppressive elements of sonic life, or noise pollution, that the Canadian sonic subject has now been taught to notice and detest:

"First we want to listen," Schafer tells us in a section on acoustic design. "Then we want to make judgments. And the more informed our judgments are, the better."[55] In listening for alternatives, this new subject will hear that some of those great sonic reservoirs—old foghorns, mills, nonindustrial farming sounds—are disappearing. But what is crucial to both Gould's and Schafer's project is that the Canadian subject does not, as yet, entirely hear what there is to hear—that encouragement and training are needed. All of these exercises depend, in other words, on a temporal displacement for the duration it takes us gradually to learn how to hear.[56]

The "greatest disparagement of what John Coltrane is doing," Baraka suggests, "must come from those who *cannot hear* what he is doing" (*BM*, 57). It was certainly the case that musicologists trained in the Western tradition often had a hard time describing both blues and jazz, assuming both to be merely bad adaptations or distortions of Western scales and tonal systems. The point for Baraka when *It's Nation Time* was released in 1972, however, was not convincing white critics of Coltrane's merits but institutionalizing his sound: training African Americans not merely to hear its values but to live them. Sonic tuning had shifted, and narrowed, its context. Baraka's record was a narrowcast not in the sense of Ginsberg's countermedia module VW poems, where specifying the space of address allowed one both to put the (vulnerable because abstracted) body back in the picture and to render it unfit for military service; nor did *It's Nation Time* depend on the kind of narrowing of physical context that allowed Larry Eigner to deprogram normative radio time; nor, finally, was the Black Nationalism of Baraka's record—like Olson's—either a counterhistory of the nation or an insistence on the time and process of research. What was narrow about *It's Nation Time* was more than the fact that it addressed itself not to the American nation of 1972 as a whole but to the Black nation of the future. It's that this future was engineered, sonically excavated we might say, out of materials—from air-raid sirens to Broadway musicals—instrumental in policing boundaries and framing desire within the Jim Crow United States of Baraka's early adulthood. In reducing the size of his audience, Baraka also proposed to teach subjects how to hear a crucial difference inside the sonic dimensions of the social regimes that had kept these reactionary institutions in place.

This question of how (and when) one might become a sound citizen within a Black or Canadian nation gives us, perhaps, a stronger, more fascinating thread than the ironic relationship between Canadian claims toward national autonomy and the revelation of an underlying imperial infrastructure, manned in part by Sergeant Jones. If we have, again, known for some time that even real nations rely on imaginary notions of belonging and that such belonging is necessarily more attenuated in the case of imaginary nations, then these perhaps implausibly linked case studies highlight the temporal displacements required in such imagining. But they do something more: while there are many plausible objections to comparing Canadian sound studies with the radicalizing forces within African American culture that, during the same period, were articulating models for a Black nation, the two movements did, in the 1960s and 1970s, turn to the marginalized sense of hearing not merely as a rallying point for self-identification but as a field of expertise—site-specific audio research—that might detoxify, deprogram, or reframe existing sonic institutions, propose new models of subjectivity more attentive to their sonic surroundings, and in so doing renegotiate social and intellectual imbalances.

Notes

Audio Research

1. William S. Burroughs, "The Invisible Generation," in *The Ticket That Exploded* (New York: Grove Press, 1967), 213. While Burroughs himself did not appear in the anthology, his Beat cohort did—Allen Ginsberg, Jack Kerouac, Gregory Corso, and Peter Orlovsky.

2. Larry Eigner, *The Collected Poems of Larry Eigner*, vol. 2, 1958–1966, ed. Curtis Faville and Robert Grenier (Stanford, CA: Stanford University Press, 2010), 357; subsequent citations of Eigner's poem are to this edition and cited parenthetically as *EP*. This poem is from November 1959.

3. I consider Allen Ginsberg's view of the tape recorder as a means for registering thought without typing in the first part of Chapter 1; for the media theorists, this "ability to make contact from a distance" is a feature of recorded music stressed, for instance, by Douglas Kahn (who attributes it to John Cage) in the very first sentence of his introduction to his edited collection: Douglas Kahn and Gregory Whitehead, eds., *Wireless Imagination: Sound, Radio, and the Avant-Garde* (Cambridge, MA: MIT Press, 1992), 1. Similarly, N. Katherine Hayles emphasizes the "evolving subjectivity [that] emerges from the instabilities produced when voices are taken out of bodies and bodies find themselves out of voices." "Voices out of Bodies, Bodies out of Voices: Audiotape and the Production of Subjectivity," in *Sound States: Innovative Poetics and Acoustical Technologies*, ed. Adalaide Morris (Chapel Hill: University of North Carolina Press, 1998), 75. For the avant-gardists, see my account of Charles Bernstein later in the introduction.

4. To those of us whose ears have been trained on public radio, with its practice of spatially situating the field reporter within a representative audioscape, the first part of this proposal may seem unremarkable—for in fact it is a dominant characteristic of contemporary radio to begin each field report with an evocation of the singular (and preferably exotic) sounds that frame each region of the globe considered capable of producing news. But this was not always so: in the 1950s and 1960s a far higher proportion of broadcast radio was produced in, and thematized the audio effects of, the nonspace of the studio. More important, in as much as they stress their sonic representativeness, the consumption-ready scene setters of the NPR field report are finally quite different from the odd environmental ambiences I study here.

5. As Pater says, "Although each art has its incommunicable element, its untranslatable order of impressions, its unique mode of reaching the 'imaginative reasons,' yet the arts may be represented as continually struggling after the law or principle of music, to a condition which music alone completely realizes; and one of the chief functions of aesthetic criticism, dealing with the products of art, new or old, is to estimate the degree in which each of those products approaches, in this sense, to musical law." "The School of Giorgione," in *The Renaissance*, ed. Donald L. Hill (Berkeley: University of California Press, 1980), 109.

6. James Holzman, *James Jesus Angleton, the CIA and the Craft of Counterintelligence* (Amherst: University of Massachusetts Press, 2008), 215; subsequent references are cited parenthetically as *JA*.

7. Fredric Jameson, *The Political Unconscious: Narrative as a Socially Symbolic Act* (Ithaca, NY: Cornell University Press, 1981), 9, 9–10.

8. This should suggest the extent to which I at once sympathize with the project of surface reading (as a mobilization of description over and against symptomatic reading's claims always to see *through* a text to its real meaning elsewhere) but also part ways in understanding description as in no sense self-evident. I have spelled this out in more detail in "lowercase theory and the site specific turn," *ASAP Journal* 2, no. 3 (2017): 653–76.

9. Michael Davidson, *Ghostlier Demarcations: Modern Poetry and the Material World* (Berkeley: University of California Press, 1997). Davidson's chapter, which has been generative for my own thinking, is titled "Technologies of Presence: Orality and the Tape-voice of Contemporary Poetics."

10. In *All Poets Welcome: The Lower East Side Poetry Scene in the 1960s* (Berkeley: University of California Press, 2003), Daniel Kane uses tape recording as evidence about particular poems and poets and the social dynamics at various reading series and events.

11. Tomás Uraoyán Noel, *In Visible Movement: Nuyorican Poetry from the Sixties to Slam* (Iowa City: University of Iowa Press, 2014).

12. Raphael Allison, *Bodies on the Line: Performance and the Sixties Poetry Reading* (Iowa City: University of Iowa Press, 2014), 11.

13. Ibid., 3, 7.

14. As Middleton puts it, "The persistence of these momentary ascendancies of poetry in an everyday world that threatens at every instant to flood back in and reclaim the space for its everyday function suggests . . . [that] these supposed flaws [are in fact] part of the act. . . . The myriad distractions that mitigate against the ideal are stage villains representing resistant conditions of the contemporary culture in the drama of poetry's tentative appearance and overcoming of inertia and opposition, when space, time, and poetry collude to produce a temporary dream of triumph for the power of poetry over the noise, routine, and institutions of everyday life each time a poetry reading is held." *Distant Reading: Performance, Readership, and Consumption in Contemporary Poetry* (Tuscaloosa: University of Alabama Press, 2005), 31. A previous version of Middleton's essay on the poetry reading appeared in Charles Bernstein, ed., *Close Listening: Poetry and the Performed Word* (New York: Oxford University Press, 1998).

15. Fredric Jameson, "Metacommentary," in *The Ideologies of Theory, Essays* 1971–1986, vol. 1, *Situations of Theory* (Minneapolis: University of Minnesota Press, 1988), 10.

16. Charles Bernstein, ed., "Introduction," in *Close Listening: Poetry and the Performed Word* (New York: Oxford University Press, 1998), 6.

17. Émile Benveniste, "The Notion of 'Rhythm' in Its Linguistic Expression," in *Problems in General Linguistics*, trans. Mary Elizabeth Meek (Coral Gables, FL: University of Miami Press, 1971), 281, 286. The essay was first published in 1951. I thank Lisa Robertson (whose writing on and recordings of sound have been generative for my own thought) for calling my attention to this essay; on her sound work, see Lytle Shaw, "Robertson's Research," in *The Fate of Difficulty in the Poetry of Our Time*, ed. Charles Altieri and Nicholas D. Nace (Evanston, IL: Northwestern University Press, 2017), 299–308.

18. Benveniste, "The Notion of 'Rhythm,'" 287.

19. Bernstein, *Close Listening*, 9, 10.

20. Ibid., 10.

21. For other, significantly different, versions of a Language writing poetics, see, for instance, Barrett Watten, *Total Syntax* (Carbondale: Southern Illinois University Press, 1985); and Lyn Hejinian, *The Language of Inquiry* (Berkeley: University of California Press, 2000).

22. Bernstein, *Close Listening*, 10, 21, 11, 18, 11. See, by way of comparison, Morton Feldman's claims about his concern with "sound itself" in his article "The Anxiety of Art," in *Give My Regards to Eighth Street: Collected Writings of Morton Feldman*, ed. B. H. Friedman (Cambridge, MA: Exact Change, 2000), 22. On Feldman, see Ryan Dohoney, "The Anxiety of Art: Morton Feldman's Modernism, 1948–1972" (PhD diss., Columbia University, 2009).

23. Bernstein, *Close Listening*, 21.

24. Questioning the traditional elevation of history over the other modes, Denis Diderot, in his 1765 "Notes on Painting," offers one of the earliest defenses: "Genre painters and history painters don't openly avow the contempt they feel for each other, but one senses it. The latter regard the former as minds of limited scope, lacking ideas, poetry, grandeur, elevation, and genius, who slavishly pursue a nature they dare not loose from view a single moment. Poor copyists whom they'd readily compare to a craftsman at the Gobelins [and] specialists in trivial subjects." *Diderot on Art*, vol. 1, *The Salon of* 1765 *and Notes on Painting*, trans. John Goodman (New Haven, CT: Yale University Press, 1995), 229–30. "The genre painter, on his side," Diderot continues, "regards history painting as a genre of phantasy, devoid of verisimilitude or truth, in which extravagance is the norm; which has nothing in common with nature" (230). While the terms Diderot uses to establish the contrast are linked to realism and the quotidian rather than to temporality proper, he makes it clear in his reading of Vernet (in the six "sites" and seventh picture in Diderot's "Salon of 1767") that genre painting can also have ties to modes of temporal arrangement that complicate the singular event-status of most history painting.

25. Quoted in Peter Burke's introduction to a contemporary republication of Burck-

hardt's 1860 *The Civilization of the Renaissance in Italy*, trans. S. G. C. Middlemore (New York: Penguin, 1990), 6.

26. Amiri Baraka, *Black Music* (New York: William Morrow, 1968), 61–62; subsequent references are cited parenthetically as *BM*.

27. Hayden White, *Metahistory: The Historical Imagination in Nineteenth-Century Europe* (Baltimore: Johns Hopkins University Press, 1973), 7.

28. In his classic essay "Everyman His Own Historian," Carl Becker suggests that "to establish the facts is always in order, and is indeed the first duty of the historian; but to suppose that the facts, once established in all their fullness, will 'speak for themselves' is an illusion." He continues: "Left to themselves, the facts do not speak; left to themselves they do not exist, not really, since for all practical purposes there is no fact until some one affirms it. The least the historian can do with any historical fact is to select and affirm it. To select and affirm even the simplest complex of facts is to give them a certain place in a certain pattern of ideas, and this alone is sufficient to give them a special meaning" (251). *Everyman His Own Historian* (New York: F. S. Crofts, 1935), 249, 251.

29. See, for instance, Jason Camlot, "The Sound of Canadian Modernisms: The Sir George Williams University Poetry Series, 1966–74," *Journal of Canadian Studies* 46, no. 3 (2012): 28–59. Camlot documents that "Robert Creeley, Michael McClure, Charles Reznikoff, Ted Berrigan, David Bromige, Robert Duncan, Allen Ginsberg, Kenneth Koch, Jackson Mac Low and Jerome Rothenberg" all traveled to Montreal and were recorded there by machines that were part of the university's language laboratory (30–31). While this phenomenon has been studied most often in a Canadian context, where the ideological pressures were less, we know that the poets in *Narrowcast* also were recorded by machines on loan from university language laboratories: Olson at Berkeley; Baraka and Ginsberg at San Francisco State, for instance.

30. Bernadette Mayer, *Memory* (Plainfield, VT: North Atlantic Books, 1975), 111.

31. Mayer asks, "What's the relation of things that stand out, things that seem interesting (like a sentence from a tape I made, the tape was 7 hours long, but this sentence would always stand out: 'The food of the mother is better than the food of the fatter father.' . . .)—what's the relation of this type of event to the rest & how to develop moments as, 'standing out' like language does, like language ideas do." *Studying Hunger* (New York and Bolinas, CA: Adventures in Poetry and Big Sky, 1975), 7.

Chapter 1

1. Allen Ginsberg, *The Fall of America: Poems of These States*, 1965–1971 (San Francisco: City Lights, 1972). Ginsberg, at the beginning of the tapes, mentions the date as December 17, 1965. We learn from Michael Schumacher's biography that Ginsberg's van was paid for by a Guggenheim grant and that he stayed in Los Angeles for three weeks. *Dharma Lion: A Biography of Allen Ginsberg* (New York: St. Martin's, 1992), 458. Schumacher tells us that Ginsberg had "readings scheduled in Kansas the first week of Febru-

ary, [with] his trip there involving a swing through Arizona, New Mexico, and Texas. . . . The first night on the road, they camped in the snow in the Arizona desert, and from there it was on to Albuquerque for a brief visit with Robert Creeley, who was now teaching at the nearby University of New Mexico" (459).

2. Barry Miles tells us that Peter Orlovsky drove and that Peter's brother Julius and Steven Bornstein went along as well. *Ginsberg: A Biography* (New York: Simon and Schuster, 1989), 381, 383.

3. This was not the first portable tape recorder. Ampex has had one in production since 1949. While the first models were still bulky, the smaller Model 600 (18 × 12 × 9 inches), introduced in 1954, "was used extensively as a broadcast 'on the scene' recorder." Eric D. Daniel, ed., *Magnetic Recording: The First 100 Years* (New York: IEEE Press, 1999), 88.

4. As Jane Kramer explains, "The manager, whose name was Charles Rothschild, handled Ginsberg's friend Bob Dylan and a good many other performers. . . . While Ginsberg took care of invitations from college literary magazines and fledgling poetry centers, Rothschild booked him for maximum exposure—at places like the Westbury Music Fair in Long Island, where he split the bill with the Butterfield Blues Band, and at the Santa Monica Auditorium, where he went on with the Fugs." *Allen Ginsberg in America* (New York: Vintage, 1970), 96–97.

5. Jack Kerouac, *On the Road* (1957; repr., New York: Penguin, 1991), 134–35.

6. Ginsberg, *Fall of America*, 24, 1.

7. Though "Wichita Vortex Sutra" is the best known of these poems, it comes in a series of poems that use the city name, the concreteness of place, as a way to anchor instances, locations for the production of Americanness, while at the same time connecting this system to its effects beyond the space of the nation. For an account of this poem in relation to Robert Smithson's concepts of site and nonsite, see Lytle Shaw, *Fieldworks: From Place to Site in Postwar Poetics* (Tuscaloosa: University of Alabama Press, 2013), 121–22.

8. The paper component alone of Ginsberg's stretches over "three-feet high," the poet himself stated proudly at one point. Herbert Mitgang, *Dangerous Dossiers: Exposing the Secret War against America's Greatest Authors* (New York: Donald Fine, 1988), 266. That paper stack now sits with the other Ginsberg papers at Stanford University (though a few sections are reproduced in Fales Special Collection in Bobst Library at New York University). Via the Allen Ginsberg Project, and because of the FBI's new website, it is possible to read much of Ginsberg's file online.

9. "Poetry and eloquence are both alike the expression or utterance of feeling. But if we may be excused the antithesis, we should say that eloquence is *heard*, poetry is *over*heard." John Stuart Mill, "Thoughts on Poetry and Its Varieties," in *Collected Works of John Stuart Mill, Vol.* 1, ed. John Robson (Indianapolis, IN: Liberty Fund, 2006), 348.

10. John Stuart Mill, "What Is Poetry?," *Monthly Repository*, January 1833, 66. My thanks to Andrea Brady who, in a talk at NYU from her forthcoming book, *Poetry and Bondage*, called this early version of the essay to my attention.

11. As Olson says, "If a contemporary poet leaves a space as long as the phrase before it, he means that space to be held, by the breath, an equal length of time. . . . Observe him, when he takes advantage of the machine's multiple margins, to juxtapose. . . . But what I want to emphasize here, by this emphasis on the typewriter as the personal and instantaneous recorder of the poet's work, is the already projective nature of verse as the sons of Pound and Williams are practicing it. Already they are composing as though verse was to have the reading its writing involved, as though not the eye but the ear was to be its measurer, as though the intervals of its composition could be so carefully put down as to be precisely the intervals of its registration." *The Selected Writings of Charles Olson*, ed. Robert Creeley (New York: New Directions, 1966), 22–23.

12. Schumacher, *Dharma Lion*, 457–58.

13. Cited in Clark Coolidge, *Now It's Jazz: Writing on Kerouac and the Sounds* (Albuquerque, NM: Living Batch Press, 1999), 54. This can be contrasted with two other Kerouacian modes: memory blowing and babble flow. Of the former, Kerouac writes, "All of it is in my mind, naturally, except that language that is used at the time it is used" (51); of babble flow, Coolidge explains, "Pressure off words so they pile and collide in and he hears them in mind as if spoken by another. Words, then, are fresh solids of the just heard" (55).

14. On this point, I thank J. D. Connor ("Icon, Index, Transcript: Lessons from Louis Armstrong and the Oral History Association," paper presented to the Modern Language Association, Austin, Texas, January 2016) for alerting me to the ways in which the previous question was also played out within debates about the status of recordings within oral history, where the recording themselves were at first seen just as efficient ways of producing text but gradually came to be understood—at least by some practitioners—as the final cultural documents themselves. On this debate, see Roland J. Grele, ed., *Envelopes of Sound: The Art of Oral History* (Chicago: Precedent, 1985); and, in the context of ethnopoetics, Dennis Tedlock, who writes, "It is not only the voice of the storyteller that is set free by sound recording, but also the ear of the mythographer. Even as the story is being told, the ear already takes in a broader spectrum of sounds than the anxious ear that tried to hear how each word might be *spelled.*" *The Spoken Word and the Work of Interpretation* (Philadelphia: University of Pennsylvania Press, 1983), 3.

15. Ginsberg, *Fall of America*, 8, 37, 1, 14, 29, 15, 30.

16. The context is as follows: "Well, The FUGS have been on a coast to coast concert tour . . . stayed in the Berkeley–SF area for three weeks. Ginzap was on a couple of concerts with us—the Zap is now billed as folk rock mantra-ist. We are on the way to the Creeley conspiracy in Placitas." Charles Olson Papers, University of Connecticut, Storrs, Box 211; subsequent references are cited parenthetically as OC.

17. See Daniel Kane, *Do You Have a Band? Poetry and Punk Rock in New York City* (New York: Columbia University Press, 2017).

18. A little over halfway into Andy Warhol's novel *A*, a work based on taping Warhol superstar Ondine for twenty-four hours, the main characters pause to wonder about the final medial basis of the project on which they are then at work. Having just listened

to music, Ondine asks about its presence in the novel, whereupon Warhol objects: "But how can I put a piano in the uh [book]?" When Ondine suggests that it would be "very easy," Warhol mentions that *A* will be transcribed from the tape. Apparently Ondine has up until this moment imagined *A as* the recording itself, not as a transcription, and therefore asks the quite reasonable question: "What do you mean transcribe this? . . . Why don't we make the book a tape?" *A: A Novel* (1968; repr., New York: Grove, 1998), 257.

19. Allen Ginsberg, *Spontaneous Mind: Selected Interviews,* 1958–1996, ed. David Carter (New York: Harper, 2001), 32–33.

20. For instance, "I said to myself, Wham, listen to that man laugh. That's the West, here I am in the West." Kerouac, *On the Road,* 19. It is impossible in *On the Road* to be visible yet not a perfect embodiment of a place.

21. Ginsberg, *Fall of America,* 1, 56, 24, 56. At moments, Ginsberg locates print as a similar problem, though it receives far less attention than radio: "the money munch / war machine, bright lit industry / everywhere digesting forests & excreting soft pyramids / of newsprint" (46).

22. Ibid., 46.

23. The meta-anthropological tribe of Cliffords, for instance, are mostly agreed on this. Where they part ways is whether this inevitable participation of the observer, in itself, fatally compromises the activity of fieldwork: James Clifford suggesting that it does, Clifford Geertz arguing that the move to a post-fieldwork understanding of the discipline has been less productive, decisive, and beneficial than fieldwork's critics imagined. See James Clifford, "On Ethnographic Authority," in *Writing Culture: The Poetics and Politics of Ethnography,* ed. James Clifford and George E. Marcus (Berkeley: University of California Press, 1986). For Geertz's view, see "The State of the Art," in *Available Light: Anthropological Reflections on Philosophical Topics* (Princeton, NJ: Princeton University Press, 2000).

24. Davidson, *Ghostlier Demarcations,* 197.

25. Ginsberg writes in the notebook that his "Auto Poesy Nebraska," dated February 15, 1966, is "transcribed from tape." The first lines, "Turn right next corner," become the intro for "Wichita Vortex Sutra." Allen Ginsberg Papers, Stanford University, Box 20.

26. While Ginsberg does acknowledge in his jacket blurb for *The Fall of America* that he also transcribes and sings (whose status is unclear in relation to recording and writing), he always stresses the tape recording first: "Beginning with 'long poem of these States,' *The Fall of America* continues *Planet News* chronicle tape-recorded scribed by hand or sung condensed, the flux of the car bus airplane dream consciousness Person during Automated Electronic War years, newspaper headline radio brain auto poesy & silent desk musings, headlights flashing on road through these States of consciousness."

27. On the development of cybernetics, see Peter Galison's brilliant article, "The Ontology of the Enemy: Norbert Wiener and the Cybernetic Vision," *Critical Inquiry* 21 (1994) 228–66. Galison suggests that Wiener's war work in the antiaircraft industry provided the basis not just for a theory of feedback but for also for theories of the human/

machine relationship, as well as for a model of humanity's relation to nature: "In the course of characterizing the enemy pilot's actions and designing a machine to forecast his future moves, Wiener's ambitions rose beyond the pilot, even beyond the World War. Step by step, Wiener came to see the predictor as a prototype not only of the mind of an inaccessible Axis opponent but of the Allied antiaircraft gunner as well, and then even more widely to include the vast array of human proprioceptive and electro-physiological feedback systems. The model then expanded to become a new science known after the war as 'cybernetics,' a science that would embrace intentionality, learning, and much else within the human mind. Finally, the [antiaircraft] predictor, along with its associated engineering notions of feedback systems and black boxes, became, for Wiener, the model for a cybernetic understanding of the universe itself" (229).

28. Norbert Wiener, *The Human Use of Human Beings: Cybernetics and Society* (1950; repr., New York: Avon, 1967), 35.

29. Immediately after World War II Wiener himself made a very public break with military work, seeking actively to resist the instrumentalization of his research. For accounts of this, see the second volume of his autobiography, *I Am a Mathematician: The Later Life of a Prodigy* (Cambridge, MA: MIT Press, 1956), 293–313; and Flo Conway and Jim Siegelman, *Dark Hero of the Information Age: In Search of Norbert Wiener, the Father of Cybernetics* (New York: Basic Books, 2005), esp. 237–94.

30. Frank O'Hara, *The Collected Poems of Frank O'Hara*, ed. Donald Allen (New York: Knopf, 1972), 499.

31. A document in his folder dated April 25, 1958, for instance, mentions that the "subject resides 104 East Third Street, New York City with his employment unknown." Amiri Baraka (LeRoi Jones) FBI File, accessible through William Maxwell's F.B. Eyes Digital Archive: http://digital.wustl.edu/fbeyes/.

32. According to Hettie Cohen (soon to be Hettie Jones), however, the story is slightly different. Working in a Greenwich Village record store one afternoon, Cohen discovers that Jones is a fast typist. She asks him where he learned, and he elaborates: "In the Strategic Air Command, but they threw me out . . . for reading *Partisan Review*." *How I Became Hettie Jones* (New York: Grove, 1990), 27.

33. Baraka FBI File.

34. "OSI records further reflect that on February 14, 1956, Mrs. STEPHEN LUCAS, wife of the owner of the L & S Market, 124 ½ West Kinney Street, advised that the subject was employed at the L & S Market as a part-time clerk after school hours and during summer and Christmas vacation periods while a student in high school and college. She stated her records reflect he was employed by them intermittently from 1951 to 1954. During the time she knew him, she never knew him to belong to any subversive organization" (ibid.).

35. One indication of this comes on October 9, 1970: "In view of the prominence of Jones at the Congress of African Peoples (CAP) in Atlanta, Georgia, in September, 1970, this investigation must be intensified. Target informants on the activities of Jones [line and a half blacked out] investigation necessary to determine in detail his current

activities. . . . Submit reports in this case as often as necessary, depending on the extent of Jones' activities, but at least quarterly. This case should receive aggressive, imaginative attention" (ibid.).

36. Such pirated tapes of speeches include one on February 17, 1968, at Wilson Auditorium in Cincinnati—sent to the Bureau on February 28, 1968. This, again, was not simply a tape of the event made by the university: "tape was made through a confidential source whose identity cannot be revealed." Another was made on May 18, 1969, in Detroit, at the Shrine of the Black Madonna, Central United Church of Christ, 7625 Linwood Avenue (an FBI document from later that month tells us); here an agent "used a concealed recording device to record a public speech by Le Roi Jones" (ibid.). I take up the Bureau scholar's reading of this event in Chapter 4.

37. "Greatest thing was last Fri," he writes, "when some friends and I had something funny planned, and a uniformed high officer policeman shows up early in the morning . . . 10 or so, comes in (I almost slammed the door it shook me so) and says to me 'We have reason to believe that you are a member of a group that plans to demonstrate in Times Square.' He then produces a leaflet that sure enough I had helped draft, but there were no names or anything on it! Just a thing calling for Negroes (it was distributed in Harlem) to show up in TS and get their heads bent. The man continued, after I asked him why he came to me, 'The point is that if you do show up in TS, in any capacity, *even on your way to buy a hotdog,* you'll be arrested.'" Amiri Baraka, *Amiri Baraka and Edward Dorn: The Collected Letters,* ed. Claudia Moreno Pisano (Albuquerque: University of New Mexico Press, 2013), 109.

38. "Now shit," Baraka explains to Dorn, "the motherfuckers are even working inside around me. I thought that FBI shit on the radio (Levine, ex agent . . . you read about it) where the cat says 1/5 of Communist Party aqui are FBI agents, and that they contribute the largest single share to the party! . . . Anyway, the other thing we had thought to do was further thwarted, BECAUSE WHEN WE GOT THERE THERE WERE SIX SQUAD CARS SITTING IN FRONT OF WHERE WE WERE TO GO . . . and this was just to make some kind of disturbance" (ibid.).

39. Jones, *How I Became Hettie Jones,* 206. We know from Ginsberg's file that the FBI did in fact conduct surveillance on all those who had become involved with the Fair Play for Cuba movement, including Ginsberg.

40. Baraka, *Amiri Baraka and Edward Dorn,* 121.

41. William Maxwell, *F.B. Eyes: How J. Edgar Hoover's Ghostreaders Framed African American Literature* (Princeton, NJ: Princeton University Press, 2015), 24, 8, 9.

42. This level of production seems to have required novel research methods. Rather than send its spies to work in rare book rooms, for instance, the FBI seems simply to have lifted the entire collections—books, manuscripts, correspondence together: "Following the 1919 invasion of the Russian People's House in Manhattan, trucks were requisitioned to remove dangerous treasure: not crates of firearms, but reams of writing. Entire institutional libraries were swallowed by Hoover's, twenty-five tons worth in New York in January 1920 alone" (ibid., 50).

43. Many of these books were written by several authors other than Hoover, including Robert Adger Bowen. "Even though *Masters of Deceit* (like Hoover's earlier book, *Persons in Hiding*) was ghostwritten, it was," Richard Gid Powers tells us, "as much a reflection of Hoover's ideas and feelings as if he had actually written it himself. Hoover's style of thought and expression so permeated the Bureau that the FBI's writers could emote in a manner indistinguishable from Hoover's, complete with his characteristic patterns of speech and thought." *Broken: The Troubled Past and Uncertain Figure of the FBI* (New York: Free Press, 2004), 238. Still, Hoover's writings must be seen as popularizations in relation to much of the actual interpretation done by the Bureau. We know, for instance, that other FBI writers made a scrupulous distinction between empirical authors and speakers in service of unscrupulous ends: Why? Because that scrupulousness was seen, finally, as more effective: authors *were not* the same as speakers, and conflating them would confuse the analysis of power.

44. If Hoover's widely distributed books on communism represented a popularization of the Bureau's concerns, they also pointed to methodological problems that even the subtlest of Bureau spies could not immediately overcome: that to weave together biographical analyses of empirical authors with close rhetorical and political unpackings of difficult texts necessarily resulted in hybrid, discontinuous critical texts that could not help resembling the modernism the Bureau distrusted. As Maxwell puts it, "Punitive, quotidian, and conventionally literary forms of textuality mingled between cardboard covers, the interior resembling the montage modernism the Bureau disliked everywhere outside its D. C. office." *F.B. Eyes*, 65.

45. Ginsberg, *Fall of America*, 29. Chief counsel for the Church Committee, Frederick A. O. Schwarz Jr., writes, "After King criticized the FBI for lax civil-rights enforcement in November 1961, Hoover became obsessed with King, and sought approval for wiretaps." *Democracy in the Dark: The Seduction of Government Secrecy* (New York: New Press, 2015), 67–68. The justification behind which the Bureau hid was the claim that Stanley Levinson, a King adviser, was affiliated with the Communist Party. However, the Bureau knew that Levinson was not tied to the party. Instead, they returned to the dead dossier to establish a *plausible* case for opening a new line of surveillance on King. "Hoover had 'scrambled' to find more current evidence against Levinson. But his agents found the opposite. The FBI's New York office told headquarters that they had 'interviewed their best fourteen informants, only to find that not a single one recognized Levinson's name or photograph.' The agents told Hoover it was useless" (69).

46. Maxwell tells us further that during "the FDR years, 1933–45, the FBI's annual budget bulged from 2.7 to 45 million dollars, and its workforce of special agents grew from 266 to some 5,000." *F.B. Eyes*, 77.

47. Ibid., 81. Schwarz confirms this: "After Franklin Roosevelt, who opened the door to FBI investigations into 'subversives,' became Hoover's first enabler, Herbert Brownell, Eisenhower's attorney general, added to Hoover's power by secretly permitting Hoover to use bugs on his own authority." Schwarz, *Democracy in the Dark*, 66.

48. See Ed Sanders, *Fug You: An Informal History of the Peace Eye Bookstore, the Fuck*

You Press, the Fugs, and Counterculture in the Lower East Side (New York: Da Capo, 2011), 305.

49. We know from Ginsberg's FBI file that the Bureau inquired about his phone in 1965, during a period in which he had, more than before, moved from "bizarre but not dangerous" to a more consistent person of interest. "On March 15, 1965 [blank] Security Supervisor, New York Telephone Company, 104 Broad Street, New York City, advised SA JAMES M. ANDERSON that telephone number OR 3-3638 formerly listed at 704 East Fifth Street, New York City, was now located at 408 East Tenth Street, Apartment 4C, New York City. This phone, residential service, was connected in February, 1964, in the name of PETER A. ORLOVSKY, who was described in their files as an unemployed hospital attendant. An additional listing for this telephone was given as ALLEN A GINS-BERG." It seems plausible that Sergeant Anderson's inquiry into Ginsberg's phone at his Tenth Street Apartment was ultimately connected with some kind of surveillance. Allen Ginsberg FBI File, https://vault.fbi.gov/irwin-allen-ginsberg.

50. Mitgang tells us, "In a memorandum from Hoover to the Secret Service in 1965, Ginsberg was cited as an 'Internal Security—Cuba' case, and a potential threat to the president of the United States. On the document, stamped *Secret*, Ginsberg was listed as 'potentially dangerous' and a 'subversive,' with 'evidence of emotional instability (including unstable residence and employment record) or irrational or suicidal behavior,' as having made 'expressions of strong or violent anti-U.S. sentiment,' and as having 'a propensity for violence and antipathy toward good order and government.' All such items were checked on a form in his file." *Dangerous Dossiers*, 267.

51. Holzman explains, "President Johnson was convinced, as President Nixon would be after him, that the antiwar demonstrations were directed by agents of the Soviet Union, disguised as non-Communist leftists" (*JA*, 248). It was under this belief that the White House put pressure on the CIA to provide more extensive and detailed reporting on the role of foreign connections with American dissident activities.

52. Mitgang, *Dangerous Dossiers*, 267. The case was framed in relation to "antirioting laws" in 1968 by the Chicago office of the FBI. "[Name blacked out] advised he observed GINSBERG at Grant Park in front of the Conrad Hilton Hotel in conversation with associates. GINSBERG chanted unintelligible poems in Grant Park on August 28, 1968." Allen Ginsberg FBI File. Ginsberg explained that the "unintelligible poems" were William Blake's "The Grey Monk."

53. William C. Sullivan, *The Bureau: My Thirty Years in Hoover's FBI* (New York: Norton, 1979), 163. For Sullivan, it was therefore a problem that, unlike the situation in England, France, Holland, Israel, and other countries, a single agency like the FBI handled both criminal and intelligence work.

54. See Mark Riebling, *Wedge: From Pearl Harbor to 9/11: How the Secret War between the FBI and the CIA Has Endangered National Security* (New York: Touchstone, 1994).

55. Sullivan continues, "Though Hoover used [a flimsy link between the New Left and the Communist party] as a wedge to drive us into investigating the New Left, the connection wasn't real, and the only people who believed in it were [American Com-

munist party leader] Gus Hall and J. Edgar Hoover (I have my doubts about Hall). The New Left never had any important connection with the Communist party; as a matter of fact, the New Left looked on Hall and the Communist party as a joke—hidebound, retrogressive, and outside the mainstream of revolutionary action." *The Bureau*, 148.

56. Holzman tells us, "In the [FBI's] New Left program . . . approximately thirty-nine percent of all actions attempted to keep targets from speaking, teaching, writing, or publishing" (*JA*, 240).

57. See Frances Stonor Saunders, *The Cultural Cold War: The CIA and the World of Arts and Letters* (New York: New Press, 1999).

58. Sherman Kent, *Writing History* (1941; repr., New York: Appleton, 1967), 34.

59. Ibid., 34–35.

60. Ibid., 35.

61. William R. Johnson, *Thwarting Enemies at Home and Abroad: How to Be a Counterintelligence Officer* (Washington, DC: Georgetown University Press, 2009), 84.

62. Ibid., 86–87.

63. Ibid., 87.

64. Ginsberg himself commented directly on this use of the Bureau's time and energy: "While J. Edgar Hoover denied for decades the existence of organized crime, he devoted the energies of his intelligence agency to eavesdropping on Martin Luther King, Jr.'s bedrooms and to myriad-paged surveillance of white Negro Abbie Hoffman's psycho-political gaga." *Deliberate Prose: Selected Essays, 1952–1995*, ed. Bill Morgan (New York: Harper, 2000), 30. While, as Maxwell mentions, wiretapping stretched back to the 1920s and flourished under FDR, it came back into prominence in the 1960s in part through Hoover's antipathy to Martin Luther King Jr. By 1963 "microphone surveillance of King's hotel rooms was," as Gid Powers notes, "producing reels of tape documenting what the Bureau called 'entertainment': sounds of King partying, drinking, and having sex." *Broken*, 255.

65. Allen Ginsberg, *Planet News, 1961–1967* (1968; repr., San Francisco: City Lights, 1992), 117.

66. Ibid., 125.

67. Ibid., 124.

68. But if Ginsberg himself resisted understanding his new work as entirely a matter of recording, some of his audience had other ideas. Ginsberg gave readings in Wichita, Kansas City, Topeka, and Lawrence. As he wrote to his father about a reading in Lawrence at the University of Kansas—sponsored by the Philosophy, not the English, Department, "The chancellor warned that he would stop me if I said dirty words, and so the vice squad came armed with tape recorders, but *they* left weeping." Kramer, *Allen Ginsberg*, 96. However much Ginsberg may have exaggerated the reaction of the audio surveillance vice squad, his poems of this period and project—especially "Wichita Vortex Sutra," composed in Kansas at that point—did have palpable effects on audiences.

69. On *Ramparts*, see Peter Richardson, *A Bomb in Every Issue: How the Short, Unruly Life of "Ramparts" Magazine Changed America* (New York: New Press, 2009).

70. Warren Hinckle, John Schneer, and Sol Stern, "The University on the Make, or How MSU Helped Arm Madame Nhu," *Ramparts*, April 1966, 11–22. The article was introduced by Stanley Sheinbaum, a Michigan State University faculty member.

71. Even Angleton's detractors cite his record of keeping double agents out of the CIA: although it is not absolutely certain that there were no double agents during Angleton's tenure, his record has been considered "blemish-free," especially "compared to the horrifying security gaffes of the British, German, and French services." Thomas Powers, *The Man Who Kept the Secrets: Richard Helms and the CIA* (New York: Knopf, 1979), 67.

72. Johnson, *Thwarting Enemies*, 9–10.

73. Other English professors at Yale at the time who operated as "contact points" for the OSS included the influential masters of two colleges, John Dudley French, master of Jonathan Edwards College, and Samuel B. Hemingway, master of Berkeley College. Robin W. Winks, *Cloak and Gown: Scholars in the Secret War*, 1939–1961 (New York: William Morrow, 1987), 38.

74. The spring 1948 issue of *Furioso*, for instance, contains a warm review by Andrews Wanning of the 1947 New Directions reissue of *Seven Types*. Amiri Baraka in the air force in Puerto Rico in the mid-1950s turns to New Criticism to escape his oppressive experience of serving the American state: "I read Empson's *Seven Types of Ambiguity* and plowed into all the fashionable literary McCarthyism coming out then, as my entrance and baptism into the world of serious letters." *The Autobiography of LeRoi Jones/Amiri Baraka* (Chicago: Lawrence Hill Books, 1997), 167; future references are cited parenthetically as *AB*.

75. *Furioso* also published reviews and essays by Maynard Mack, Cleanth Brooks, John Crowe Ransom, Wayne Booth, Edmund Wilson, Kenneth Burke, Leslie Fiedler, Malcolm Cowley, Richard Ellmann, Leo Marx, M. H. Abrams, and Reuben Brower.

76. David C. Martin, *Wilderness of Mirrors* (New York: Harper, 1980), 12. On Pearson's circle, see Eliot Weinberger, *Outside Stories* (New York: New Directions, 1992), 52. Weinberger also claims that Angleton, during his time at the OSS, recruited two more Yale graduates to the CIA: Joyce biographer Richard Ellmann; and 1938 winner of the Yale Younger Poets award, Edward Weismiller.

77. It is not exactly that "tapes" were decoded (since both the German Enigma and the Lorenz encryption systems sent their messages via radio) but that in order to decrypt the Lorenz, in particular, it became necessary to build what was in effect the first computer ever, Colossus, which used tapes. Enigma messages were sent by a standard Morse code radio transmitter.

78. Angleton was now operating in the immediate context in which Alan Turing, for instance, was decoding the German Enigma machines at Bletchley Park (*JA*, 40). On Turing and operations at Bletchley Park, see Andrew Hodges, *Alan Turing: The Enigma* (New York: Simon and Schuster), 1983.

79. Allen Ginsberg, *Poems All over the Place—Mostly 'Seventies* (Cherry Valley, NY: Cherry Valley Editions, 1978), 46.

80. Immediately after the war Angleton spent several years in Italy, then moved to

Washington and developed a social scene that included artists Anne Truit (*JA*, 219) and Kenneth Noland. He likely knew Olson as well.

81. As David Martin tells us, "On November 21, 1955, Angleton recommended to Richard Helms, the number two man in the Operations Directorate, that 'we gain access to all mail traffic to and from the USSR which enters, departs or transits the United States through the Port of New York.'" *Wilderness of Mirrors*, 69.

82. Ibid., 70.

83. Ibid., 18.

84. "The Agency was also," Holzman notes, "reading telegraphs: In the early 1960s . . . RCA Global and ITT World Communications began to store their international paid message traffic on magnetic tapes, *and these were turned over to the NSA*. . . . Telegrams to or from, or even mentioning, U.S. citizens whose names appeared on the watch list in the late sixties and early seventies, would have been sent to NSA analysts, and many would subsequently be disseminated to other agencies. . . . It is estimated that NSA . . . selected about 150,000 messages a month for NSA analysts to review" (*JA*, 175).

85. Tim Weiner argues against Angleton's judgment that Nosenko was a plant. *Legacy of Ashes: The History of the CIA* (New York: Doubleday, 2007), 230–32. But more recent scholars, including Holzman, suggest that Angleton may have been correct that Golitsyn was authentic and Nosenko was not. But because the FBI had already based significant policy decisions on the judgment that Nosenko was authentic, the Bureau was not receptive to contrary claims. As Angleton's deputy, Newton Miller, puts it, "You had a bunch of CIA guys throwing darts at the FBI's sources.' . . . The . . . interagency dispute over Nosenko's bona fides crystallized twenty years of difference over CIA philosophy. Angleton's pattern-recognition method, which found in the study of poetry a relevance to the detecting of strategic deceptions, was set squarely against Hoover's criminal-evidentiary approach" (*JA*, 215).

86. Angleton's method of reading was directly opposed to that of the FBI. This difference was also important when the Agency and the Bureau were, based on claims made by Golitsyn, both investigating the possibility of moles: whereas Angleton would let the suspects try to incriminate themselves, with the later plan of turning them into double agents, the Bureau would quickly confront the suspect, obliterating the possibility of self-incrimination (*JA*, 211).

87. See, for instance, Rebecca Lowen, *Creating the Cold War University: The Transformation of Stanford* (Berkeley: University of California Press, 1997); and Winks, *Cloak and Gown*. As one CIA article puts it, "The president of the university is the initial point of contact; the contacter needs his blessing for the exploitation of university personnel and records. Lesser officials and faculty members also tend to be more cooperative when they know that the president is aware of the intelligence collection activity and approves of it. The deans of the schools, the dean of students, and the department chairmen are worth cultivating, for most of the day-to-day activity of the university filters through them. They can, for instance, provide information on special research projects, foreign travel of faculty members, visiting foreign scholars, foreign graduate students,

and other points of intelligence interest. "H. Bradford Westerfield, ed., *Inside the CIA's Private World: Declassified Articles from the Agency's Internal Journal*, 1955–1992 (New Haven, CT: Yale University Press, 1995), 59.

88. "The more names known to secret intelligence," Holzman explains, "the greater the chance that any query submitted to the Registry would result in a 'hit.' This is part of the librarianship of counterespionage, unglamorous, but an essential component of professionalism" (*JA*, 181). Offering us a vivid picture of the material dimensions of this project, Holzman explains: "The ever-expanding list of citizens teaching, writing, and publishing during the 1960s were typed on the Bureau's specially ordered paper—thicker than that used by other government agencies—requiring vast supplies of (ordinary) manila file folders, which in their turn filled the gray drawers of filing cabinets, which, in ever proliferating numbers, created a crisis of storage" (*JA*, 240).

89. Something similar happened with the FBI, beginning with the break-in in Media, Pennsylvania, on March 8, 1971, that exposed COINTELPRO and led to its dissolution and to the Church Committee. See Betty Medsger, *The Burglary: The Discovery of J. Edgar Hoover's Secret FBI* (New York: Vintage, 2014).

90. However different their politics might have been, this group of literary CIA agents whose training in the 1930s and 1940s would allow them to become the cosmopolitan surveillance theorists of the 1950s and 1960s shared with many of the more famous Yale critics a set of key references within the Anglo-American orbit of New Criticism. The point is not that this somehow makes the poststructuralists complicit or even strictly parallel: what the two groups *did* with their referents was of course extremely different.

91. While both the Bureau and the Agency were struggling to find new interpretive paradigms that might organize the exponentially larger amounts of data they were gathering, it was the Agency's illegal gathering operations that were suddenly brought to light.

92. Jameson, *The Political Unconscious*, 31–32.

93. Perhaps sensing this as a potentially contentious area, Jonathan Culler asks Jameson about his relation to feminism in an interview. Jameson's response is, in part, to recode feminism: "Obviously we have learned many things from feminism, but people have also been changed by the very changes in social temperature from which the feminist movements themselves sprang, so all this is hard to sort out. I have to say that much of the political force of feminism comes from its collective dimension, its status as the culture and the ideology of a genuine social group." Fredric Jameson, Leonard Green, Jonathan Culler, and Richard Klein, "Interview: Fredric Jameson," *Diacritics* 12, no. 3 (1982): 91.

94. Jameson, *The Political Unconscious*, 102. Noting in passing that "a totalistic stance has not . . . had only revolutionary political implications," Martin Jay goes on to claim about totality that, just within Western Marxism, "the major subterranean quarrel of this subterranean tradition has been waged over this concept's implications." *Marxism and Totality: The Adventures of a Concept from Lukács to Habermas* (Berkeley: University of California Press, 1984), 13–14.

95. Jameson himself, not surprisingly, also had (has) an FBI dossier. What is surprising, however, is that the writer Philip K. Dick may have reported Jameson to the Bureau as a potential communist—this after Jameson, along with several friends including Peter Fitting, paid the novelist a visit in May 1974 in his home in Fullerton, California. Dick seems to have understood the visit as an attempt to tape-record him agreeing with Marxist interpretations of his work—masterminded by Stanislaw Lem (a Polish science fiction writer whom Dick believed was a Soviet agent) and Darko Suvin (editor of *Science Fiction Studies*, whom Dick believed was part of Lem's Soviet clique). See Jason P. Vest, *The Postmodern Humanism of Philip K. Dick* (Lanham, MD: Scarecrow Press, 2009), 102; and Jeet Heer, "Marxist Literary Critics Are Following Me!," *Lingua Franca* 11, no. 4 (2001): 26–31. Jameson himself, however, believes "there is a very real question of whether [Dick] ever actually sent the letter to the FBI. He thought they were after him, and I think he wanted to be careful to document his contacts with this alleged soviet 'clique' (his word). Needless to say, neither Suvin nor Lem were present, and he was very nice to us, I think we even went out to dinner with him." Frederic Jameson, e-mail to the author, May 22, 2017.

96. "Angleton," Holzman tells us, "having been trained at Yale in the analytical techniques of New Criticism, applied those techniques to the analysis of the somewhat unusual text, comparing it with others in the standard manner of literary-influence studies" (*JA*, 236).

97. Ginsberg, *Planet News*, 112.

98. Ibid., 110.

99. Kramer, *Allen Ginsberg*, 95.

100. Ginsberg, *Planet News*, 111.

101. Ibid., 114, 113.

102. Ginsberg was eventually able to wrest his file from the US government and learn, for instance, that "under a variety of covers, personnel attached to the 113th infiltrated a number of organizations and rallies organized to protest the Democratic National Convention [Chicago, 1968], including a Lincoln Park rally addressed by Panther leader Bobby Seale, [and] a sunrise meeting conducted by poet Allen Ginsberg ('other than singing and meditation the meeting was uneventful')." Frank J. Donner, *The Age of Surveillance: The Aims and Methods of America's Political Intelligence System* (New York: Knopf, 1980), 313.

103. Among writers and poets associated with the New Left, there were Ginsberg himself, Ken Kesey, Richard Brautigan, Lawrence Ferlinghetti, Nat Hentoff, Jerome Rothenberg, and Gary Snyder. There were also a lot of writers whose work was not immediately associated with the counterculture: Richard Kostelanetz, Thomas Parkinson, Djuna Barnes, John Berryman, and George Santayana. Finally, *Ramparts* published a number of writers who had appeared in the pages of Angleton's *Furioso*, including Peter Viereck, Leslie Fiedler, and Richard Ellmann.

104. Angleton would have known from his own editing of *Furioso* the difficulty of assigning a single, fixed political stance to a magazine that even includes literature: his

had, after all, published Ezra Pound and John Crowe Ransom alongside Bertolt Brecht, Pablo Neruda, and communist poet John Wheelwright. Angleton had also printed, in issue 4, Archibald MacLeish's elegy to the Spanish republic, "The Spanish Dead." Then there were writers, like Auden—also included in the magazine—who began close to communism and moved steadily right. How, then, might Angleton's own firsthand experience of the complexity of a magazine's politics have affected his analysis of *Ramparts*?

105. As Holzman puts it, "The investigation of *Ramparts* was, if anything, a greater violation of the CIA charter than the matters reported by *Ramparts*. If someone at the time had suggested that the CIA was investigating over three hundred Americans merely because of their connection with a magazine, the report would no doubt have been discounted as typical 'conspiracy theory' paranoia" (*JA*, 235).

106. Gary Snyder, review of *The Ticket That Exploded*, by William S. Burroughs," *Ramparts*, December 1967, 87–90.

107. Burroughs, *The Ticket That Exploded*, 205, 213.

108. Ibid., 213.

109. Ibid., 215.

110. Ibid., 217.

111. Ibid., 209, 207, 207. About the massive power of audio editing, Burroughs remarks, "You can edit a recorded conversation retaining material which is incisive witty and pertinent[;] you can edit a recorded conversation retaining remarks which are boring flat and silly" (ibid., 206).

112. Snyder, review of *The Ticket That Exploded*, 90. This composite subjectivity based on audio splicing is very similar to what Burroughs and Brion Gysin call "the third mind" and elaborate in the collaborative book of that title, *The Third Mind* (New York: Seaver, 1978).

113. Snyder, review of *The Ticket That Exploded*, 90.

114. William S. Burroughs, *Electronic Revolution* (1971; repr., Bonn, Germany: Expanded Media, 1998), 14.

115. In fact, not only the CIA but also special groups of agents working directly under Nixon did this. As Anthony Summers notes, during a 1972 "reading of the names of the 48,000 Americans who had been killed in Vietnam" that occurred at the Washington Monument, "mingling with the protesters were ten men from the Nixon White House, on a mission to provoke fights and disrupt the rally." *Official and Confidential: The Secret Life of J. Edgar Hoover* (New York: Putnam, 1993), 10.

116. The letter was composed by William Sullivan; see William Maxwell, *F.B. Eyes*, 1–5.

117. David Cunningham, *There's Something Happening Here: The New Left, the Klan, and FBI Counterintelligence* (Berkeley: University of California Press, 2004), 116.

118. As Cunningham puts it, "Whenever the Bureau tried to spread misinformation through the creation of faked 'underground' leaflets, they necessarily had to imitate the language of New Left adherents. An interesting dynamic would emerge as obscene language would often be censored within the memo itself even though it was understood

that it would be required in the Bureau-generated materials eventually distributed" (ibid., 100–101).

119. Memo from Cincinnati to director, June 29, 1970 (ibid., 239).

120. "The harm COINTELPRO did to law-abiding citizens cannot be overestimated. COINTELPRO destroyed reputations, got teachers fired, broke up marriages, sabotaged political campaigns, falsely labeled intended victims as government informers to encourage violent reprisals against them, and provoked 'numerous beatings and shootings.' All of this was done secretly, without any authorization either by statute or by anybody outside the Bureau in the executive branch." Schwarz, *Democracy in the Dark*, 73.

121. "There exists widespread suspicion, though the evidence remains inconclusive, that the small group of men who lowered the flag prior to the Grant Park police action were either under cover Chicago police officers or FBI informants." Cunningham, *There's Something Happening Here*, 56.

122. A large collection of Ginsberg audio recordings can be heard at PennSound: http://writing.upenn.edu/pennsound/x/Ginsberg.php. The Allen Ginsberg Project also makes a great deal of material available: http://allenginsberg.org/.

Chapter 2

1. Dragon's character references the real technology and intelligence transfer from Nazi Germany to Cold War America known as Operation Paperclip. Two Nazi intelligence agents above all seem related: Reinhard Gehlen (1902–79), active in the Soviet Campaign, who avoided trial at Nuremburg by stashing away what became the central archive of materials relating to the Soviet Union (and thus was of extreme value to the United States), and later, after extensive debriefing in the United States, established the Gehlen Organization in West Germany, which was the central German spy network until it was taken over by the government in 1956; the other was Otto von Bolschwing (1909–82), who became the main American representative of the Gehlen Organization and worked closely with the CIA. Neither of them was an albino. See James Critchfield, *Partners at Creation: The Men behind Postwar Germany's Defense and Intelligence Establishments* (Annapolis, MD: US Naval Institute Press, 2003); Annie Jacobsen, *Operation Paperclip: The Secret Intelligence Program That Brought Nazi Scientists to America* (New York: Little, Brown, 2014); and Christopher Simpson, *Blowback: America's Recruitment of Nazis and Its Effects on the Cold War* (New York: Weidenfeld and Nicolson, 1988).

2. "In the Vietnam era," Frank J. Donner tells us, "the release of secret information by officeholders served as a channel of bureaucratic protest both against governmental policies and against the secrecy with which they were formulated. The spread of opposition to the war and the increasingly adverse role of the press institutionalized the anonymous press leaks by government insiders, a contemporary *trahison des clercs*. And ready access to copying machines gave the practice a new, documentary dimension. The monitoring and prevention of leaks quickly became an intelligence concern entrusted to

a specially created unit, the Plumbers." *Age of Surveillance*, 249. For more on the documentary dimension of copying at this moment, see Lisa Gitelman, *Paper Knowledge: Toward a Media History of Documents* (Durham, NC: Duke University Press, 2014), chap. 3.

3. In fact, it was (and is) not only whistle blowers who leaked documents but also a wide range of governmental workers at every level, all the way up to the president. As Frederick A. O. Schwarz tells us, for instance, about the Pentagon Papers, perhaps the single most important leak of the period, "When the Pentagon Papers began to appear in print, Nixon's first reaction was glee. The stories embarrassed his Democratic predecessors. Nixon actually demanded that *more* material be leaked, particularly about the Kennedy administration's secret role in the assassination of Vietnamese president Ngo Dinh Diem. The president told his aides, 'Now that it's being leaked, we'll leak out the parts we want.' But Henry Kissinger, appealing to Nixon's manhood, advised him that China would not respect a leader who allowed leaks." *Democracy in the Dark*, 157.

4. On the political valences of Eastwood's roles in the late 1960s and early 1970s, see above all J. Hoberman's excellent *The Dream Life: Movies, Media, and the Mythology of the Sixties* (New York: New Press, 2004).

5. Eigner writes on April 27, 1971, to David and Maria Gitin: "Doubt if I told you a film-making and sociologist colleague of brother's whom I met in August, Asst. Prof. of Research in Architecture at Wash . . . U, early Nov. as he was leaving for plane back here asked ma cd he do a documentary of me, and always agreeable she said yes, which I later seconded (just escapist and extrovert). His idea e.g. is to use your reading. Thursday, March 18 filming here." Larry Eigner Papers, Box 1, Folder 2, Archives & Special Collections at the Thomas J. Dodd Research Center, University of Connecticut Library; subsequent references are cited parenthetically as EC. Here and throughout my transcriptions of Eigner's letters I have, for clarity, filled in some of Eigner's more ambiguous abbreviations.

6. "Larry Eigner," *Contemporary Authors Autobiography Series*, vol. 23 (Detroit, MI: Gale, 1996), 41.

7. Eigner was himself living in Berkeley when this poem was published there fifteen years later. The poet lived in Swampscott from 1930 until a few months after his father's death in 1978, when he moved to Berkeley, first to a group household for people with disabilities. This proved unworkable, and a year later Eigner went to live with the poets Robert Grenier and Kathleen Frumkin in a house on McGee Avenue in Berkeley provided by Eigner's brother Richard. Grenier and Frumkin lived with Eigner until 1989; the last seven years of the poet's life (he died in 1996) were spent in the same house but with different caregivers.

8. Realized in 1980, the Tuumba edition "is a version of the aborted Pierrepont Press edition of April, 1969. It follows a typescript prepared by Robert Grenier." Larry Eigner, *Flat and Round* (Berkeley, CA: Tuumba, 1980), n.p.

9. Eigner did blazon this on subsequent book jackets. I am quoting, though, from Andrea Wyatt, *A Bibliography of the Works by Larry Eigner, 1937–1969* (Berkeley, CA: Oyez, 1970), 2.

10. Concerned perhaps that this description might disturb readers, she continues: "Instinctively our pride cries out against this—until perhaps pride breaks, and we look again, and see there is no contempt for man in this attention given to a pebble, only the sense that both are strange, unknowable, unpredictable" (ibid., 5).

11. Watten, *Total Syntax*, 186. Watten continues: "At the same time that it constitutes a reality in language it allows for a maximum distance between things in the world. The poem is a judgment of these two possibilities, one that is achieved simultaneously with the calling of things into existence in the act of naming" (ibid.).

12. Because Johnson tapped his own phone, it is now possible to listen to these conversations about escalation in Vietnam, including a detailed one about Operations Double Eagle (the largest amphibious operation of the war) and Masher (a search-and-destroy mission) with an unidentified general that occurs on the exact day (February 15, 1966) that Ginsberg composed the first part of "Wichita Vortex Sutra." After listening to the general's description, his estimate of the total number of men to be employed by the height of the operation in June (sixty thousand) and the current number of men involved (thirty thousand), Johnson inquires: "That as fast as you can we get 'em there?" Recording 9640, titled "White House Situation Room." The first two years of these tapes have been transcribed and edited in Michael R. Beschloss, ed., *Taking Charge: The Johnson White House Tapes, 1963–1964* (New York: Simon and Schuster, 1997); the audio archive is available at http://millercenter.org/scripps/archive/presidentialrecordings/johnson.

13. In fact, the 1965 location of NORAD was the relatively nondescript Chidlaw Building on 221 East Bijou Street; however, by April 20, 1966, NORAD had moved into the more properly Bond-villainesque Cheyenne Mountain Complex.

14. Bertolt Brecht, "The Radio as an Apparatus of Communication," in *Brecht on Theatre: The Development of an Aesthetic*, ed. and trans. John Willett (New York: Hill and Wang, 1992), 52. The article was first published in 1932. Brecht continues: "The radio would be the finest possible communication apparatus in public life, a vast network of pipes. That is to say, it would be if it knew how to receive as well as to transmit, how to let the listener speak as well as hear, how to bring him into a relationship instead of isolating him. On this principle the radio should step out of the supply business and organize its listeners as suppliers" (ibid.).

15. This statement appeared most prominently in Donald Allen, ed., *The New American Poetry, 1945–1960* (New York: Grove, 1960), 436. It was also included, in the same year, in Eigner's book *On My Eyes*, a collaboration with the photographer Harry Callahan (Highlands, NC: Jonathan Williams, 1960). But this framing via radio was repeated frequently. Eigner gives, for example, another version of it in a draft of his career narrative used in a 1971 Guggenheim application, elaborating slightly by stressing that "my brother, who called me to hear it, happened onto the last minute or two of the first or second broadcast of Cid Corman's 'This is Poetry' program. I started what turned out to be a rewarding correspondence (my opening letter to him offered one point of criticism at least, as I remember, I had the impression his delivery wasn't stentorian enough to do

right by Poetry), in which I learned some and got introduced to things, the ice breaking considerably as I tried as usual to understand what [was] said and written (to me especially) and yet because of this soon learned to relax hidebound and too earnestly and seriously held ideas. Robert Creeley, who came on Corman's program, corresponded with me during the next five years . . . and I had a few letters from, and later on personal exchanges with, Charles Olson." Letter to Richard and Beverly Eigner and David and Maria Gitin, February 11, 1971 (EC).

16. Seth Forrest, "The Body of the Text: Cerebral Palsy, Projective Verse and Prosthetics in Larry Eigner's Poetry," *Jacket* 36, 2008, http://jacketmagazine.com/36/forrest-eigner.shtml. Forrest frames the first part of the problem nicely: "Besides the thin membrane of the porch windows, Eigner's connection to the outside world comes through electronic boxes, television and radio."

17. Larry Eigner Papers, Box 2, Folder 23, University of Connecticut, Storrs.

18. Charles Olson, *The Maximus Poems*, ed. George Butterick (Berkeley: University of California Press, 1983), 2; subsequent citations are to this edition and cited parenthetically as *MP*.

19. "We very much hope," Creeley continues, "Emerson, out in Ohio, comes thru with some recordings Olson made this past summer for his show, & there will be those, if he can get them to us. Otherwise, our own attempts." Letter to Larry Eigner, December 1950 (EC).

20. What is perhaps less well known (although Forrest notes it) is that, like Eigner, Creeley considered his contact with Corman's radio program (also generated by a chance encounter with it over the air and a subsequent letter) as a central, formative moment in his career. As Creeley writes, "In 1950 Cid Corman, the subsequent editor of *Origin*, had a radio program in Boston called *This Is Poetry*, which by a fluke of air waves I heard one night in Littleton, N.H. The guest was Richard Wilbur, who read with such graceful accents I was filled with envious ambition to read also, although I had none of his qualifications; and some weeks later, after correspondence with Cid which that night began, I convinced him I was good enough, or he was tolerant enough, and so I read one Saturday night while I was in Boston showing chickens at the Boston Poultry Show. Literary history is like that, and this event would be altogether unnotable, were it not that a magazine which I then tried to start (with much the same motives), but could not get printed, was absorbed in the first two issues of Cid's *Origin*—and that among the contacts so contributed were Charles Olson, Paul Blackburn and Denise Levertov." Robert Creeley, *A Quick Graph: Collected Notes and Essays* (San Francisco: Four Seasons, 1970), 161.

21. Letter to David Gitin, September 14, 1970 (EC). Eigner spells it "whelk" here and later—perhaps intentionally casting the soporific Muzak purveyor as a sea snail.

22. Ibid. A media environment can also be productive under the right conditions: "One thing that makes books seem dispensable is radio and tv, which are now more effective here in taking me out of myself." Letter to Maria Gitin, February 13, 1971 (EC). In addition to this displacement, Eigner suggests a kind of education that happens by

activating one's role as consumer: "You always really learn, so it sticks, by enough doing. Like watching the 12 hour dramatized biog. of the duke of marlborough I recollected some things and came across others in the dictionary that stay with me. Otherwise things just pass thru you whether tv radio or page plugs into you. Like a foreign tongue." Letter to David and Maria Gitin, April 27, 1971 (EC).

23. Letter to David Gitin, September 14, 1970 (EC).

24. That said, Ginsberg's attention in *Indian Journals* is already directed toward the problems of language that will become central in *The Fall of America*. And thus we might read the passage Eigner evokes on the first pages—titled "Premonition Dream" and about India as a hallucinatory vision of "my promised land"—against Ginsberg's own later critiques of precisely such visions: "Poetry XX Century like all arts and sciences is developing into examination-experiment on the very material of which it's made. They say 'an examination of language itself' to express this turnabout from photographic objectivity to subjective-abstract composition of words à la Burroughs. . . . Now poetry instead of relying for effect on dreaminess of image or sharpness of visual phanopoeia— instead of conjuring a vision or telling a truth, stops. Because all visions & all truths are no longer considerable as objective & eternal facts, but as plastic projections of the maker & his language." *Indian Journals* (San Francisco: City Lights, 1970), 38.

25. Letter to David Gitin, May 30, 1970 (EC).

26. In a May 19, 1971, letter to the Gitins, Eigner writes: "2 or 3 weeks ago ma made her latest discovery with the furniture when she moved box of books from St. Louis from chair out here to bookcase top. Most convenience I ever had—fleeting realization of advantages of compartmentalized bookshelves before but this brought some real imaginative interchange entre nous, while I did most of the thinking aloud. It wasn't till 5 days ago, though, that i realized cognized up/down motion with my arm is easier, far easier, than push/pull—this suddenly when Dad noticed the 2 nice green plastic containers which 3 or 4 days earlier had replaced the cardboard box" (EC).

27. In another 1959 poem Eigner treats the newspaper as an explicit part of his immediate landscape, while at the same time undermining its claims to provide the news: "paper / rugs / even today / 'news' the ads / present confiding tomorrow" (*EP*, 316). Like the rugs, walls, or windows, the paper is a physical feature of immediate existence that seems to justify itself through the unpersuasive claims that it delivers "news," which, according to Eigner, is compromised not only by discrete advertisements within the paper but also by the larger sense that the entire address of the paper is a temporal advertisement, an attempt to control time by dictating its terms and concerns, the "present confiding tomorrow"—the would-be authoritative (though intimate—a confidence) claim today about what will be significant tomorrow.

28. Establishing accurate models with which to understand the acoustic effects of air's movement through architecture was a central problem confronting modern architects and engineers. Attempting to set office furniture for ideal acoustics, however, they discovered a somewhat surprising model that might be taken to bear on Eigner's poetics: "The great difference in loudness of sound with and against the wind," notes Wallace

Clement Sabine, the father of modern architectural acoustics, "is not due to the fact that the sound has been simply carried forward or opposed by the wind, but rather to the fact that its direction has been changed and its wave front distorted." *Collected Papers on Acoustics* (New York: Dover, 1964), 122. Wind, in other words, is less a force of sonic acceleration than one of disjunction and distortion. In a sense, Eigner considered the media bleed from his parents' television and radio similarly to how he took in the shifting audio effects of his neighborhood, as they were generated by wind. Sabine describes this "wave front" earlier: "If a sound is produced in still air in open space it spreads in a spherical wave diminishing in intensity as it covers a greater area. The area of a sphere being proportioned to the square of the radius, we arrive at the common law that the intensity of sound in still air is inversely proportional to the square of the distance from the source" (118). For more on Sabine, see Emily Thompson's excellent study *The Soundscape of Modernity: Architectural Acoustics and the Culture of Listening in America, 1900–1933* (Cambridge, MA: MIT Press, 2002).

29. Letter to David Gitin, May 30, 1970 (EC).

30. On the emergence of genre and landscape painting, see Georg Wilhelm Friedrich Hegel, *Hegel's Aesthetics: Lectures on Fine Arts, Vol. 1,* trans. T. M. Knox (Oxford: Clarendon, 1988); Max Friedländer, *Landscape, Portrait, Still-Life* (New York: Philosophical Library, n.d.); and Christopher Wood, *Albrecht Altdorfer and the Origins of Landscape* (London: Reaktion, 1993).

31. Arguably, this conflict emerged long before its full explosion in the nineteenth century. The challenges to history painting's management of time mounted by seventeenth-century genre and especially landscape painting are the subject of my manuscript "New Grounds for Dutch Landscape," of which just one section has been published: "Van Goyen's Puddles," *AA Files* 65 (2012): 76–86.

32. In "Notes on Painting" Diderot writes: "There's great skill involved in knowing how to animate dead things" as genre painters are supposed to do; "imitators of dead, brute nature must be called genre painters; imitators of sentient, living nature must be called history painters; and so the quarrel is resolved. But if we allow these terms to retain their generally accepted connotations, I see that genre painting has almost all the difficulties of history painting; that it calls for just as much intelligence, imagination, and even poetry . . . because it depicts the things that are most familiar and best known to us, there are more judges of it, and better ones." Diderot, *Diderot on Art,* 231, 230.

33. On Eigner in the context of disability studies, and on the problematic of dependency in particular, see Michael Davidson, *Concerto for the Left Hand: Disability and the Defamiliar Body* (Ann Arbor: University of Michigan Press, 2008); on dependency, see also Libbie Rifkin, "'Say Your Favorite Poet in the World Is Lying There': Eileen Myles, James Schuyler and the Queer Intimacies of Care," *Journal of Medical Humanities* 38 (2017): 79–88.

34. Olson's mother in fact died in 1950, but Connie Olson, the poet's first wife, must have played an *immense* role in maintaining the domestic "field" so that Charles could spend, in the early 1950s, upward of eight hours a day simply in correspondence with

Robert Creeley ("the figure of outward"), above and beyond all of his other letter writing, reading, and poetry production. Their ten-volume correspondence covers a bit over two years.

35. Letter to David and Maria Gitin, November 7, 1972 (EC).

36. "A phrase often in her mouth for years was," Eigner explains in a January 31, 1971, letter to his friends the Gitins, "even if I were in the white house I'd still be a little boy to her" (EC).

37. Later on Eigner will have several other secretaries, most notably Robert Grenier, who approaches Eigner in 1970 and works with him continuously until Eigner's death in 1996.

38. Letter to David and Maria Gitin, August 12, 1971 (EC).

39. As Eigner puts it to the Gitins in a letter dated April 28, 1971, "Grenier my 2nd or 3rd poet/secretary—they've just popped up. Real leisurely he is, while the others, Andrea Wyatt and Jon. Green from Bard College, it was a Project. He's quite as willing to type unsparingly for BRICOLEUR as for something to show Laughlin [for] New Directions" (EC).

40. Alan Davies and Richard Dillon, "One into Zero Goes Zero Times," review of *Anything on Its Side*, by Larry Eigner, *Chicago Review* 26, no. 3 (1974): 188–89. Though the review appears to be collectively composed, the authors use the first person singular.

41. On the technological dimensions of early radio, see especially Sungook Hong, *Wireless: From Marconi's Black-Box to the Audion* (Cambridge, MA: MIT Press, 2001).

42. As Douglas explains, after the Japanese bombing of Pearl Harbor, "an estimated 60 to 90 million Americans—the largest audience up to that time—listened to Roosevelt's fireside chat as he told the country, 'We are now in this war. We are in it—all the way.'" *Listening In: Radio and the American Imagination* (Minneapolis: University of Minnesota Press, 2004), 188. US population at that point was 133.4 million.

43. As Bruce Lenthall puts it in his analysis of the fireside chats, "Radio made it possible for listeners to re-envision the impersonal relationship between politician and citizen in twentieth-century America as an intimate one." *Radio's America: The Great Depression and the Rise of Modern Mass Culture* (Chicago: University of Chicago Press, 2007), 84. Lenthall also details how Roosevelt relied on radio more broadly: "He gave twenty national broadcasts in 1933, and only four of them were considered fireside chats" (89). He offers statistics to confirm (while adding a level of detail to) Douglas's claim about the size of Roosevelt's audience: "A 1939 poll found that 38 percent of Americans claimed they listened to Roosevelt's major radio addresses. And for highly significant chats, listenership could run much higher: 79 percent of Americans heard the president's address following the bombing of Pearl Harbor" (90).

44. See Jason Loviglio, *Radio's Intimate Public: Network Broadcasting and Mass-Mediated Democracy* (Minneapolis: University of Minnesota Press, 2005).

45. Burroughs was not merely a lunatic fringe, either; he was following many of the experimental protocols of the US state, which had been looking into the effects recorded voice could have in breaking down subjects during interrogation.

46. R. Murray Schafer, "Radical Radio," in *Voices of Tyranny, Temples of Silence* (Indian River, Ontario: Arcana, 1993), 135. "Western broadcasting," he writes elsewhere in the same essay, "is governed and tyrannized by an instrument we have accepted as inviolable, though it belongs to no other society but ours: the clock" (134).

47. As Douglas puts it, in documenting the enormous growth in FM stations over the course of the 1960s and early 1970s, the FM "ethos rested on a contempt for what had come to be called mass culture: a disdain for the 'vast wasteland' of television and for the formulaic, overly commercialized offerings of radio, and a scorn, first on the part of older intellectuals and later on the part of the counterculture, for the predictability and mindlessness of mainstream popular music." *Listening In*, 259.

48. This disruption was, however, gradually contained. "As in other industrial practices," Douglas tells us, the eclectic and imaginative curation that had first marked FM radio "gave way to automation, which became greatly enhanced by computerization. As early as the mid-1970s, an estimated one-seventh of FM stations were automated, with the numbers continuing to grow. Automation meant that a station could stay on the air for hours with virtually no human intervention. The process was simple. The sequence of music was provided on tape, and prerecorded comments from DJs for a four-hour show (which they could tape in fifteen minutes) could be inserted at the appropriate times" (ibid., 280).

49. Letter to David and Maria Gitin, September 16, 1971 (EC).

50. Larry Eigner, *areas / lights / heights: Writings* 1954–1989, ed. Benjamin Friedlander (New York: Roof, 1989), 26.

51. Letter to Maria Gitin, February 13, 1971 (EC).

52. This seems closely related to the dynamic in Beckett's novel *The Unnamable*, which begins, "Can it be that one day, off it goes on, that one day I simply stayed in, in where, instead of going out, in the old way, out to spend day and night as far away as possible, it wasn't far." *Three Novels: Molloy, Malone Dies, The Unnamable* (New York: Grove Press, 1991), 291.

53. Postcard to his mother, February 21, 1983. Eigner Papers, Box 21, Stanford University.

54. As frustrated as Eigner could be with his mother's media environment, threats, and poor secretarial work, he was also an extremely devoted correspondent once he moved across the country, writing to her more or less weekly from the West Coast. Eigner's letters also tell the story of his remarkable curiosity. To all his family members he wrote multicolumn, multiorientation letters—often with poems nested in, set off often within tiny columns of commentary running along the margin of one side of a page, and frequently switching directions somewhere near the middle. In these letters, one sees a highly constructed, customized sense of graphic space that contributed centrally to their effect, which was at once playfully open to accident and invention while also layered and complex. Creeley, for instance, writes of Eigner's letters' "lovely characteristic density." Postcard to Eigner, February 27, 1988 (ibid., Box 9).

55. As Cage puts it in "Lecture on Nothing," seeming to speak of Eigner: "But beware

of / that which is / breathtakingly / beautiful, / for at any moment / the telephone / may ring / or the airplane / come down in a / vacant lot / A piece of string / or a sunset / possessing neither / each acts / and the continuity / happens." *Silence: Lectures and Writings by John Cage* (1961; repr., Middletown, CT: Wesleyan University Press, 1973), 111.

56. Eigner touches on such endings in a February 12, 1972, letter to David and Maria Gitin: "I used to try long poems, but no longer, my ego is [diminished] in the lush tropical present or great crisscross railroad yard of hurtling goods. I let a poem's end come as it may, part of the figure it makes, though when there's an unexpected offshoot or lengthening, just as, I guess, you'd like to go on living forever. Well—too bad and yet no tragedy—poems long and short keep going out of my head, displaced by other poems and things" (EC).

57. The prose is collected in Larry Eigner, *Country / Harbor / Quiet / Act / Around*, ed. Barrett Watten (Berkeley, CA: This, 1978).

58. Ron Silliman, ed., *In the American Tree: Language, Realism, Poetry* (Orono, ME: National Poetry Foundation, 1986), xv, xvii. Tempering Grenier's polemical epithet with a dose of bland pluralism, Silliman continues: "Neither speech nor reference were ever, in any real sense, the enemy. But, because the implicit 'naturalness' of each, the simple seemingly obvious concept that words should derive from speech and refer to things, was inscribed within all of the assumptions behind normative writing, the challenge posed by *This* [a foundational magazine edited by Robert Grenier and Barrett Watten] was to open a broad territory of possibility where very different kinds of poets might explore and execute a wide range of projects" (xvi).

59. While it might often seem as though Eigner's work is descriptive of the ongoing characteristics of this world, at times it appears as though he is in fact *willing* this entire cosmos into being—controlling it like an engineer or model builder, and at times narrating his own sound track. "BE SILENT," Eigner commands in a 1959 poem: "with the verse / turning // the world / looks like a hurricane / the curtain falls" (*EP*, 300). Here the "turning" achieved by verse is equally the agent of the world's moving, the hurricane arriving, the curtain falling. The point is not merely that Eigner's project is somehow "subjective" rather than objective but that his ongoing thematization of the agency of his attention highlights the way that description is ultimately a form of involvement with the thing described, and thus any repeatedly depicted environment, like Bates Road in Swampscott, comes into focus through the singular kinds of attention he brings to it. This is what situates Eigner as the maker of such a durational diorama, not merely its attendant. This sense of making is also what underlies many of his metadescriptive passages.

60. We can see this now because for the last thirty years or so, since perhaps the late 1980s or early 1990s, since the end of the Cold War, experimental poetry has *not* been able to position the temporalities of daily life or disjunction as effective antidotes to administered time. While we can acknowledge that avant-garde devices of defamiliarization have half-lives and thus cannot work their offices indefinitely, this process of exhaustion has been affected more radically from the outside—by the fact that time is

now administered very differently from how it was from the 1950s to the 1980s. With the effective obliteration of the opposition between work and leisure, in short, the dialectical temporal frame that guided so much of this older poetry can no longer operate with the power it once did.

61. The *March of Time* existed in both filmic and radio formats. As Howard Blue tells us of the radio version, the "program was the brainchild of Fred Smith" of Cincinnati station WLF, "who wanted to provide radio with an alternative source to the wire services" and "came up with the idea of dramatizing the news to give it an immediacy that would bring listeners right into the events they were hearing. In pursuit of his plan, he contacted *Time*'s Roy Larson, and proposed a collaboration." Howard Blue, *Words at War: World War II Era Radio Drama and the Postwar Broadcasting Industry Blacklist* (Lanham, MD: Scarecrow Press, 2002), 161. It is important to note, too, that the program used actors: "For most of its run, *The March of Time* featured a core company of ten New York actors, including Orson Welles, all of whom imitated the most regular newsmakers. Art Carney regularly played the role of Franklin Delano Roosevelt, finely imitating his patrician accent. Ted de Corsia mastered the voices of Benito Mussolini and Pierre Laval; Agnes Moorehead and Jeanette Nolan imitated Eleanor Roosevelt; Dwight Weist did renditions of Adolf Hitler, Joseph Goebbels, William Randolph Hearst, and Father Charles Coughlin, among others" (ibid.).

62. Alan Brinkley, *The Publisher: Henry Luce and His American Century* (New York: Knopf, 2010), 183.

63. Ibid.

64. Robert Herzstein, *Henry R. Luce: A Political Portrait of the Man Who Created the American Century* (New York: Scribners, 1994), 117–18.

65. Largely center right, *March of Time* was, in the film reel world, flanked on the far right by the Hearst film shorts and on the left by the popular front.

66. C. Wright Mills, *White Collar: The American Middle Classes* (1951; repr., New York: Oxford, 2002), 149.

67. In *Time*'s first year of publication New York senator Franklin Delano Roosevelt had objected that the magazine had "made statements in regard to events which are not wholly fact." Luce was prone to writing of the "Roosevelt Depression." Herzstein, *Henry R. Luce*, 50, 88.

68. Ibid., 81.

69. Eigner Papers, Box 21, Folder 3, Stanford University. Joseph Eigner taught at Washington University in St. Louis; the letter is thanking him for sending Zukofsky's *Autobiography*. Interestingly, this instance is prefaced by "I too," suggesting that Joe may have been doing the same.

70. "Belated thanks (I'm really by now loafing and taking things easy 80–90% of the time) for that check from LA Weekly," Eigner writes, for instance, to Clayton Eshleman on December 30, 1984 (ibid., Box 9).

71. Letter to his sister-in-law, Janet Eigner, July 2, 1963 (ibid., Box 21).

72. On Luce's regime, see Robert Vanderlan, *Intellectuals Incorporated: Politics, Art,*

and Idea inside Henry Luce's Media Empire (Philadelphia: University of Pennsylvania Press, 2010).

73. Herzstein, *Henry R. Luce*, 128, 147.

74. Brinkley, *The Publisher*, 124.

75. Ibid., 131.

76. Herzstein, *Henry R. Luce*, 253.

77. "The opening passage of every issue was an account of the president's week, no matter how trivial his activities. Receiving tickets to a World Series game that the president had no intention of attending was as noteworthy as signing legislation. Accepting the honorary presidency of the Camp Fire Girls attracted as much attention as his consideration of American membership in the World Court" (ibid., 131).

78. Luce was in fact going to call it "We Americans" but was persuaded to change the title by John Shaw Billings (ibid., 179).

79. *Life Magazine*, February 17, 1941, 61.

80. Ibid.

81. Ibid.

82. Ibid., 63.

83. Robert Smithson, *Robert Smithson: The Collected Writings*, ed. Jack Flam (Berkeley: University of California Press, 1996), 37.

84. Clark Coolidge, whose own recording for the same series, *Polaroid*, was done September 24, 1974, wrote on October 15, 1974, to Eigner: "I went down to UConn a couple of weeks ago to read, & record for Michael Koehler's S. Press tape Editions, my long (100 minute) work, POLAROID. George Butterick was most pleasant & helpful to set up a small last minute sorta-'private' reading in the special collections room, where it felt a bit strange to keep stopping for reel-changes (that work has a certain momentum that's harder to sustain after any sort of break, I found), but went well enough I think.... Michael tells me he has recorded you as well for this series & I look forward to hearing you there. He seems to have done a fine job of gathering American poets (Creeley, Duncan, Snyder, etc.) for tape publication. Something no American has yet done to my knowledge (though there've been many attempts thru the years)." Eigner Papers, Box 8, Stanford University.

85. The recording can be heard on PennSound: http://writing.upenn.edu/pennsound/x/Eigner.php. Raphael Allison claims that "Eigner at the microphone performs a somatic immediacy that has been virtually scrubbed from this reception." *Bodies on the Line*, 152.

86. If one follows Charles Bernstein's line of argumentation about recorded poetry, perhaps the uncertainty we see here about where to locate interpretive authority was not a problem unique to Eigner but rather a more fundamental dilemma that attended any recorded voicing in relation to its would-be textual source: for Bernstein, again, it is not a matter of whose voicing should provide a measure or standard pacing, or even whether a single authorial voicing ought to serve as a model for later understandings of

a text; rather, it is the more fundamental question of whether readings should be heard as referring back to ontologically prior and in some sense determining texts.

87. As in many of Eigner's letters about recording, there is a great deal of attention to the recording and playback apparatus, to the physical situation of listening: "Kitchen table is round and just the right height etc. Didnt think of less favorable conditions. . . . It's to be kept on one table or another in a corner of the livingroom, fairly small the table, where it'll be pretty much at arms-length for me, it looks like." Letter to David and Maria Gitin, January 31, 1971 (EC). The tape recorder is always understood by Eigner as part of an architectural setting for daily activities—an interior landscape at once sonic and visual.

88. Just before this, Eigner writes: "This month the panasonic brother got for the folks (and myself) revived, ma . . . (at the last minute got me to try reciting Keep me still . . .—long experience with nerves I've had), and today Defense-Dep..t economist cousin came over to show them how to work it" (ibid.).

89. Similarly, Eigner suggests that when he can remember his own pronunciation at the time of composition—"sometimes it has come back to me"—this *ought* to be the final arbiter of how to recite the poems (ibid.).

90. As Eigner puts it in the same letter, "Only 2 complete poems, PARTS OF SALEM and 'Keep me still . . . ,' or only the first, really, when it comes to wholes (besides the 1st or 2 from. . . *Fragments*) have lain in my head over the yrs, so in looking back I'm doubtful myself how to say thngs" (ibid.).

91. Ibid.

92. He continues: "A first print this was, and a letter from Henny come ten days ago said they've improved the sound [again] some more as well as making subtitles more visible, something he said wd be done before the show started" (ibid.).

93. Eigner describes his own performance as follows: "Allen then I do 'Birthday' and before that (he at least) 'Open' from *On My Eyes*. I solo a longish one ('Whitman's cry at starvation'—see WORK #5), head down, partly as I recall from effort to see ts or maybe page in my lap, ok it seemed on 2nd viewing when I decided to figure it is, I was glad of the words anyway—" (ibid.).

94. As Eigner puts it, "A boner (big one, no doubt) is where Allen or somebody else . . . says I dictate to my mother and brother Joe who are the only people who can understand me, an error repeated in the catalogue description Henny flashed on me after supper here—so staying up till 2am I rewrote it, the enclosed, as I had 2 yrs ago done to his 1st draft, a revision accepted at the time, but which when I asked abut Aug 25 he said was too long" (EC).

Chapter 3

1. "Olson had to argue himself out of Washington, and out of the terms of Western history too," Robert von Hallberg suggests; "he wanted a clean slate, but needed an alibi for so broad an erasure—Truman sufficed." *Charles Olson: The Scholar's Art* (Cam-

bridge, MA: Harvard University Press, 1978), 6–7. Ross takes on, among other things, the cartographic dimensions of Olson's thought, claiming that what his "empiricist point of view ignores . . . is that it is just as surely the map itself, with its historically innovative representations of space, which makes the fact of space and the idea of expansionism possible. The map, then, *creates* our conventional space, which is why it is indeed the instrument of modern political internment." *The Failure of Modernism: Symptoms of American Poetry* (New York: Columbia University Press, 1986), 114. For Yépez, it is Olson's trip to and writings about Mexico that encode his imperialism. While Yépez takes aim at a wide range of Olsonian ideas (in at times a scattershot way not entirely unlike Maximus's own rantings), the baseline is the wry suggestion that "Olson's speculations about the Maya are repeatedly crude or brutal, worthy of any *surfer* or *marine* visiting Mexico as a tourist." *The Empire of Neomemory*, trans. Jen Hofer, Christian Nagler, and Brian Whitener (Oakland, CA: Chain Links, 2013), 125.

2. "As early as January of 1945," George Butterick explains, "shortly before [Olson] would abandon party politics and declare his independence in the poem 'The K,' itself a 'telegram' announcing his decision (written in Key West in February 1945, it was originally titled 'Telegram'), the groundwork for *Maximus* was laid." *A Guide to the Maximus Poems of Charles Olson* (Berkeley: University of California Press, 1978), xx, xxi.

3. Alan Gilbert notes this in his "Charles Olson and Empire, or Charles Olson Flips the Wartime Script," http://writing.upenn.edu/epc/authors/olson/blog/Olson_and_Empire.pdf,1. Tom Clark calls the pamphlet "a sophisticated manipulation of patriotic feeling that managed to convert sadness over great loss of life into a rousing call to arms." *Charles Olson: The Allegory of a Poet's Life* (New York: Norton, 1991), 79.

4. See Shaw, *Fieldworks*, chaps. 2, 4.

5. Daniel Belgrad, *The Culture of Spontaneity: Improvisation and the Arts in Postwar America* (Chicago: University of Chicago Press, 1998), 24.

6. Why Spanish speakers died in disproportionate numbers in Bataan was already a linguistic question. The army needed Spanish speakers to function in the Philippines: "Bataan was a National Guard tragedy. The first soldiers ready, they were the first to go. Unlike the regular army, the Guards were home town units, local soldiers, local leaders. The threat of war was too great to allow time to regroup them. They went to the Philippines as they were. The 200th and 515th Coast Artillery of New Mexico were sent because they could talk Spanish and above all because they were the crack anti-aircraft units the Filipino people needed. On April 9th, it was all over. The glory of Bataan is the nation's but the grief is in the homes of the small towns of America—from Harrodsburg, Kentucky to Salinas, California, on the faces of this New Mexican mother, these Kentucky parents. . . . New Mexico gave the fullest measure of devotion—one quarter of the 9000 men from the mainland lost." Charles Olson, *Spanish Speaking Americans in the War* (Washington, DC: Office of War Information, 1943), n.p.

7. On the history of Muzak and its inventor, Major General George Owen Squier, see Joseph Lanza, *Elevator Music: A Surreal History of Muzak, Easy-Listening and Other Moodsong* (New York: St. Martin's, 1994), 22–30.

8. This strategy of describing a problem that only one's own poetry can solve has a rather distinguished genealogy, including, among many others, the Wordsworth of "Lines Left upon a Seat in a Yew-Tree" and the Whitman of "American Vistas."

9. As historians of the discipline note, the status of the recordings themselves remained an issue. Among those early anthropologists using wax cylinder recordings for the Bureau of American Ethnology, for instance, the "records themselves were," as Erika Brady tells us, "valued only as a means to derive written transcriptions in phonetic orthography, English textual translations, or musical transcriptions in standard notation more easily from the collected material. It was these 'derived texts,' not the cylinders themselves, that represented the primary basis for descriptive and analytical work in folklore and anthropology." *A Spiral Way: How the Phonograph Changed Ethnography* (Jackson: University Press of Mississippi, 1999), 62. Brady's account of the sound anthropology of the 1890s gets further developed in Jonathan Sterne's now classic *The Audible Past: Cultural Origins of Sound Reproduction* (Durham, NC: Duke University Press, 2003). Less studied has been the sonic poetics of the midcentury group of ethnopoetic-oriented anthropologists and poets (including Dennis Tedlock, Jerome Rothenberg, and Nathaniel Tarn) that formed in conscious dialogue with Charles Olson, on the one hand, and emergent linguistic anthropology associated with figures like Dell Hymes, on the other.

10. In his study of the formation of area studies, for instance, Zachary Lockman quotes the 1963 speech from Harvard professor and national security adviser McGeorge Bundy cited earlier: "It is a curious fact of academic history that the first great center of area studies in the United States [the School of Advanced International Studies, SAIS] was not located in any university, but in Washington, during the Second World War, in the Office of Strategic Services. In very large measure the area study programs developed in American universities in the years after the war were manned, directed, or stimulated by graduates of the OSS—a remarkable institution, half cops-and-robbers half faculty meeting." *Field Notes: The Making of Middle Eastern Studies in the United States* (Stanford, CA: Stanford University Press, 2016), x. While Lockman grants, especially up to the late 1960s, the overlap between universities and intelligence-gathering agencies, he nonetheless suggests that it is "simplistic to depict area studies in the United States as in essence a product or servant of the national security state built during the Cold War" because, after the late 1960s, many academics in area studies departments became radicalized (ibid.).

11. David Price, *Anthropological Intelligence: The Deployment and Neglect of American Anthropology in the Second World War* (Durham, NC: Duke University Press, 2008), 55, 55–56, 56; see also Regna Darnell, *Invisible Genealogies: A History of Americanist Anthropology* (Lincoln: University of Nebraska Press, 2001).

12. Price, *Anthropological Intelligence*, 56.

13. Annegret Fauser, *Sounds of War: Music in the United States during World War II* (New York: Oxford University Press, 2013), 54, 18.

14. There had, in fact, been occasional points of contact between marching bands and avant-garde music: the sound of two such bands moving in opposite directions

had, Henry and Sidney Cowell tell us, provided "the germ of [Charles] Ives' complicated concept of polyphony." *Charles Ives and His Music* (1955; repr., New York: Oxford University Press, 1969), 144. Despite Schoenberg's explicit approval of Ives's music, the former's flustered "I guess" suggests that Ives's resources were considered aberrant and that ambitious composers would do well not to offer their services to military bands.

15. Certainly this enlistment happened among Axis musicians as well. As Alex Ross tells us, there is the example of Hindemith "attempting to regain the trust of the authorities, promising to write a work in honor of the Luftwaffe." *The Rest Is Noise: Listening to the Twentieth Century* (New York: FSG, 2007), 319.

16. Fauser, *Sounds of War*, 15.

17. Henry Cowell, "Shaping Music for Total War," in *Essential Cowell: Selected Writings on Music by Henry Cowell, 1921–1964*, ed. Dick Higgins (New York: McPherson, 2001), 307.

18. In other cases, entire departments simply began under the pressures of war: "[Stanford] university had hired its first anthropologist in 1943 to enable it to fulfill its contract with the army to train soldiers in language and area study." Lowen, *Creating the Cold War University*, 203.

19. Cowell, *Essential Cowell*, 307.

20. In the specific music context, see Fauser, *Sounds of War*; and Martin Iddon, *New Music at Darmstadt: Nono, Stockhausen, Cage, and Boulez* (Cambridge: Cambridge University Press, 2013).

21. On the radio work of the OWI, see, for instance, Blue, *Words at War*.

22. Rather than merely sell Coke, CBS was also broadcasting during the war two major radio programs that, under the direction of their commentator Deems Taylor, were in fact crucial to the war effort: *America Preferred* and the "intermission commentaries for the CBS broadcasts of the New York Philharmonic Orchestra." Fauser, *Sounds of War*, 69. It was on *America Preferred* that, as Fauser notes, a major debate between Taylor and Thomas Mann's daughter Erika was aired, with Erika Mann suggesting that Nazi sympathizers like Richard Strauss ought to be struck from musical programs, and Deems proposing that it was precisely by our ability to uncouple music from immediate politics, and associate it instead with a larger universal culture, that we demonstrated our superiority to the Nazis (70–73).

23. Miles writes: "In the total silence, broken only by the click of the fridge thermostat and our own voices, so clear and loud without traffic noise or transistor rock to hide and dull them. There was so much to say. On the first night we did nothing but talk. The Nagra remained in its travelling case. Charles must rank along with Wilde and Strachey as a great conversationalist." Charles Olson, *Charles Olson Reads from Maximus Poems IV, V, VI*, LP (New York: Folkways, 1975).

24. Letter from Miles to Olson, October 1, 1968 (OC). Miles concludes: "We could record you there or bring you here as you please. I naturally know your books very well and would be very very happy if you would like to be involved in this venture. It really is time that poetry got up off the page and into people's heads. If they can't attend a

reading then a record is the best way of reaching them—and far more of them" (OC, Box 177).

25. The countercultural flair of the series was important to Miles. After returning to London, he writes, for instance, to Olson on March 3, 1969: "I recorded an album with Charles Bukowski in Los Angeles using portable equipment as with you and did three albums in the studio in San Francisco: one with Lawrence Ferlinghetti using a lot of music, one with Michael McClure and Free Wheelin' Frank of the Hells Angels (McClure seeing himself very much as a pop star and singing such great numbers as 'Allen Ginsberg for President Waltz' and a few Blake songs, Frank did some fine Hells Angels poems) and an album with Richard Brautigan—Don Allen's best selling author (in fact Don reads a poem on the album and also does a duet with David Schaff)" (OC, Box 177).

26. Miles, liner notes, *Charles Olson Reads from Maximus IV, V, VI*.

27. Here is but one such account: "A couple of times in the spring of 1965 I found Olson in the café across from the main gates of the State University of New York at Buffalo, and asked him a few direct questions about the earlier *Maximus* poems. . . . After the second session, Olson leaned across the booth table, his eyes round in his glasses, and said, 'How would you like to be my scholar?'" Ralph Maud, *Charles Olson at the Harbor* (Vancouver, BC: Talonbooks, 2008), 206.

28. One of the best readings of this event is offered by Libbie Rifkin, who remarks that "Olson's performance wasn't entirely off the map"; instead, it was "predicated on the accumulation of a certain amount of social capital, both individual and collective" among the assembled poets. *Career Moves: Olson, Creeley, Zukofsky, Berrigan, and the American Avant-Garde* (Madison: University of Wisconsin Press, 2000), 23.

29. Ibid., 19.

30. For text, see the Zoe Brown transcription in *Reading at Berkeley* (San Francisco: Coyote, 1966), 15; in the recording, minute 53. The reading has been retranscribed by Ralph Maud for Charles Olson, *Muthologos: Lectures and Interviews* (Vancouver, BC: Talonbooks, 2010), but this passage remains unchanged.

31. A similar exchange occurred later in the reading as more listeners walked out: "Gee, we—You know this is what Socrates did, goddamn it! And this is why Plato became a writer. I hope you all go! I'll be left here alone, goddamn it, proving my point. That the establishment of the future society depends upon this kind of discourse." Olson, *Muthologos*, 40.

32. Watten, *Total Syntax*, 130. Other moments in the reading confirm the sense that this performance was imagined politically: "I mean I think this is a political occasion; from my point of view I am addressing a convention floor" (42:27); "And I wouldn't mind proving tonight that I belong where I have been—in Madison Square Garden . . . dig this" (44:06). The recording is available on PennSound: https://media.sas.upenn.edu/pennsound/authors/Olson/Olson-Charles_Complete-Recording_Intro-Robert-Duncan_UC-Berkeley_7-23-65.mp3.

33. Morris explains that the initial recording was made on a Wollensak reel-to-reel. One might have expected that this same device would then sit inside the actual box.

However, the device was placed inside the base on which the box rested. This displacement seems to have been result of 1961 reel-to-reel recorders not being small enough to fit inside the box Morris could build with one 4 × 8 sheet of walnut. For Morris, the amount of lumber he could carry in one trip was the dominant frame for the project. I thank Renee Brown of the Castelli Gallery and Robert Morris himself for answering my questions. Brown, e-mail to the author, September 14, 2017. At the Seattle Art Museum, where the piece now lives, this hiccup is solved by beaming the sound into a small speaker inside the box, which now rests on the ground.

34. For an excellent account of Ralph Ellison's pursuit of (and writing about) high-fidelity acoustics, see Alexander G. Weheliye, *Phonographies: Grooves in Sonic Afro-Modernity* (Durham, NC: Duke University Press, 2005), 106–44.

35. Douglas, *Listening In*, 266.

36. The countries mentioned include Greece, Italy, England, Spain, Germany, France, Ireland, Switzerland, Holland, Russia, Syria, Egypt, Lebanon, Turkey, Israel, Iran, Iraq, India, Japan, China, Mexico, Peru, Brazil, Sierra Leone, Tunisia, Mozambique, Uganda, Iceland, Sweden, Norway, Greenland, Jamaica, Haiti, Barbados, and the Dominican Republic.

37. Baraka writes of the mid-1950s: "Dylan Thomas was also very heavy in those days downtown. People passing through [Steve] Korret's house talked of 'Dylan.' One black poet there lilted some of Thomas' verses and then some of his own which were amazingly similar" (*AB*, 169).

38. For an account of Caedmon, see Jacob Smith, *Spoken Word: Postwar American Phonograph Cultures* (Berkeley: University of California Press, 2011).

39. Are listeners who hear this dimension just eliding the mediation that makes accent, too, a sign and not a natural reflection of place? Many sound theorists would argue yes. My argument here is not about the truth or falsity of this link between spoken language and location but merely about the believed perceptibility of the link.

40. Nor is it the case that the record was made to emphasize a kind of live, one-take quality. As Miles writes to Olson on May 7, 1969, "I have almost finished leading, editing and timing each track, editing out mistakes and repeats and choosing the best tracks of those poems that we did special versions of. I think its going to be a very good one" (OC).

41. On the first of these sonic frames—the space of a particular room—one thinks, for instance, of Alvin Lucier's 1969 *I Am Sitting in a Room*, in which a brief recording is played back and rerecorded until it breaks down into the sonic frequencies of the room in which it occurs.

42. Tedlock, *The Spoken Word*, 4. He continues: "Performance-oriented sociolinguists and folklorists call the mythographer away from a text-centered approach, urging that verbal art be studied in the contexts of its production, but if we come to think of everything that is fixed on a tape as our primary text, we need no longer feel torn between text and context" (ibid.).

43. Olson half apologizes for it in his brief introduction: "And it's very local in its

reference, but the point is that that not get in the way, as well as the enormous use of dates" (6:15). How on earth could that not get in the way? Or, we might ask, "in the way" of what? Aren't the names and the dates themselves very much "the way" here?

44. The fact that Olson reverses the dates in his last stanza, which reads "'set' by 1725, & living up through 1775" (*MP*, 322), seems to undermine the entire temporal scheme of his poem; still, this is not corrected.

45. In his 1962 lecture at Goddard College in Vermont, Olson responds to the question of whether he minds being tape-recorded: "No. As a matter of fact I'm going to just watch it like a fire—let's sit here and watch that tape [laughter]. What happens if it just goes on and I don't say anything? Who knows? See, that's the problem with reading, it gets to be kind of a bore, because it, it's become a performing art. You feel as though you have an audience and you're supposed to do a concert or something, and I don't think I believe in verse in this respect at all. As a matter of fact, I know I don't." *Charles Olson at Goddard College, April 12–14, 1962*, ed. Kyle Schlesinger (Victoria, TX: Cuneiform Press, 2011), 1. I thank John Melillo for bringing this to my attention.

46. Alan Gilbert sees this part of the archive as extending the project of *Spanish Speaking Americans*, which is that of disseminating "a New Deal agenda. . . . Given the pervasiveness of fascist sympathies Olson and fellow researchers found in US newspapers and even on US radio, it's not surprising that the OWI felt a need to propagandize the war effort in foreign language speaking communities in the original language of these communities." *Charles Olson and Empire*, 11. Gilbert is right, I think; but the research also perhaps worked to alert Olson to the dynamics of forming alternative social and political networks through publications.

47. Those five languages were at the head of the survey, since the United States had the most foreign-born citizens from those countries (using the 1930 census as its measure). Obviously the report was most concerned about citizens from Axis countries: at the time there were just under 2.2 million Germans and 1.8 million Italians. The graphs also measured circulation of the foreign-language papers: 530,000 for German papers, 516,000 for Italian. Olson's division also carefully reported on the foreign-language newspapers of the next sixteen most populous groups of foreign-born citizens in the United States, which were, in order, Swedish, French, Norwegian, Russian, Hungarian, Slovak, Czech, Greek, Danish, Lithuanian, Finnish, Portuguese, Serbo-Croat, Slovene, Japanese, and Ukrainian.

48. Other documents in Olson's OWI archive deal explicitly with foreign-language radio programs. A summary of a July 25, 1940, meeting of the representatives of such programs, for instance, notes the collective sentiment that "it would be helpful if stations . . . would explain to the public that the foreign language broadcasts are not foreign broadcasts, but are American broadcasts in a foreign language [necessary because] in many areas as much as two-thirds of the population . . . were born in a foreign country." Directors of these stations were urged to make "special efforts . . . to scrutinize [them] to see that they express only the highest ideals of Americanism" and that such programs had "a special trust to perform in the public service" (OC). Granted, this organization

has a financial stake in continuing these broadcasts. But it might nonetheless seem surprising that the Foreign Language Division would accommodate itself to such broadcasters, working to maintain foreign-language radio outlets at a moment when many perceived threats to national unity were violently suppressed. Perhaps the explanation is similar to the dynamic involved in Olson's *Spanish Speaking Americans in the War* pamphlet: the practical recognition that the presence of multiple languages among the American population necessitates sonic tuning *within* foreign languages rather than the attempt to shut them down and pretend that the United States could operate solely within English.

49. As Olson's archive suggests, the broad-lens sociological surveillance we encountered in James Angleton's reading of *Ramparts* was not simply a *new* mode of reading developed solely under the pressure of increasing information as the Bureau and the Agency began to monitor wider and wider swaths of the New Left. Rather, it seems to have been a well-established principle of government reading that, nonetheless, presented some problems for the New Critically trained Yale critics within the CIA, attached as they were to finer-grained analysis, pattern recognition, and monumental works of what I termed "monographic surveillance" that could be understood to develop only in relation to the increased importance of the truth value of testimony from single figures like Nosenko and Golitsyn. We might complicate the picture offered in Chapter 1 by seeing this literary surveillance mode not as the Agency's default orientation but as a midcentury, high Cold War mutation of what had been (and would become again) the dominantly historical and sociological model of reading associated both with the Bureau and the Agency, as it had been with the OWI during World War II.

50. Michael Denning, *The Cultural Front: The Laboring of American Culture in the Twentieth Century* (New York: Verso, 1996), 82.

51. The table of contents includes analysis of the following foreign nationality groups in the United States: Albanian, Arab, Armenian, Austrian, Belgian, Bulgarian, Carpatho-Russian, Czechoslovak, Danish, Dutch Estonian, Finnish, French, German, Greek, Hungarian, Icelandic, Irish, Italian, Latvian, Lithuanian, Norwegian, Polish, Portuguese, Rumanian, Russian, Spanish, Swedish, Ukrainian, Yugoslavian—all of European descent.

52. Ellery Sedgwick Jr., from a Catholic background, was apparently an exception, as in a way was F. O. Matthiessen (1902–50)—though neither had nearly as much power as Miller or Murdock, who was assistant dean of Harvard College from 1919 to 1924 and dean of the Faculty of Arts and Sciences from 1931 to 1936. The most famous of the group, Miller published works during Olson's time at Harvard, including *Orthodoxy in Massachusetts* (1933) and the first volume of *The New England Mind* (1939). Presumably Miller was already teaching Jonathan Edward by then, though his monograph on Edwards would not come out until 1949, four years before the second volume of *The New England Mind.* The main work of Murdock was on the Mather family: *Increase Mather: The Foremost American Puritan* (1925); *Selections from Cotton Mather* (1926); the Wigglesworth edition came out in 1929. Murdock also edited an edition of Michael

Wigglesworth's *The Day of Doom* and would publish *Literature and Theology in Colonial New England* (1949), as well as writings on Henry James.

53. See especially William Carlos Williams, *In the American Grain* (1925; repr., New York: New Directions, 1956).

54. In fact, as David Damrosch remembers, one easy critique (mounted often by intimidated students) was that de Man's French was poor, delivered as it was in a Belgian accent. "Head to Head or Tête-à-Tête? The (Un)translatability of World Literature," panel debate with Emily Apter, Modern Language Association, Austin, Texas, January 2016.

55. See especially Christine Mitchell, "Again the Air Conditioners: Finding Poetry in the Institutional Archive," *Amodern* 4, March 2015. http://amodern.net/article/again-air-conditioners/; and Camlot, "The Sound of Canadian Modernisms."

56. By 1946 "plastic disc player/recorders such as the SoundScriber (first advertised in the *Modern Language Journal* in October 1946) were in use at Yale University and other schools." Warren Roby, "Technology in the Service of Foreign Language Learning: The Case of the Language Laboratory," in *Handbook of Research on Education Communications and Technology*, ed. David Jonassen and Marcy Driscoll (Mahwah, NJ: Lawrence Erlbaum, 2004), 523–41.

57. The 1940–41 *Harvard President's Report* mentions a "Modern Language Center" in Harvard Union, in the appendix to the *Library Report*. Throughout the war it apparently had a hard time getting books from Europe, but by 1947–48 it is in full swing (adding 915 books). Some of our information comes from these reports, but there is also an article by Petter B. Taub in the *Harvard Crimson* (December 13, 1949) that describes the institution's move in 1946 to "Cannon House," the residence of a former professor that was given to the university. See http://www.thecrimson.com/article/1949/12/13/now-in-fourth-year-modern-language/. My thanks to Ross Mulcare and David Alworth of Harvard University for their help in unearthing this history.

58. De Man's later dissertation director, Harry Levin, was closely involved with the language center: in the 1947–48 *Harvard President's Report*, we find out that "the first lecture of the Cervantes IV Centenary series, *Cervantes and Melville*, by Harry T. Levin, Chairman of the Department of Comparative Literature at Harvard, was given at the Museum on October 23, under the auspices of the Modern Language Center" (314). Renato Poggioli, also on de Man's dissertation, was likewise close to the center, serving on its administrative committee.

59. On Kissinger's negotiations with de Gaulle, see Niall Ferguson, *Kissinger 1923–1968: The Idealist* (New York: Penguin, 2015), 718–19; subsequent references are cited parenthetically as *K*.

60. Stéphane Mallarmé, *Selected Poems*, ed. Mary Ann Caws, trans. Hubert Creekmore (New York: New Directions, 1982), 53. I select these lines because they appear in de Man's famous essay "Lyric and Modernity," in *Blindness and Insight: Essays in the Rhetoric of Contemporary Criticism* (Minneapolis: University of Minnesota Press, 1971), 175. On de Man's time at Harvard, two new sources are available: *The Paul de Man Note-*

books, ed. Martin McQuillan (Edinburgh: Edinburgh University Press, 2014; and *The Post-Romantic Predicament*, ed. Martin McQuillan (Edinburgh: Edinburgh University Press, 2012). The latter of these makes available much of the writing de Man did as a graduate student at Harvard, including extended treatments of Mallarmé. We learn in his 1960 essay "Mallarmé" that de Man understands the poet's work as structured around three primary texts: "Hérodiade," "Igitur," and, of course, "Un coup de dés." *The Post-Romantic Predicament*, 37. "The attempt to interpret Mallarmé primarily in terms of [this triad] (rather than in terms of more finished and 'successful' works such as 'L'après-midi d'un faune,' or 'Prose pour des Essintes' or 'Toast funèbre') is necessary and rewarding." This collection also includes "Stefan George and Stéphane Mallarmé," composed in 1952, while de Man was working for Kissinger, which is not quite as strict with its canon, although it is strict in its explanation of suffering, which de Man takes as fundamental to both poets. "One thing we can be sure of from the start: whatever the nature of this suffering may be, it originated in the poetic act itself. Extra aesthetic or sentimental perturbations were of no concern to them" (182).

61. Indeed, Kissinger eventually complained that his German no longer functioned as a language of statecraft: "Strange as it may seem . . . my vocabulary in German is not good enough to speak extemporaneously on a complicated subject. Because my secondary and higher education was in English, all my thinking on international and military affairs has been in English also. (I have a superb German vocabulary for soccer, if that should interest any audiences)" (*K*, 487).

62. Paul de Man, "Walter Benjamin's 'The Task of the Translator,'" in The *Resistance to Theory* (Minneapolis: University of Minnesota Press, 1986), 84. De Man continues: "The process of translation, if we can call it a process, is one of change and of motion that has the appearance of life, but of life as an afterlife, because translation also reveals the death of the original. Why is this? What are those death pangs, possibly birth pangs, of the original? It is easy to say to some extent what this suffering is not. It is certainly not subjective pains, some kind of pathos of a self, a kind of manifestation of a self-pathos which the poet would have expressed as his sufferings. This is certainly not the case, because, says Benjamin, the sufferings that are here being mentioned are not in any sense human" (85).

63. He had not yet begun writing his dissertation on Mallarmé and Yeats.

64. Among the articles de Man will translate are a string his posthumous critics might like to understand as reminders of the darker period of his early life from which he had recently emerged—Raymond Aron, "On Treason" (*Confluence* 3 [1954]); Erick Lueth, "The German Jews: A Problem in Political Morality" (1 [1954]); Jules Monnerot, "Intellectual Nihilism and the Crisis of Authority" (4 [1954]). Essays that seem more directly linked to the major concerns of his later years, though perhaps here pitched in a less rigorous, more journalistic mode, include Max Bense's "On the Language of Philosophy" (1 [1954]), and Julián Marías, "The Novel as a Means of Knowledge" (2 [1954]).

65. From Kissinger's end, the magazine could be traced in part to his work between 1950 and 1952, when he traveled extensively in Europe and Asia. He had been sent, for

instance, to Korea to study the "psychological impact" of American military occupation (*K*, 267); he had also been a consultant in Germany, discovering that the Germans in the West hated Americans even more than they hated the Soviets (*K*, 269–70). So *Confluence* was conceived, explicitly, in this context of American foreign relations, as an engine of what we call area studies—a magazine designed to intervene in public debate—primarily in Europe but gradually in Asia as well, to build an anticommunist consensus. Kissinger published Reinhold Niebuhr, André Malraux, Raymond Aron, Hannah Arendt, Ralph Ellison, Ernst Jünger, and Karl Jaspers—but also I. A. Richards, while John Crowe Ransom and later Allen Tate were on the advisory board.

66. Seeking to complicate the anti-Semitism above all reading of de Man's wartime journalism, Fredric Jameson, for instance, cites but seeks to distance de Man somewhat from wartime anticommunism: "The exclusive emphasis on anti-Semitism ignores and politically neutralizes its other constitutive feature in the Nazi period: namely, anticommunism. [The] very possibility of the Judeocide was absolutely at one with and inseparable from the anticommunist and radical right-wing mission of National Socialism. . . . But put this way, it seems at once clear that De Man was neither an anticommunist nor a right-winger." *Postmodernism, or, The Cultural Logic of Late Capitalism* (Durham, NC: Duke University Press, 1991), 256–57.

67. Rudolf Vogel, "Press and Radio in Germany," *Confluence* 1, no. 4 (1952): 15–23. Two providers of French summaries are listed (the other is Lee Van Horn), but the summaries are not individually credited.

68. Ibid., 15.

69. The technology was invented by Fritz Pfleumer in 1928, improved over the 1930s—in collaboration first with AEG (Allgemeine Elektricitäts-Gesellschaft) and then with IG Farben—and deployed throughout the war. See David Morton, *Off the Record: The Technological and Cultural History of Sound Recording in America* (New Brunswick, NJ: Rutgers University Press, 2000).

70. Vogel, "Press and Radio in Germany," 16, 18. While Vogel seems to be evoking a live master, there is debate about the extent to which the very RCA ad campaign that introduced that phrase was seeking to evoke "the persistence of the voices of the dead." As Jonathan Sterne points out about the initial ad, which used a dog named Nipper listening to the phonograph, "Many contemporaries who viewed that picture considered Nipper to be positioned on a coffin. Although RCA began cropping the picture higher and higher, eventually eliminating any clear detail about the surface on which the dog sits, the original picture remains at least ambiguous in this respect." *The Audible Past*, 302.

71. Vogel, "Press and Radio in Germany," 16–17. The fact that much Western European radio programming was musical makes this equation even more complex. There is a minor critical literature on the attempt at once to de-Nazify German music (no more Wagner, a lot of serialism via institutions like the Darmstadt International Summer Courses for New Music) and to keep it separate from Soviet musical regimes. While the full musical story is beyond my scope, I note that recent scholarship on postwar German musical programming has questioned some of the earlier, broad-brush claims

about American control of both airwaves and concert series. "In truth," Martin Iddon writes, "Frances Stonor Saunders's regularly cited claim that the courses [at the famous Darmstadt school] were 'a bold initiative of the American military government' is almost certainly without foundation, at least as far as the years before currency reform [1948] are concerned." *New Music at Darmstadt*, 19.

72. Thus, occupied Germany becomes a patchwork of conflicting broadcast fiefdoms; at first these operate more or less in proportion to the geographical parceling of the country. But after a radio allocation conference in Copenhagen that redistributes medium-wave frequencies, "none of the three Western Powers lived up to their obligation under international law as possessors of uncontested sovereignty in their respective zones of occupation. As a result, the Federal Republic lost most of the good broadcasting frequencies and pre-eminence in the medium-wave field passed to the Soviet zone" (*New Music at Darmstadt*, 17). While such dynamics would later reverse, what is important here is the widespread belief that regimes of broadcasting simply *produce* reflective political cultures.

73. Commenting on the *Ramparts* revelation of CIA funding, which would cycle back to CIA-funded radio projects like Radio Free Europe and Radio Liberty, Tim Weiner notes (in a way that suggests that, despite US claims about freedom, Vogel was not exactly wrong), "The radios were arguably the most influential political-warfare operations in the agency's history. The CIA had spent close to $400 million subsidizing them, and it had reason to believe that millions of listeners behind the iron curtain appreciated every word they broadcast. But their legitimacy was undercut when they were revealed as the CIA's frequencies." *Legacy of Ashes*, 271.

74. On Elliott, see Walter Isaacson, *Kissinger: A Biography* (New York: Simon and Schuster, 1992). Kissinger had actually taken an introduction to French course his first semester at Harvard in the fall 1947 (*K*, 227) and "continued to serve as a reserve CIC officer, which consumed a considerable amount of his vacation time" (*K*, 223).

75. See Louis D. Rubin Jr.'s introduction to the 1962 reprinting of *I'll Take My Stand: The South and the Agrarian Tradition, by Twelve Southerners* (New York: Harper, 1930).

76. Isaacson tells us that Elliott "won a Rhodes Scholarship, gloried in Oxford's tutorial system, and donned the mantle of athlete-poet-scholar [he had been an all-American tackle at Vanderbilt] with great majesty. At Harvard, he swung for the fences at departmental softball games, wrote and published florid poetry, and propounded philosophical notions with more fervor than reflection" (*Kissinger*, 62). "During his time at Balliol College," Ferguson adds, "Elliott mingled in literary circles with Robert Graves and W. B. Yeats" (*K*, 230).

77. As Ferguson puts it, "At times, Elliott's enthusiasm for all things British verged on self-parody, as in his radio lecture on 'The British Commonwealth Spirit.' He lobbied vainly for more than a decade to establish an American version of the 'Round Table' he had encountered as a Rhodes scholar at Balliol. He lamented the American decision not to back the United Kingdom during the Suez Crisis, arguing that Nasser had been the aggressor in nationalizing the canal company. Even in the late 1950s, Elliott was still hostile to Arab, Asian, and African nationalism, assuring Nixon that

colonial peoples were not yet ready for 'the responsibilities of modern statehood'" (*K*, 261).

78. This connection was still in place in the late 1960s and early 1970s. As Tim Weiner notes, "As a preemptive act of self-protection [with Nixon's entry into the White House in 1969, CIA director Richard] Helms had created a committee of Wise Men called the Covert Operations Study Group to report to the president-elect on the value of the clandestine service—and to protect it from attack. The group was led by Franklin Lindsay, once Frank Wisner's right-hand man, housed at Harvard, and convened in secret; its foremost members were Richard Bissell and Lyman Kirkpatrick. It included half a dozen Harvard professors who had served the White House, the Pentagon, the State Department, and the CIA. Three of them were close enough to their colleague Henry Kissinger to know he would be the next president's national security adviser no matter who won the race." *Legacy of Ashes*, 293.

79. The letter with the offer is from Walter I. Hughes, Outpost Personnel, and dated June 17, 1944 (OC).

80. "As early as 1950 . . . in a report to the Senate drawn up for the Office of Production Management," Elliott was, Ferguson tells us, "urging 'peacetime psychological warfare' as an alternative to military intervention" (*K*, 263).

81. From the beginning of *Confluence*, Elliott is listed as the director; Kissinger, the editor. While his fellow graduate students seem to have delighted in referring to him as "Henry Ass-Kissinger," it appears that Kissinger was in fact the driving force of both the magazine and the summer program, which operated as a kind of real-time and real-space analog to the discursive world built by *Confluence*. Hugh Wilford, *The Mighty Wurlitzer: How the CIA Played America* (Cambridge, MA: Harvard University Press, 2009), 124. In a scandal similar to the *Ramparts* revelation discussed in Chapter 1, so the Harvard Summer School's secret patron was also discovered in the late 1960s. Wilford notes, "In 1967, when the *New York Times* reported that Harvard had acknowledged receiving some $456,000 in disguised subsidies from the CIA between 1960 and 1966, of which $135,000 went to the foreign seminar, Kissinger explicitly denied having known the true source of the money" (127). Most historians do not believe Kissinger's claim to have been unaware that the CIA was funding his magazine.

82. To this end, Kissinger focused on countries whose position within the Cold War remained ambiguous or undetermined. Thus, Britain, Switzerland, and all of Scandinavia were excluded on the grounds that they had firmly established democratic cultures (*K*, 273). But among the people included, the list of those that went on to powerful careers was impressive: "Yasuhiro Nakasone of Japan in 1953, Valéry Giscard d'Estaing of France in 1954, Yigal Allon of Israel in 1957, Bülent Ecevit of Turkey in 1958, Leo Tindemans of Belgium in 1962, and Mahathir Bin Mohammad of Malaysia in 1968." Isaacson, *Kissinger*, 71.

83. On the later Yale school, see Marc Redfield's extremely insightful *Theory at Yale: The Strange Case of Deconstruction in America* (New York: Fordham University Press, 2016).

84. While Nixon is the US president most famous for taping his conversations, in fact he was preceded in this by Johnson, Kennedy, Eisenhower, Truman, and even FDR. Kennedy seems to have been the first to document his own illegal activities. As Tim Weiner explains, "On Monday, July 30, 1962, John F. Kennedy walked into the Oval Office and switched on the brand-new state-of-the-art taping system he had ordered installed over the weekend. The very first conversation he recorded was a plot to subvert the government of Brazil and oust its president, Joao Goulart." *Legacy of Ashes*, 189.

85. Certainly not all recordings were immediately transcribed—some involved low-priority concerns; others, illegal activities about which the White House did not want to multiply records. More surprisingly, however, quite a bit of presidential tape recording proved to be inaudible: the supposedly fool-proof and objective record promised by reel-to-reel recording turned out to contain artifactual gaps, hums, and inarticulate bodily noises that baffled transcribers—as was the case in the Kennedy tapes, where "the large majority of the tapes crackle, rumble, and hiss. Conversation is as hard to make out as on a factory floor or in a football stadium during a tight game." Ernest R. May and Philip D. Zelikow, eds., *The Kennedy Tapes: Inside the White House during the Cuban Missile Crisis* (Cambridge, MA: Harvard University Press, 1997), xii–xiii. Thus, "significant passages remained only partly comprehensible" despite the editors commissioning "a team of court reporters from the firm of Atlantic Transcriptions, Inc." and asking "an expert in audio forensics to improve the sound quality of most of the tapes" (xiii).

86. As Anthony Summers notes, "The way Edgar secured a man's allegiance, and by contrast silenced potential enemies, was ruthless. FBI agents were forever on the alert to record human failings. 'We had a general instruction,' said former senior agent Curtis Lynum, 'to record anything we might need in the future, in what we called a 'Zero file.''" "After Edgar's death, by one official count, the Bureau was holding 883 files on senators, 722 on congressmen. Some are still withheld, others have been shredded." *Official and Confidential*, 196, 197.

87. In a sense, this is similar to the Agency's and Bureau's taping of foreign diplomats and consulates, including friendly ones, without a prior suspicion about a particular conflict but instead with a curiosity about any potential conflict or useful piece of information. Such surveillance, I am suggesting, has a different, more complex, relation to the kind of research on subjects the state wants to neutralize.

88. Seymour Hersh, *The Price of Power: Kissinger in the Nixon White House* (New York: Summit, 1983), 16; subsequent references are cited parenthetically as *H*.

89. As Hersh explains, "Kissinger . . . kept his link to domestic intelligence through his excellent liaison with Hoover, and he was among the few non-CIA officials to receive full briefings on that agency's illegal domestic spying program. The program, known as Project Chaos, had been set up in 1967 under President Johnson, and it grew under Nixon and Kissinger." Kissinger was supplied "with a steady stream of highly classified reports on American radicals, many of them based on information from CIA agents who infiltrated dissident groups abroad and in the United States" (*H*, 209).

90. See Medsger, *The Burglary*.

91. Victor Marchetti and John D. Marks, *The CIA and the Cult of Intelligence* (New York: Dell, 1974). Beyond surveillance, Marchetti and Marks more fundamentally demonstrated state-sponsored violence against foreign governments and individuals. The book is also an amazing period demonstration of the aesthetics of redaction, since about a third of it is censored, and the authors *show* these omissions.

92. On the relation between this transitional moment in surveillance culture and its terrifying afterlife in which we all live, see especially Lloyd C. Gardner, *The War on Leakers: National Security and American Democracy, from Eugene V. Debs to Edward Snowden* (New York: New Press, 2016).

93. Kissinger, Hersh tells us, "apparently did not learn of the taping until May 1973, along with other senior members of the Watergate-besieged White House staff, and once again was outraged at someone else's successful use of his methods" (*H*, 316).

94. Sullivan, *The Bureau*, 218.

95. Ibid., 218–19.

96. Hunter S. Thompson, *The Great Shark Hunt* (New York: Warner, 1979), 338.

97. Hayden White, e-mail to the author, April 24, 2017.

98. In 1972, White had coauthored two books (both with Willson Coates, the first also with J. Salwin Schapiro): *The Emergence of Liberal Humanism in Western Europe: From the Italian Renaissance to the French Revolution* and *The Ordeal of Liberal Humanism: An Intellectual History of Western Europe* (New York: McGraw Hill, 1966 and 1970); edited or coedited two collections: *The Uses of History: Essays in Intellectual and Social History* (Detroit, MI: Wayne State University Press, 1970), and *Giambattista Vico: An International Symposium* (Baltimore: Johns Hopkins University Press, 1969); and finished the manuscript of another monograph, *The Greco-Roman Tradition*, which, together with *Metahistory*, would also appear in 1973.

99. Hayden White, "The Burden of History," *History and Theory* 5, no. 2 (1966): 111–34. I am quoting from the essay as reprinted in *Tropics of Discourse: Essays in Cultural Criticism* (Baltimore: Johns Hopkins University Press, 1978), 29. While *Tropics of Discourse* would not come out until 1978 (and White's equally influential *The Content of the Form* would not be published until 1987), key essays from both collections were composed quite a bit earlier, stretching well back into the 1970s and even, as in the case of "The Burden of History," the 1960s.

100. In "The Value of Narrativity in the Representation of Reality," an essay first published in *Critical Inquiry* in 1980 and presumably in draft in the late 1970s, White wrote: "Historians do not *have* to report their truths about the real world in narrative form. They may choose other, nonnarrative, even antinarrative, modes of representation, such as the meditation, the anatomy, or the epitome." This essay was reprinted in *The Content of the Form: Narrative Discourse and Historical Representation* (Baltimore: Johns Hopkins University Press, 1987), 2.

101. Apparently the LAPD did not feel it necessary for the student to register for White's class under an assumed name. White remembers that the student in question earned a B in the class at a time when that was a good grade.

102. Hayden White, e-mail to the author, April 24, 2017.

103. Ibid.

104. White, *Content of the Form*, 13.

105. As White puts it, "Well, I am not so sure it was a win; the Court ruled only that we had standing to bring a case of misuse of taxpayers' funds for an activity by the police that could have a chilling effect on free speech. The LAPD continued to do this kind of work, as did the FBI and now that the Patriot Act has been installed, God knows how many other agencies are involved in it (166 agencies in Homeland Security?)." E-mail to author, April 24, 2017.

106. White, *Tropics of Discourse*, 60.

107. Ibid., 54. Unlike narratives, plots for White are limited. As he put it in "Interpretation and History" (echoing the themes of *Metahistory*), "What the historian must bring to his consideration of the record are general notions of the *kinds of stories* that might be found there" (60).

108. White, *Content of the Form*, 20. "Needless to say," as White puts it, he did not attack the officer. And yet, as White's scholarship suggests, two versions of this event were in play, and there was in this sense a very basic need for him to speak up: whatever people who know White or read his work may assume about the gentlemanly, mild-mannered metahistorian, the very fact that Chief Davis could appear on television brandishing a ripped officer's jacket, supposedly the relic of White's assault on an officer, suggests that it was in fact necessary for White to undo the work of Davis's narrative before White could successfully persuade his readers and listeners of his version of the event.

109. Ibid., 13.

110. Let me give White the last word. After my e-mail correspondence with him, I called him and conducted a forty-minute follow-up phone interview on May 16, 2017. Extremely genial, he concluded, nonetheless: "I don't trust interviews; even when you have recording equipment [which I did not]. Because (I'm a Derridean on this) once you start writing you get swept up in it, carried along, and you begin to bend the evidence."

111. The original link on the National Security Archives site, http://nsarchive2. gwu.edu/NSAEBB/NSAEBB123/index.htm, has been removed, but most of the transcript is available at the Allen Ginsberg Project: http://allenginsberg.org/2009/02/kissinger-tapes/.

112. Antiwar activists Rennie Davis (b. 1941) and David Dellinger (1915–2004); African American civil rights and antiwar activist Ralph Abernathy (1926–90), who rose to prominence especially after the assassination of Martin Luther King Jr. in 1968.

113. Paul de Man, "Literary History and Literary Modernity," in de Man, *Blindness and Insight*, 152.

Chapter 4

1. Scott's grandson, Peter Dale Scott (b. 1929), could himself be a figure in this book:

he is both a poet and a historian of the secret state, or as he calls it, "deep state" (with separate books on the CIA's relation to the mafia, the JFK assassination, and the American war machine, among others).

2. Creeley, *A Quick Graph*, 227–28.

3. Ibid., 228.

4. "Writers who have collaborated with Schafer include Robin Blaser, bpNichol, Steve McCaffery, Paul Dutton, Brian Fawcett, The Horsemen and Owen Sound." Steve McCaffrey, with bpNicholl, introduction to "R. Murray Schafer: A Collection," special issue, *Open Letter*, 4th ser. (1979): 5.

5. Of this larger project, Lisa Robertson writes (in the context of her own sonic fieldwork in Paris): "They were botanists of the sensorium, intrepidly combing deepest Europe for fugitive samples of a lapsed authenticity to bring home to the new world's universities and studios. I follow them with combined gratitude and disbelief." *Nilling: Prose Essays on Noise, Pornography, the Codex, Melancholy, Lucretius, Folds, Cities and Related Aporias* (Toronto: Book Thug, 2012), 68.

6. American sound artist Bernie Krause provides perhaps a parallel origin. His works from the late 1960s on (especially the 1970 LP *In a Wild Sanctuary*, with Paul Beaver) were also fundamental to the formation of sound studies; his work is also devoted more directly and entirely to the sounds nature makes without humans. During this period, however, Krause did not popularize and extend his project through theoretical writings, radio programs, and university research projects the way Schafer did. On his work, see *Into a Wild Sanctuary: A Life in Music and Natural Sound* (Berkeley, CA: Heyday, 1998); and *The Great Animal Orchestra: Finding the Origins of Music in the World's Wild Places* (New York: Little, Brown, 2012).

7. Schafer, "Radical Radio," 144.

8. Unlike most other community soundmarks, the Vancouver air horns are deemed oppressive when heard nearby and seem to require a safe distance. These horns, which played the first three notes of the Canadian national anthem, were added to celebrate the country's centennial in 1967. Schafer records them close up to demonstrate their "ear-splitting" effect on the downtown, "three blocks from the public library," and then moves his recording point two miles away to demonstrate how much better they sound at this distance.

9. R. Murray Schafer, Howard Broomfield, Bruce Davis, Peter Huse, Barry Truax, and Adam Woog, *Soundscapes of Canada*, 1974 (my transcription).

10. Branden Joseph, "Interview with Paolo Virno," trans. Alessia Ricciardi, *Grey Room*, no. 21 (Fall 2005): 33.

11. David Grubbs, *Records Ruin the Landscape: John Cage, the Sixties, and Sound Recording* (Durham, NC: Duke University Press, 2014), 80.

12. Like "The Search for Petula Clark," this essay was first published in *High Fidelity*. I am quoting from *The Glenn Gould Reader*, ed. Tim Page (New York: Knopf, 1984), 300; subsequent references are cited parenthetically as *GG*.

13. See Kevin Bazzana, *Wondrous Strange: The Life and Art of Glenn Gould* (New York: Oxford University Press, 2004), 292.

14. I thank J. D. Connor for turning me on to Gould's prose and Lisa Robertson for pointing me toward Gould's sound documentaries.

15. John Szwed, *Alan Lomax: The Man Who Recorded the World* (New York: Penguin, 2010), 127.

16. See Otto Friedrich, *Glenn Gould: A Life and Variations* (Toronto: Lester and Orpen Dennys, 1990), 179–80.

17. Glenn Gould, *The Idea of North* (my transcription).

18. Jones, *How I Became Hettie Jones*, 47.

19. William S. Burroughs's family business, the Burroughs Corporation, was in charge of linking information from the radar stations to the central computers within SAGE; IBM oversaw the system as a whole. Computerization was necessary not merely to convert the radar feeds into a blinking image; it was also crucial in synthesizing information from different radar sources: mobile ships and planes, fixed ground installations, and offshore platforms. Once all of this information was collected, actual threats then had to be distinguished from the enormous volume of "friendly" air traffic.

20. However odd it is that the strategic idea of north does not enter into Gould's sound documentary, however much he may have succumbed to Canadian nationalist ideas of autonomy, there is no question that Gould was uniquely positioned to understand some of the key dynamics of the Cold War. At almost the exact moment of the Dew Line's completion, in 1957, Gould was the first major Western musician to tour the Soviet Union. Friedrich, *Glenn Gould*, 62. He visited both Moscow and Leningrad in the spring of 1957, where Gould's beloved Bach was at the time largely off limits because of his association with theology. Gould also introduced Russian audiences (especially students at the Moscow conservatory) to modernist composers, including Alban Berg, Arnold Schoenberg, Anton Webern, and Ernst Krenek. He played the first for the concert and the latter three for the students (64). As risky as the trip itself and Gould's musical selections were, the virtuoso pianist had, before entering Soviet airspace, checked with his southern neighbor to be sure that this trip to the other side of the Cold War would not bar him from further concerts in the United States.

21. The University of Connecticut Eigner Archives contain three 1959 and 1960 letters from Jones to Baraka.

22. In his essay "Cuba Libre," Jones mentions that he left New York on July 20. In Amiri Baraka, *Home: Social Essays* (Hopewell, NJ: Ecco, 1998), 13.

23. Jones refers to the trip in a letter to Eigner: "Am on my vacation now . . . sitting and drinking too much, &c. Wife & I off to Cuba, 19th of July at the invitation of *Lunes de Revolucion* (official literary mag there). I'll ask Castro some straight questions (It's ok, I've got a beard, he won't, I hope, shoot me . . . but one never knows . . . do one??)." In another letter he refers to the Allen anthology: "Anyway, D Allen seems to be getting his anty just about in shape, . . . & I really believe Jan or Feb shd see its debut. (we all hope!) (EC).

24. "So: it stands: I'll get back probably in January for Jan 1 celebraccion. How long, &c. I have no idea. And, of course, complexion of Cuba-Us relations will have alot to do with final disposition of trip. They cd stop us. (As the embassy folks called as soon as we got into Habana and sd we ought to 'drop by.' Of course I didn't." Jones to Olson, November 1960 (OC, Box 165).

25. Ibid. He continues: "Got to talk to Fidel . . . who is beautiful & I'm sure true. Ditto Che Guevarra [*sic*], who is genuine cowpoke, & quiet voice like Gary Cooper. A.G. & I invited back next month for some knd of writers conference. Sartre coming back, also DeBeauvoir, Neruda, Robbe-Grillet, &c., . . . I asked them to send you an invitation . . . tho I didn't know if you'd be able to go &c. but you shd hear from them" (ibid.).

26. Ibid.

27. LeRoi Jones to Larry Eigner, 1959 (no month or day) (EC).

28. Gloucester's Charles Olson, after all, both began the anthology and was given the most pages. "There's small chance that Sorrentino Oppenheimer & I might be going up to see Chas this wkend," Jones writes to Eigner; "if so we'll drop by yr place . . . OK??" Though that weekend ultimately did not work out, it is possible LeRoi Jones did visit Larry Eigner in Swampscott (EC).

29. There he joined the 73rd Strategic Reconnaissance Squadron, later called the 73rd Bombardment Squadron, which seems to have been absorbed into the more famous 72nd. The poet was part of the "'Ready' crew, which meant we were among the actual strike force of any bombing mission" (*AB*, 170).

30. Alas, at the time Baraka was in the military the SAC command control center had not yet been sunk in its granite bunker and existed in a less dramatic aboveground location in Colorado Springs. Its new home, the Cheyenne Mountain Complex, would be fully operational in 1967, the year of Gould's trip north.

31. Baraka continues: "Sometimes we took off and came right back. Sometimes we'd go and land somewhere else and stay a few days. Sometimes we'd go right back to the barracks. And I was the only guy on my crew with the big awkward .45 automatic and a shoulder holster. Putting a parachute on over that getup was painful and dangerous. The rest of the crew had .38s, small and compact and buckled on at the waist" (*AB*, 171).

32. About the specific bombers, Baraka notes: "Those planes (B-36s) were not comfortable like commercial airliners. They were cold and drafty. Colder than air conditioning! An hour or so out, my nose would start running. I'd have on my flight jacket, but the whole flight I'd be freezing to death. My feet felt like ice cubes" (ibid.).

33. See, for instance, the bureaucratized apocalypse theorized in Herman Kahn's *On Thermonuclear War* (Princeton, NJ: Princeton University Press, 1960). Kahn jettisons "not particularly illuminating" terms like "intolerable," "catastrophic," and "total destruction" (ix)—for specialists' recent calculations in which only a quarter to half of the US population gets wiped out in a Soviet nuclear strike. I read Kahn in relation to 1960s artists, especially Smithson, in Lytle Shaw, "The Utopian Past," in *The Present Tense through the Ages: On the Recent Work of Gerard Byrne* (Cologne: Koenig Books,

2007). Another theorist (and advocate) of manageable nuclear war was Henry Kissinger, especially in his 1957 book *Nuclear Weapons and Foreign Policy* (New York: Harper, 1957).

34. I take the qualification "(but not mechanical)" to modify the happening, not the means of listening: that is, while the happening is not mechanical, the listening is.

35. Malcolm X died on February 21. The reading was in connection with a symposium on his book *Blues People*. He also read "Western Front," with its attack on Ginsberg, and "Ghosts," with its potential aerial bombardment images.

36. This recording is available on PennSound's Amiri Baraka page: http://writing.upenn.edu/pennsound/x/Baraka.php.

37. Amiri Baraka, *Black Magic: Sabotage, Target Study, Black Art—Poetry 1961–1967* (Indianapolis: Bobbs-Merrill, 1969), 10. The poem begins: "They now gonna make us shut up" before the second stanza continues: "They now gonna line you up, ask you about God. Nail / your answers on the wall, for the bowling alley owners / to decide" (ibid.).

38. Ibid., 116.

39. The musicians are Sonny Murray, percussion; Albert Ayler, tenor saxophone; Don Cherry, trumpet; Henry Grimes and Louis Worrell, bass. Baraka wrote the liner notes, which also appear in *Black Music*.

40. Amiri Baraka and Sun Ra, *A Black Mass*, LP (Newark, NJ: Jihad, 1968); Amiri Baraka, *It's Nation Time*, LP (Newark, NJ: Jihad, 1972).

41. This LP was recorded at Astral Recording Studios, Inc., in Harlem. It was engineered by Luis Gonzales and produced by Woodie King. About thirty musicians play on the record.

42. Baraka FBI File.

43. In comparison to its printed form in the pamphlet put out by Third World Press in 1970, where it appears as the last of three poems (after "The Nation Is Like Ourselves" and "Sermon for Our Maturity"), the recording adds verses.

44. Amiri Baraka and Fundi, *In Our Terribleness (some elements and meaning in black style)* (Indianapolis, IN: Bobbs Merrill, 1970), n.p. I am quoting from the book to register how Baraka scores the words on the page but have checked that the poem as printed also functions as a reliable transcription of the recording.

45. Side one's last song, "Wha's Gonna Happen," answers its call with "land's gonna change hands."

46. I note in passing that Baraka's *The System of Dante's Hell* (New York: Grove, 1965) might also be read in relation to this question of the sound of "hell's actual voice."

47. The critical literature on Coltrane, like that on Baraka's music writing, is vast. Here I will less do justice to either than attempt to make a more limited, but I hope surprising, point about Coltrane's function for Baraka.

48. This dynamic is comparable to the one Fred Moten tracks in his extremely rich analysis of Baraka's 1966 essay "The Burton Greene Affair," where the desire for a return to an African cultural/musical/ontological tradition arguably goes through Heideggerian ontology and nationalism. Moten then links this perhaps unexpected German mo-

ment to the name Johannes Koenig (which Baraka used in some music criticism in the early 1960s) as a third (often ignored) phase in the transformational itinerary claimed in the self-renaming from LeRoi Jones to Amiri Baraka. As Moten puts it, "The transition from LeRoi Jones to Johannes Koenig to Amiri Baraka . . . marks, would bridge [a] cut; but just like the way home seems to go through Germany, like the way back to the ground of metaphysics is a middle passage, like the way back to Afro-spirit is through *Geist* and *anima* in spite of the invocations of the east, the way back to Euro-spirit is scored with the boom of an other rhythm." *In the Break: The Aesthetics of the Black Radical Tradition* (Minneapolis: University of Minnesota Press, 2003), 138.

49. As Baraka says of another song on the record, also linked in 1961—in this case more directly—with dominant and oppressive values that were stifling the nascent civil rights movement, "I didn't realize until now what a beautiful word *Alabama* is. That is one function of art, to reveal beauty, common or uncommon, uncommonly. And that's what Trane does" (*BM*, 66).

50. Ibid., 225.

51. Jones, *How I Became Hettie Jones*, 143–44.

52. William S. Burroughs, *Roosevelt after Inauguration* (San Francisco: City Lights, 1979), 16–17. One wonders what Charles Olson, a Roosevelt appointee, thought of this piece. We know, however, that Ed Dorn wrote directly and repeatedly to Jones about his objections to Burroughs's writing as he encountered it in *The Floating Bear*, pronouncing it politically suspect, in thrall to the existing forms of power.

53. Frank O'Hara, *Standing Still and Walking in New York*, ed. Donald Allen (San Francisco: Grey Fox, 1983), 157.

54. "All communities larger than primordial villages of face-to-face contact (and perhaps even these) are imagined," says Benedict Anderson in his classic book, *Imagined Communities: Reflections on the Origin and Spread of Nationalism* (New York: Verso, 1991), 6. "Communities," he continues, "are to be distinguished, not by their falsity/generousness, but by the style in which they are imagined." Anderson also stresses temporal displacements as a key feature of this process: "If nation-states are widely conceded to be 'new' and 'historical,' the nations to which they give political expression always loom out of an immemorial past, and, still more important, glide into a limitless future" (11–12).

55. *Soundscapes of Canada*, episode 8.

56. While Canada operates for Schafer as the immediate and pressing context in which new forms of listening must be explored, and the *Soundscapes of Canada* project becomes the exemplary training exercise in which this activity is undertaken, it is not accidental that this exploration was conceived from the start as part of a World Soundscape Project. The goal seems to have been to begin locally and then use the methods established to expand the frame geographically.

Bibliography

Allen, Donald, ed. *The New American Poetry, 1945–1960*. New York: Grove, 1960.

Allison, Raphael. *Bodies on the Line: Performance and the Sixties Poetry Reading*. Iowa City: University of Iowa Press, 2014.

Anderson, Benedict. *Imagined Communities: Reflections on the Origin and Spread of Nationalism*. New York: Verso, 1991.

Angleton, James Jesus, and Reed Whittemore, eds. *Furioso*. New Haven, CT: Furioso Press, 1939–53.

Baraka, Amiri [LeRoi Jones]. *Amiri Baraka and Edward Dorn: The Collected Letters*. Edited by Claudia Moreno Pisano. Albuquerque: University of New Mexico Press, 2013.

———. *The Autobiography of LeRoi Jones/Amiri Baraka*. Chicago: Lawrence Hill Books, 1997.

———. *Black Magic: Sabotage, Target Study, Black Art—1961–1967*. Indianapolis, IN: Bobbs-Merrill, 1969.

———. *Black Music*. New York: William Morrow, 1968.

———. *Home: Social Essays*. 1966. Reprint, Hopewell, NJ: Ecco, 1998.

———. *It's Nation Time*. Chapbook. Chicago: Third World Press, 1970.

———. *It's Nation Time*. LP. Newark, NJ: Jihad, 1972.

———. *The System of Dante's Hell*. New York: Grove, 1965.

Baraka, Amiri, and Fundi. *In Our Terribleness (some elements and meaning in black style)*. Indianapolis, IN: Bobbs-Merrill, 1970.

Baraka, Amiri, and Sun Ra. *A Black Mass*. LP. Newark, NJ: Jihad, 1968.

Bazzana, Kevin. *Wondrous Strange: The Life and Art of Glenn Gould*. New York: Oxford University Press, 2004.

Becker, Carl. *Everyman His Own Historian: Essays on History and Politics*. New York: F. S. Crofts, 1935.

Beckett, Samuel. *Three Novels: Molloy, Malone Dies, The Unnamable*. New York: Grove Press, 1991.

Belgrad, Daniel. *The Culture of Spontaneity: Improvisation and the Arts in Postwar America*. Chicago: University of Chicago Press, 1998.

Benveniste, Émile. *Problems in General Linguistics.* Translated by Mary Elizabeth Meek. Coral Gables, FL: University of Miami Press, 1971.

Bernstein, Charles, ed. *Close Listening: Poetry and the Performed Word.* New York: Oxford University Press, 1998.

Berrigan, Ted. *The Sonnets.* 1964. Reprint, New York: Grove, 1967.

Beschloss, Michael R., ed. *Taking Charge: The Johnson White House Tapes, 1963–1964.* New York: Simon and Schuster, 1997.

Blue, Howard. *Words at War: World War II Era Radio Drama and the Postwar Broadcasting Industry Blacklist.* Lanham, MD: Scarecrow Press, 2002.

Brady, Andrea. "Poetry and Bondage." Manuscript in progress.

Brady, Erika. *A Spiral Way: How the Phonograph Changed Ethnography.* Jackson: University Press of Mississippi, 1999.

Brecht, Bertolt. *Brecht on Theatre: The Development of an Aesthetic.* Edited and translated by John Willett. New York: Hill and Wang, 1992.

Brinkley, Alan. *The Publisher: Henry Luce and His American Century.* New York: Knopf, 2010.

Burckhardt, Jacob. *The Civilization of the Renaissance in Italy.* Translated by S. G. C. Middlemore. Introduction by Peter Burke. 1860. Reprint, New York: Penguin, 1990.

Burroughs, William S. *Electronic Revolution.* 1971. Reprint, Bonn, Germany: Expanded Media, 1998.

——. *Roosevelt after Inauguration.* 1965. Reprint, San Francisco: City Lights, 1979.

——. *The Ticket That Exploded.* New York: Grove Press, 1967.

Burroughs, William, and Brion Gysin. *The Third Mind.* New York: Seaver, 1978.

Butterick, George. *A Guide to the Maximus Poems of Charles Olson.* Berkeley: University of California Press, 1978.

Cage, John. *Silence: Lectures and Writings by John Cage.* 1961. Reprint, Middletown, CT: Wesleyan University Press, 1973.

Camlot, Jason. "The Sound of Canadian Modernisms: The Sir George Williams University Poetry Series, 1966–74." *Journal of Canadian Studies* 46, no. 3 (2012): 28–59.

Clark, Tom. *Charles Olson: The Allegory of a Poet's Life.* New York: Norton, 1991.

Clifford, James, and George Marcus, eds. *Writing Culture: The Poetics and Politics of Ethnography.* Berkeley: University of California Press, 1986.

Coltrane, John. *My Favorite Things.* LP. New York: Atlantic, 1961.

Connor, J. D. "Icon, Index, Transcript: Lessons from Louis Armstrong and the Oral History Association." Paper presented to the Modern Language Association, Austin, Texas, January 2016.

Contemporary Authors Autobiography Series, vol. 23. *Larry Eigner.* Detroit, MI: Gale, 1996.

Conway, Flor, and Jim Siegelman. *Dark Hero of the Information Age: In Search of Norbert Wiener, the Father of Cybernetics.* New York: Basic Books, 2005.

Coolidge, Clark. *Now It's Jazz: Writing on Kerouac and the Sounds.* Albuquerque, NM: Living Batch Press, 1999.

Cowell, Henry. *Essential Cowell: Selected Writings on Music, 1921–1964.* Edited by Dick Higgins. Kingston, NY: McPherson, 2001.

Cowell, Henry, and Sidney Cowell. *Charles Ives and His Music.* 1955. Reprint, New York: Oxford University Press, 1969.

Creeley, Robert. *A Quick Graph: Collected Notes & Essays.* Edited by Donald Allen. San Francisco: Four Seasons, 1970.

Critchfield, James. *Partners at Creation: The Men behind Postwar Germany's Defense and Intelligence Establishments.* Annapolis, MD: US Naval Institute Press, 2003.

Cunningham, David. *There's Something Happening Here: The New Left, the Klan, and FBI Counterintelligence.* Berkeley: University of California Press, 2004.

Damrosch, David. "Head to Head or Tête-à-Tête? The (Un)translatability of World Literature." Panel debate with Emily Apter, Modern Language Association, Austin, Texas, January 2016.

Daniel, Eric D., ed. *Magnetic Recording: The First 100 Years.* New York: IEEE Press, 1999.

Darnell, Regna. *Invisible Genealogies: A History of Americanist Anthropology.* Lincoln: University of Nebraska Press, 2001.

Davidson, Michael. *Concerto for the Left Hand: Disability and the Defamiliar Body.* Ann Arbor: University of Michigan Press, 2008.

———. *Ghostlier Demarcations: Modern Poetry and the Material Word.* Berkeley: University of California Press, 1997.

Davies, Alan, and Richard Dillion. "One into Zero Goes Zero Times." Review of *Anything on Its Side,* by Larry Eigner. *Chicago Review* 26, no. 3 (1974). 188–91.

De Man, Paul. *Blindness and Insight: Essays in the Rhetoric of Contemporary Criticism.* Minneapolis: University of Minnesota Press, 1971.

———. *The Paul de Man Notebooks.* Edited by Martin McQuillan. Edinburgh: Edinburgh University Press, 2014.

———. *The Post-Romantic Predicament.* Edited by Martin McQuillan. Edinburgh: Edinburgh University Press, 2012.

———. *The Resistance to Theory.* Minneapolis: University of Minnesota Press, 1986.

Denning, Michael. *The Cultural Front: The Laboring of American Culture in the Twentieth Century.* New York: Verso, 1996.

Diderot, Denis. *Diderot on Art.* Vol. 1, *The Salon of 1765 and Notes on Painting.* Translated by John Goodman. New Haven, CT: Yale University Press, 1995.

Dohoney, Ryan. "The Anxiety of Art: Morton Feldman's Modernism, 1948–1972." PhD diss., Columbia University, 2009.

Donner, Frank J. *The Age of Surveillance: The Aims and Methods of America's Political Intelligence System.* New York: Knopf, 1980.

Douglas, Susan. *Listening In: Radio and the American Imagination.* Minneapolis: University of Minnesota Press, 2004.

Eigner, Larry. *Another Time in Fragments.* London: Fulcrum, 1967.

———. *areas / lights / heights: Writings 1954–1989*. Edited by Ben Friedlander. New York: Roof, 1989.

———. *around new / sound daily / means*. Audiocassette. Dusseldorf, Germany: S Press, 1975.

———. *The Collected Poems of Larry Eigner*. Edited by Curtis Faville and Robert Grenier. 4 vols. Stanford, CA: Stanford University Press, 2010.

———. *Country / Harbor / Quiet / Act / Around*. Edited by Barrett Watten. Berkeley, CA: This, 1978.

———. *Flat and Round*. Berkeley, CA: Tuumba, 1980.

Eigner, Larry, and Harry Callahan. *On My Eyes*. Highlands, NC: Jonathan Williams, 1960.

Fauser, Annegret. *Sounds of War: Music in the United States during World War II*. New York: Oxford University Press, 2013.

Feldman, Morton. *Give My Regards to Eighth Street: Collected Writings of Morton Feldman*. Edited by B. H. Friedman. Cambridge, MA: Exact Change, 2000.

Ferguson, Niall. *Kissinger 1923–1968: The Idealist*. New York: Penguin, 2015.

Forrest, Seth. "The Body of the Text: Cerebral Palsy, Projective Verse and Prosthetics in Larry Eigner's Poetry." *Jacket* 36, 2008. http://jacketmagazine.com/36/forrest-eigner.shtml.

Friedländer, Max J. *Landscape, Portrait, Still-Life*. New York: Philosophical Library, n.d.

Friedrich, Otto. *Glenn Gould: A Life and Variations*. Toronto: Lester and Orpen Dennys, 1990.

Galison, Peter. "The Ontology of the Enemy: Norbert Wiener and the Cybernetic Vision." *Critical Inquiry* 21 (1994): 228–66.

Gardner, Lloyd C. *The War on Leakers: National Security and American Democracy from Eugene V. Debs to Edward Snowden*. New York: New Press, 2016.

Geertz, Clifford. *Available Light: Anthropological Reflections on Philosophical Topics*. Princeton, NJ: Princeton University Press, 2000.

Gilbert, Alan. "Charles Olson and Empire, or Charles Olson Flips the Wartime Script." PennSound. Accessed January 11, 2018. http://writing.upenn.edu/epc/authors/olson/blog/Olson_and_Empire.pdf.

Ginsberg, Allen. *Deliberate Prose: Selected Essays, 1952–1995*. Edited by Bill Morgan. New York: Harper, 2000.

———. *The Fall of America: Poems of These States, 1965–1971*. San Francisco: City Lights, 1972.

———. *Improvised Poetics*. Edited by Mark Robison. San Francisco: Anonym, 1972.

———. *Indian Journals*. San Francisco: City Lights, 1970.

———. *Planet News, 1961–1967*. 1968. Reprint, San Francisco: City Lights, 1992.

———. *Poems All over the Place—Mostly 'Seventies*. Cherry Valley, NY: Cherry Valley Editions, 1978.

———. *Spontaneous Mind: Selected Interviews, 1958–1996*. Edited by David Carter. New York: Harper, 2001.

———. *Wichita Vortex Sutra*. CD. New York: Artemis, 2004.

Gitelman, Lisa. *Paper Knowledge: Towards a Media History of Documents*. Durham, NC: Duke University Press, 2014.

Gould, Glenn. *The Glenn Gould Reader*. Edited by Tim Page. New York: Knopf, 1984.

———. *The Idea of North*. Sound Documentary. Toronto: Canadian Broadcasting Corporation, 1967.

Grele, Ronald, ed. *Envelopes of Sound: The Art of Oral History*. Chicago: Precedent Publishing, 1985.

Grubbs, David. *Records Ruin the Landscape: John Cage, the Sixties, and Sound Recording*. Durham, NC: Duke University Press, 2014.

Harvard President's Report. Cambridge, MA: Harvard, 1941–52. http://hul.harvard.edu/lib/archives/refshelf/AnnualReportsSearch.htm.

Hayles, N. Katherine. "Voices out of Bodies, Bodies out of Voices: Audiotape and the Production of Subjectivity." In *Sound States: Innovative Poetics and Acoustical Technologies*, edited by Adalaide Morris, 74–96. Chapel Hill: University of North Carolina Press, 1998.

Heer, Jeet. "Marxist Literary Critics Are Following Me!" *Lingua Franca* 11, no. 4 (2001): 26–31.

Hegel, Georg Wilhelm Friedrich. *Hegel's Aesthetics: Lectures on Fine Art, Vol. 1*. Translated by T. M. Knox. 1835. Reprint, Oxford: Clarendon, 1988.

Hejinian, Lyn. *The Language of Inquiry*. Berkeley: University of California Press, 2000.

Hersh, Seymour. *The Price of Power: Kissinger in the Nixon White House*. New York: Summit, 1983.

Herzstein, Robert. *Henry R. Luce: A Political Portrait of the Man Who Created the American Century*. New York: Scribners, 1994.

Hoberman, J. *The Dream Life: Movies, Media, and the Mythology of the Sixties*. New York: New Press, 2004.

Hodges, Andrew. *Alan Turing: The Enigma*. New York: Simon and Schuster, 1983.

Holzman, James. *James Jesus Angleton, the CIA, and the Craft of Counterintelligence*. Amherst: University of Massachusetts Press, 2008.

Hong, Sungook. *Wireless: From Marconi's Black-Box to the Audion*. Cambridge, MA: MIT Press, 2001.

Hoover, J. Edgar. *Masters of Deceit: The Story of Communism in America and How to Fight It*. 1958. Reprint, New York: Pocket Books, 1965.

———. *A Study of Communism*. New York: Holt, 1962.

Iddon, Martin. *New Music at Darmstadt: Nono, Stockhausen, Cage, and Boulez*. Cambridge: Cambridge University Press, 2013.

I'll Take My Stand: The South and the Agrarian Tradition, by Twelve Southerners. 1930. Reprint, New York: Harper, 1962.

Isaacson, Walter. *Kissinger: A Biography*. New York: Simon and Schuster, 1992.

Jacobsen, Annie. *Operation Paperclip: The Secret Intelligence Program That Brought Nazi Scientists to America*. New York: Little, Brown, 2014.

Jameson, Fredric. *The Ideologies of Theory: Essays 1971–1986*. Vol. 1, *Situations of Theory*. Minneapolis: University of Minnesota Press, 1988.

———. *The Ideologies of Theory: Essays 1971–1986.* Vol. 2, *Syntax of History.* Minneapolis: University of Minnesota Press, 1988.

———. *The Political Unconscious: Narrative as a Socially Symbolic Act.* Ithaca, NY: Cornell University Press, 1981.

———. *Postmodernism, or, The Cultural Logic of Late Capitalism.* Durham, NC: Duke University Press, 1991.

Jameson, Fredric, Leonard Green, Jonathan Culler, and Richard Klein. "Interview: Fredric Jameson." *Diacritics* 12, no. 3 (1982): 72–91.

Jay, Martin. *Marxism and Totality: The Adventures of a Concept from Lukács to Habermas.* Berkeley: University of California Press, 1984.

Johnson, William R. *Thwarting Enemies at Home and Abroad: How to Be a Counterintelligence Officer.* Washington, DC: Georgetown University Press, 2009.

Jones, Hettie. *How I Became Hettie Jones.* New York: Grove, 1990.

Joseph, Branden. "Interview with Paolo Virno." Translated by Alessia Ricciardi. *Grey Room,* no. 21 (Fall 2005): 26–37.

Kahn, Douglas, and Gregory Whitehead, eds. *Wireless Imagination: Sound, Radio, and the Avant-Garde.* Cambridge, MA: MIT Press, 1992.

Kahn, Herman. *On Thermonuclear War.* Princeton, NJ: Princeton University Press, 1960.

Kane, Daniel. *All Poets Welcome: The Lower East Side Poetry Scene in the 1960s.* Berkeley: University of California Press, 2003.

———. *Do You Have a Band? Poetry and Punk Rock in New York City.* New York: Columbia University Press, 2017.

Kent, Sherman. *Writing History.* 1941. Reprint, New York: Appleton-Century-Crofts, 1967.

Kerouac, Jack. *On the Road.* 1957. Reprint, New York: Penguin, 1991.

Kissinger, Henry, ed. *Confluence.* Cambridge, MA: President and Fellows of Harvard College, 1952–58.

———. *Nuclear Weapons and Foreign Policy.* New York: Harper, 1957.

Kramer, Jane. *Allen Ginsberg in America.* New York: Vintage, 1970.

Krause, Bernie. *The Great Animal Orchestra: Finding the Origins of Music in the World's Wild Places.* New York: Back Bay, 2012.

———. *Into a Wild Sanctuary: A Life in Music and Natural Sound.* Berkeley, CA: Heyday, 1998.

Lanza, Joseph. *Elevator Music: A Surreal History of Muzak, Easy-Listening and Other Moodsong.* New York: St. Martin's, 1994.

Lenthall, Bruce. *Radio's America: The Great Depression and the Rise of Modern Mass Culture.* Chicago: University of Chicago Press, 2007.

Lockman, Zachary. *Field Notes: The Making of Middle Eastern Studies in the United States.* Stanford, CA: Stanford University Press, 2016.

Loviglio, Jason. *Radio's Intimate Public: Network Broadcasting and Mass-Mediated Democracy.* Minneapolis: University of Minnesota Press, 2005.

Lowen, Rebecca. *Creating the Cold War University: The Transformation of Stanford.* Berkeley: University of California Press, 1997.

Mallarmé, Stéphane. *Selected Poems.* Edited by Mary Ann Caws. Translated by Hubert Creekmore. New York: New Directions, 1982.

Marchetti, Victor, and John D. Marks. *The CIA and the Cult of Intelligence.* New York: Dell, 1974.

Martin, David C. *Wilderness of Mirrors.* New York: Harper, 1980.

Maud, Ralph. *Charles Olson at the Harbor.* Vancouver, BC: Talon, 2008.

Maxwell, William J. *F.B. Eyes: How J. Edgar Hoover's Ghostreaders Framed African American Literature.* Princeton, NJ: Princeton University Press, 2015.

May, Ernest R., and Philip D. Zelikow, eds. *The Kennedy Tapes: Inside the White House during the Cuban Missile Crisis.* Cambridge, MA: Harvard University Press, 1997.

Mayer, Bernadette. *Memory.* Plainfield, VT: North Atlantic Books, 1975.

———. *Midwinter Day.* Berkeley: Turtle Island, 1982.

———. *Studying Hunger.* New York and Bolinas, CA: Adventures in Poetry and Big Sky, 1975.

McCaffrey, Steve, with bpNichol. Introduction to "R. Murray Schafer: A Collection." Special issue, *Open Letter,* 4th ser. (1979): 5–6.

Medsger, Betty. *The Burglary: The Discovery of J. Edgar Hoover's Secret FBI.* New York: Vintage, 2014.

Middleton, Peter. *Distant Reading: Performance, Readership, and Consumption in Contemporary Poetry.* Tuscaloosa: University of Alabama Press, 2005.

Miles, Barry. *Ginsberg: A Biography.* New York: Simon and Schuster, 1989.

Mill, John Stuart. "Thoughts on Poetry and Its Varieties." In *Collected Works of John Stuart Mill, Vol. 1,* edited by John Robson, 341–66. Indianapolis, IN: Liberty Fund, 2006.

———. "What Is Poetry?" *Monthly Repository,* January 1833.

Mills, C. Wright. *White Collar: The American Middle Classes.* 1951. Reprint, New York: Oxford, 2002.

Mitchell, Christine. "Again the Air Conditioners: Finding Poetry in the Institutional Archive." *Amodern* 4, March 2015. http://amodern.net/article/again-air-conditioners/.

Mitgang, Herbert. *Dangerous Dossiers: Exposing the Secret War against America's Greatest Authors.* New York: Donald Fine, 1988.

Morton, David. *Off the Record: The Technological and Cultural History of Sound Recording in America.* New Brunswick, NJ: Rutgers University Press, 2000.

Moten, Fred. *In the Break: The Aesthetics of the Black Radical Tradition.* Minneapolis: University of Minnesota Press, 2003.

Murray, Sonny. *Sonny's Time Now.* LP. New York: Jihad, 1965.

Noel, Tomás Uraoyán. *In Visible Movement: Nuyorican Poetry from the Sixties to Slam.* Iowa City: University of Iowa Press, 2014.

O'Hara, Frank. *The Collected Poems of Frank O'Hara*. Edited by Donald Allen. New York: Knopf, 1972.

———. *Standing Still and Walking in New York*. Edited by Donald Allen. San Francisco: Grey Fox, 1983.

Olson, Charles. *Charles Olson at Goddard College, April 12–14, 1962*. Edited by Kyle Schlesinger. Victoria, TX: Cuneiform Press, 2011.

———. *Charles Olson Reads from Maximus Poems IV, V, VI*. LP. New York: Folkways, 1975.

———. *The Maximus Poems*. Edited by George Butterick. Berkeley: University of California Press, 1983.

———. *Muthologos: Lectures and Interviews*. Edited by Ralph Maud. Toronto: Talonbooks, 2010.

———. *Reading at Berkeley*. Berkeley, CA: Coyote, 1966.

———. *Selected Writings of Charles Olson*. Edited by Robert Creeley. New York: New Directions, 1966.

———. *Spanish Speaking Americans in the War*. Washington, DC: Office of the Coordinator of Inter-American Affairs, 1943.

Pater, Walter. *The Renaissance*. Edited by Donald L. Hill. Berkeley: University of California Press, 1980.

Powers, Richard Gid. *Broken: The Troubled Past and Uncertain Figure of the FBI*. New York: Free Press, 2004.

Powers, Thomas. *The Man Who Kept the Secrets: Richard Helms and the CIA*. New York: Knopf, 1979.

Price, David. *Anthropological Intelligence: The Deployment and Neglect of American Anthropology in the Second World War*. Durham, NC: Duke University Press, 2008.

Redfield, Marc. *Theory at Yale: The Strange Case of Deconstruction in America*. New York: Fordham University Press, 2016.

Richardson, Peter. *A Bomb in Every Issue: How the Short, Unruly Life of "Ramparts Magazine" Changed America*. New York: New Press, 2009.

Riebling, Mark. *Wedge: From Pearl Harbor to 9/11—How the Secret War between the FBI and the CIA Has Endangered National Security*. New York: Touchstone, 1994.

Rifkin, Libbie. *Career Moves: Olson, Creeley, Zukofsky, Berrigan, and the American Avant-Garde*. Madison: University of Wisconsin Press, 2000.

———. "'Say Your Favorite Poet in the World Is Lying There': Eileen Myles, James Schuyler and the Queer Intimacies of Care." *Journal of Medical Humanities* 38 (2017): 79–88.

Robertson, Lisa. *Nilling: Prose Essays on Noise, Pornography, the Codex, Melancholy, Lucretius, Folds, Cites and Related Aporias*. Toronto: Book Thug, 2012.

Roby, Warren. "Technology in the Service of Foreign Language Learning: The Case of the Language Laboratory." In *Handbook of Research on Education Communications and Technology*, edited by David Jonassen and Marcy Driscoll, 523–41. Mahwah, NJ: Lawrence Erlbaum, 2004.

Ross, Alex. *The Rest Is Noise: Listening to the Twentieth Century.* New York: FSG, 2007.

Ross, Andrew. *The Failure of Modernism: Symptoms of American Poetry.* New York: Columbia University Press, 1986.

Sabine, Wallace Clement. *Collected Papers on Acoustics.* New York: Dover, 1964.

Sanders, Ed. *Fug You: An Informal History of the Peace Eye Bookstore, the Fuck You Press, the Fugs, and Counterculture in the Lower East Side.* New York: Da Capo, 2011.

Saunders, Frances Stonor. *The Cultural Cold War: The CIA and the World of Arts and Letters.* New York: New Press, 1999.

Schafer, R. Murray. *The Soundscape: Our Sonic Environment and the Tuning of the World.* 1977. Reprint, Rochester, VT: Destiny, 1994.

———. *Voices of Tyranny, Temples of Silence.* Indian River, Ontario: Arcana, 1993.

Schumacher, Michael. *Dharma Lion: A Biography of Allen Ginsberg.* New York: St. Martin's, 1992.

Schwarz, Frederick A. O., Jr. *Democracy in the Dark: The Seduction of Government Secrecy.* New York: New Press, 2015.

Shaw, Lytle. *Fieldworks: From Place to Site in Postwar Poetics.* Tuscaloosa: University of Alabama Press, 2013.

———. *Frank O'Hara: The Poetics of Coterie.* Iowa City: University of Iowa Press, 2006.

———. "lowercase theory and the site specific turn." *ASAP Journal* 2, no. 3 (2017): 653–76.

———. "Robertson's Research." In *The Fate of Difficulty in the Poetry of Our Time,* edited by Charles Altieri and Nicholas D. Nace, 299–308. Evanston, IL: Northwestern University Press, 2017.

———. "The Utopian Past." In *The Present Tense through the Ages: On the Recent Work of Gerard Byrne.* Cologne, Germany: Koenig Books, 2007.

———. "Van Goyen's Puddles." *AA Files* 65 (2012): 76–86.

Silliman, Ron, ed. *In The American Tree: Language, Realism, Poetry.* Orono, ME: National Poetry Foundation, 1986.

Simpson, Christopher. *Blowback: America's Recruitment of Nazis and Its Effects on the Cold War.* New York: Weidenfeld and Nicolson, 1988.

Smith, Jacob. *Spoken Word: Postwar American Phonograph Cultures.* Berkeley: University of California Press, 2011.

Smithson, Robert. *Robert Smithson: The Collected Writings.* Edited by Jack Flam. Berkeley: University of California Press, 1996.

Snyder, Gary. Review of *The Ticket That Exploded,* by William S. Burroughs. *Ramparts,* December 1967, 87–90.

Sterne, Jonathan. *The Audible Past: Cultural Origins of Sound Reproduction.* Durham, NC: Duke University Press, 2003.

Sullivan, William C. *The Bureau: My Thirty Years in Hoover's FBI.* New York: Norton, 1979.

Summers, Anthony. *Official and Confidential: The Secret Life of J. Edgar Hoover.* New York: Putnam, 1993.

Szwed, John. *Alan Lomax: The Man Who Recorded the World.* New York: Penguin, 2010.

Taub, Petter B. "Now in Fourth Year, Modern Language Center Mixes Scholarship with Informal Atmosphere," *Harvard Crimson,* December 13, 1949. http://www.thecrimson.com/article/1949/12/13/now-in-fourth-year-modern-language/.

Tedlock, Dennis. *The Spoken Word and the Work of Interpretation.* Philadelphia: University of Pennsylvania Press, 1983.

Thompson, Emily. *The Soundscape of Modernity: Architectural Acoustics and the Culture of Listening in America, 1900–1933.* Cambridge, MA: MIT Press, 2002.

Thompson, Hunter S. *The Great Shark Hunt.* New York: Warner, 1979.

Vanderlan, Robert. *Intellectuals Incorporated: Politics, Art, and Idea inside Henry Luce's Media Empire.* Philadelphia: University of Pennsylvania Press, 2010.

Vest, Jason P. *The Postmodern Humanism of Philip K. Dick.* Lanham, MD: Scarecrow Press, 2009.

Vogel, Rudolf. "Press and Radio in Germany." *Confluence* 4 (1952): 15–23.

Von Hallberg, Robert. *Charles Olson: The Scholar's Art.* Cambridge, MA: Harvard University Press, 1978.

Warhol, Andy. *A: A Novel.* 1968. Reprint, New York: Grove, 1998.

Watten, Barrett. *Total Syntax.* Carbondale: Southern Illinois University Press, 1985.

Weheliye, Alexander G. *Phonographies: Grooves in Sonic Afro-Modernity.* Durham, NC: Duke University Press, 2005.

Weiner, Tim. *Legacy of Ashes: The History of the CIA.* New York: Doubleday, 2007.

Westerfield, Bradford H., ed. *Inside the CIA's Private World: Declassified Articles from the Agency's Internal Journal, 1955–1992.* New Haven, CT: Yale University Press, 1995.

White, Hayden. *The Content of the Form: Narrative, Discourse and Historical Representation.* Baltimore: Johns Hopkins University Press, 1987.

———. *The Greco-Roman Tradition.* New York: Harper and Row, 1973.

———. *Metahistory: The Historical Imagination in Nineteenth-Century Europe.* Baltimore: Johns Hopkins University Press, 1973.

———. *Tropics of Discourse: Essays in Cultural Criticism.* Baltimore: Johns Hopkins University Press, 1978.

White, Hayden, and William J. Bossenbrook, eds. *The Uses of History: Essays in Intellectual and Social History.* Detroit, MI: Wayne State University Press, 1968.

White, Hayden, and Willson Coates, eds. *The Ordeal of Liberal Humanism: An Intellectual History of Western Europe.* New York: McGraw-Hill, 1970.

White, Hayden, Willson Coates, and J. Salwin Schapiro, eds. *The Emergence of Liberal Humanism in Western Europe: From the Italian Renaissance to the French Revolution.* New York: McGraw-Hill, 1966.

White, Hayden, and Giorgio Tagliacozzo, eds. *Giambattista Vico: An International Symposium.* Baltimore: Johns Hopkins University Press, 1969.

Wiener, Norbert. *Cybernetics: Or Control and Communication in the Animal and the Machine.* 1948. Reprint, Cambridge, MA: MIT Press, 1961.

———. *The Human Use of Human Beings: Cybernetics and Society.* 1950. Reprint, New York: Avon, 1967.

———. *I Am a Mathematician: The Later Life of a Prodigy.* Cambridge, MA: MIT Press, 1956.

Wilford, Hugh. *The Mighty Wurlitzer: How the CIA Played America.* Cambridge, MA: Harvard University Press, 2009.

Williams, William Carlos. *In the American Grain.* 1925. Reprint, New York: New Directions, 1956.

Winks, Robin W. *Cloak and Gown: Scholars in the Secret War, 1939–1961.* New York: William Morrow, 1987.

Wood, Christopher. *Albrecht Altdorfer and the Origins of Landscape.* London: Reaktion, 1993.

Wyatt, Andrea. *A Bibliography of the Works by Larry Eigner, 1937–1969.* Berkeley, CA: Oyez, 1970.

Yépez, Heriberto. *The Empire of Neomemory.* Translated by Jen Hofer, Christian Nagler, and Brian Whitener. Oakland, CA: Chain Links, 2013.

Index